8,00

RED ZONE

FROM THE OFFENSIVE LINE TO THE FRONT LINE OF THE PANDEMIC

LAURENT DUVERNAY-TARDIF

Collins
An imprint of HarperCollins*Publishers*Ltd

Published by Collins, an imprint of HarperCollins Publishers Ltd

First edition

HarperCollins Publishers Ltd
Bay Adelaide Centre, East Tower
22 Adelaide Street West, 41st Floor
Toronto, Ontario, Canada
M5H 4E3

www.harpercollins.ca

Library and Archives Canada Cataloguing in Publication

Title: Red zone : from the offensive line to the front line of the pandemic /
Laurent Duvernay-Tardif. Names: Duvernay-Tardif, Laurent, 1991- author.
Description: First edition. Identifiers: Canadiana (print) 20220267111 |
Canadiana (ebook) 20220267162 | ISBN 9781443466004 (hardcover) | ISBN
9781443466011 (ebook) Subjects: LCSH: Duvernay-Tardif, Laurent, 1991- |
LCSH: Football players—Missouri—Kansas City— Biography. | LCSH:
Physicians—Québec (Province)—Biography. | LCSH: COVID-19 Pandemic,
2020- | LCGFT: Autobiographies. Classification: LCC GV939.D88 A3 2022 |
DDC 796.332092—dc23

Printed and bound in the United States of America

LSC/H 9 8 7 6 5 4 3 2 1

I would like to dedicate this book to all the health care workers who have devoted their lives to the care of others and have protected our community since the start of the pandemic.

CONTENTS

QUESTIONS

You've always been unsure about how long you want to play football," my friend Mitch said through a mouthful of food. "If you win, are you done?"

Point-blank. True to form. The question called for a yes—or a no.

It was late January 2020. Kansas City. That damp cold you get when the temperature hovers around freezing. Mitch and I were in my apartment, eating our way through the heaping chipotle bowls he'd brought over for old times' sake. I liked that apartment. It was the second place I'd rented in KC since I'd been drafted by the Chiefs, the local NFL franchise, in 2014: two bedrooms, comfortable, nothing extravagant. It was right downtown, 10 minutes from work, everything close by. I loved the place for its central location. You can't help but feel part of a community when you're right there, eating and sleeping at the heart of it. But I was also a sucker for the sunset view from my balcony. That peaceful moment you could snag after a gruelling day of pushing yourself to the absolute limits of your physical and mental abilities—that's the irresistible challenge, and privilege, of playing pro football—you couldn't overstate the value of that.

Especially when Flo, my girlfriend, was in town from Montreal and we could hang out there together. Decompress. Reconnect. In a city where people live and die for football, enjoying tranquil time in my apartment quickly became my way of disconnecting from football.

That day, though, I wasn't exactly relaxing. Under the brilliant coaching of Andy Reid, and with me (of all people!) on the line blocking for the otherworldly quarterback Patrick Mahomes, the Chiefs had just won their first AFC Championship since, no joke, 1970. Half a century ago. In a few days we'd be heading to Miami to play in the National Football League's annual championship game, the Super Bowl.

I was actually going to play in Super Bowl LIV. It was surreal, to say the least. "Unlikely" doesn't come close.

For most of my life, I'd never expected to play in the NFL. I never dreamed of signing a big contract, let alone finding myself recognized as one of the best right guards in the league. Mitch knew that better than anyone. Six years earlier, in my first game as a starter in the NFL, he'd played at my left side. It'd been his first game as a starter too. We saw the game the same way, adopted the same tricks for handling the pressure. *We're both in this game, we're both nervous, but we're not talking about it. We're focused: throw your hands, make sure you know the game plan, play fast and see where the cards fall. Let's do this together. Let's have fun doing it.*

We lived in the same neighbourhood, and would get together in our downtime. On Thursday nights we'd meet the rest of the offensive linemen for feasts at Bo Lings, a nearby Chinese restaurant. With a teacher father and a lawyer mother, Mitch had made it to the big time via Mizzou, the University of Missouri, one of those American colleges where they take their football really seriously. But the sport wasn't his be-all and end-all. He was outward-looking, naturally curious. Unfazed by my Québécois accent, he'd ask me what it was like growing up in Quebec; about the lengthy sailing trips my family used to take; and about our all-hands-on-deck family business ventures, from a vineyard, to an orchard, to a bakery.

All these aspects of my background made me unusual in NFL circles. But that wasn't the half of it. I'd come to football late, and learned the game CFL-style—that's the Canadian Football League, which follows different rules that significantly differ the nature of play. I'd never, as a kid—not even as a teen—watched pro sports on TV. When the game became a serious pursuit for me, and aiming for the NFL a remote possibility, I couldn't name a single superstar player except for Tom Brady. For the longest time I didn't even know what the Super Bowl was. I kept mixing it up with the Grey Cup (the CFL championship) and the NHL's Stanley Cup.

Too many cups.

On top of all that, while playing football, I was working my way through medical school. Since Mitch and I first ran out on the field together, that hadn't changed. I was a pro footballer, a starter, a full-fledged member of the Kansas City Chiefs. I was also a doctor-in-training. During our years as teammates, sometimes I'd be studying medicine in a coffee shop and Mitch would show up and quiz me on stuff in my textbook, joking that it read like another language.

Mitch now played for the Buffalo Bills. It was two years since we'd been teammates, but we were still friends. And the question he put to me that day over our chipotle was both fair and all too familiar. For years, I'd hit it at every step along the way, from family, teachers, mentors, coaches, fellow students, fellow players, old friends. Way back when I first started studying medicine, I was asked, would I give up football and focus on my studies (as most people around me expected)? Then, after I'd had the chance to become a starter in the NFL, would I think, great, I've had the chance to play pro, now I can go back to medicine full time? With each passing year, the question took on more urgency. You can only stretch out your medical training so far. Eight years in, I was pushing the limit. I was going to have to choose. And of course, when you win the AFC Championship and get a chance to play in the Super Bowl, that's a pretty nice way to hang up your cleats. As Mitch put it, "At that point, you've signed a huge contract, you've won a Super Bowl, you've kicked ass, you've done everything. Now go be a freaking doctor."

He was right. I knew this was something I'd need to think about, and that I'd need to discuss it with Flo, and with my parents. I told Mitch the truth: I didn't know what I was going to do.

But then I laughed. Or he did. We both did. Because really, right now, who cared about all that? For the next couple of weeks, medicine, the future and whatever decisions I had to make would sit on the back burner—way far back. I was a Kansas City Chiefs offensive linebacker, it was late January 2020, and in less than two weeks I'd be out on the field in Miami, decked out in Kansas City red and gold, doing my thing.

On Super Bowl Sunday.

OF COURSE, Mitch wasn't the only one with questions for me. And though I was perfectly happy to set my medical self aside during the most exciting week of my NFL career, the global media that descended on Miami in the days leading up to the big game had other ideas.

The team flew into Miami on the Monday before the Super Bowl, then we headed straight to "media night" at a local baseball stadium, our first of many marathon sessions that week taking questions from the 2,000-odd reporters and writers who cover the game each year.

"Media night" resembles a circus. It's part Halloween, part stand-up routine, part hype machine and part journalism—the last part being the smallest of all. Reporters ask players all sorts of insane questions: favourite restaurants, most embarrassing stories, books on nightstands, first-date anecdotes, anything for a laugh, along with naming which analyst would make the best lineman. I couldn't complain about all the questions, which would come at us non-stop during daily, hour-long media sessions throughout the week leading up to the game, because those interviews were part of my job. Creating the biggest sporting event in the world doesn't happen just because people love football. In order to have hundreds of millions of people in more than 50 countries watching the game, you need a *big* media machine pushing content, stories and headlines. And by far the best source of content were the 50 players on both teams. Reporters left no stone unturned; for them, every story angle was good.

That first night, dressed in identical tracksuits, we were introduced then ferried onto the field. I was not one of the team superstars, so I wasn't set up with a podium and a mic. Just a table for me. But there were so many people at my table that the Chiefs' public relations staff joked about me getting more attention than our wildly popular quarterback Pat Mahomes, who'd been named the league's most valuable player the year before.

There was an interesting mix of people there. I had media from Canada, especially from Montreal, both English and French. These Canadian and Québécois reporters had come to the Super Bowl, basically, to cover my story. The French journalists would say, "Whenever you're done talking English, we're gonna talk French." They would ask very specific, in-depth or personal questions about my life, such as: "Your parents are doing a Kansas City Chiefs special pizza at the bakery. How do you feel about that?"

The second group comprised the regular sports media, and they posed intricate, obsessive questions—as is the particular skill of sports journalists—about defensive line play, game strategy and my take on our opponents, the San Francisco 49ers. If you're not careful, that line of questioning builds extra pressure for no reason; you have to learn to take the questions head-on then set them aside (a different kind of game strategy).

The third group, which I really didn't expect, was made up of the rest of the media, which included international journalists and more general media looking for human interest stories to tie to the Super Bowl. With my French-Canadian background and medical aspirations, I was the perfect candidate for stories on broader news outlets, a fresh angle sitting right in front of them, a gift. All the reporters from France wanted to talk to me. Reporters from Europe and the UK were interested in my almost-doctor status. There was a guy from Germany keen to hash out with me the duality of football and medicine. Others were just curious about how I managed to do both, why I'd stuck with both.

As the days passed, I got used to fielding these three distinct streams of questioning, paying close attention to who was asking what, and why. Is this reporter most interested in football? Quebec? Medicine? I would tailor my answers to each situation.

Then came the question that threw me. It was Thursday, January 30, three days before kickoff. Through the bustling scrum around my table, a reporter asked, "As the NFL's only doctor-in-training, what do you think about the novel coronavirus?"

At that point, I didn't know much more than the next person about the deadly and highly contagious virus that would soon come to be called COVID-19. I'd heard about it on the news, obviously, and done a bit of research online through my phone. No one really knew the true nature and scale of the virus. No one had yet used the words *global pandemic*.

What I wanted to do was remind the journalists crowding around me: I am about to play in the most important game of my career, and I need to concentrate on that. Instead, I tried to provide a reasonable answer based on a mixture of what I'd seen in news accounts; my biology class from 2012; and my basic knowledge of viruses, how they work and how they spread. I told the journalist that scientists had settled on this particular name—the novel coronavirus—because of the crowned state of the protein structure that binds to cells and injects RNA, a ribonucleic acid that acts like a messenger for living cells to synthesize protein. I met glazed eyes, puzzled looks. I realized I'd strayed way too far into technical territory. I pulled back, reminding them that I was not a public health expert, nor a virologist. I deflected by saying that for the next 72 hours I was going to put my medical degree aside and just focus on football.

It seems incredible now when I remember how little we knew. Or what was just around the corner. None of us had any idea the extent to which this virus, which still seemed like a distant threat—a distraction, even, a question I didn't really feel like answering—would upend our lives. No way could I have predicted how personally it would affect me, how it would come to mark my life every bit as much as that year's Super Bowl, and then some.

Chapter 1

THE RUN

The Denver Broncos' stadium is a mile above sea level, where the altitude makes it more difficult to breathe. When we rolled into town, we were in the early days of a seriously bad streak: from early October to mid-November 2019, the Chiefs would lose four of six contests. Football isn't set up like, say, baseball, where a team plays several times a week and has endless chances for comebacks or new winning streaks. Until 2021, NFL teams played just 16 games during the regular season, so our losses that fall would be significant. But we didn't know that yet. We only knew that we were breathing thin air and up against the Denver Broncos, who play in our division of the American Football Conference, the AFC West, making them one of Kansas City's biggest rivals.

Coach Reid dialed up a quarterback sneak on 3rd and 1 in the second quarter. On this kind of sneak, offensive linemen like myself—the big, mostly anonymous brutes up front—are supposed to perform what's called a "wedge block." The idea is to get as low as possible in order to create a pile of bodies that amass in front of a quarterback as the opposing team tries to push forward, literally *over* the wedge we have collectively created, and earn the first down.

On this particular sneak, after the play ended, I heard Pat scream. "It's out!" he hollered. "It's out!"

Because the quarterback is so important, and also because our main job is to protect him (it's in the offensive lineman's DNA: don't let anyone touch your QB), dozens of things flashed through my mind in that moment. How badly was he hurt? Had I made a mistake? Was his season over? And, if so, would ours be over too?

I watched as the trainers helped him limp off the field to our sideline. Nobody said a word. But every alarmed face in the huddle spoke volumes. Pat later told me that when he had looked down at his right leg, his kneecap was not in the right place. It was dislocated.

It's no coincidence that we didn't run a quarterback sneak again after that.

At some point in the year, every player on every team endures some measure of pain, moving from one injury or another, some more serious than others. In this case, for the first time in his professional career, Pat, by then already on his way to becoming a truly legendary NFL quarterback, looked vulnerable, more human. His dislocated kneecap, along with other injuries, combined to limit him in some games and keep him out of others.

The season carried on; NFL seasons always do. Baltimore quarterback Lamar Jackson took control of the MVP race that fall as we faded into the background of the post-season picture. Meanwhile, the Chiefs fixed some glaring defensive issues, as Pat and other injured players nursed their wounds. We fought, scratched and even healed our way through. We didn't lose again after November 10. Still, by the time the playoffs started, it's fair to say we were not considered the favourites to make the Super Bowl, let alone to win it.

*

OUR FIRST playoff game, against the Houston Texans, was at Arrowhead Stadium in KC on January 12.

Home ground.

There's nothing like playoff football in Kansas City. Barbecue smoke wafts from the grills of tailgaters, those thousands of die-hard supporters of a franchise with as proud a history as any in the NFL. The Chiefs' founder, Lamar Hunt, remains one of the league's most significant historical figures; he's even credited with inventing the term *Super Bowl*. Then there's the snow that often flutters into Arrowhead; the deafening chants; and all those faces, along with the occasional bare chest, painted in our team colours, red and gold. When that venue is rocking, like *really rocking*, the rise in the decibel levels is comparable to that on a runway when a plane is taking off. (It's the loudest stadium in the world, according to the *Guinness Book of World Records*.)

The crowd was excited, but you could feel the tension in the air. In football, the post-season is not like that of other pro sports, where teams square off in playoff rounds of multiple games, and the winner of the best of five, say, or the best of seven advances. Instead, an NFL team's fate is decided game by game. Win and advance. Lose and go home.

In my first five seasons, we'd always gone home early. In fact, in the quarter century since 1993, the Chiefs had won all of two playoff games. *Two*. Fifty full seasons had passed since the Chiefs, a franchise as historic as any in pro football, had won a Super Bowl. Kansas City had last captured an NFL title way back in 1969, and then went on to lose post-season games for decades, often in unusual or even bizarre ways—missed kicks, bad penalty calls, unfortunate bounces—in a seemingly endless stretch of what Hunt called "buzzard's luck."

That the conference's championship trophy was named after Mr. Hunt but had to be handed to another team for all that time was not lost on anyone. In the days before the big game, reporters had descended on our locker room, either before or after practice, crowding around the cubicles of half-dressed athletes, armed with digital recording devices and TV cameras, firing questions, asking about strategy. And of course they reminded us, over and over, that we'd managed to land only one appearance in the conference championship in five decades—a contest we'd lost, late in the game, at home, to Tom Brady and the New England Patriots, the previous year.

Athletes can say they don't weight those kinds of stakes, that the infinite questions are easy to ignore. My guess, at least based on my own experience, is that they're not exactly being truthful when they say that. You can embrace the pressure to win the big games and use it to motivate you, or you can let it distract you and affect your game in a negative way, but no matter what athletes say, it does affect you. For me, winning the Super Bowl was the ultimate team accomplishment. Every year during training camp, when I felt exhausted during those three hours of practice in suffocating heat, I visualized that winning scenario and convinced myself that all the hard work would pay off in that specific moment.

I also wanted Coach Reid to win his first Super Bowl as a head coach, so that reporters could stop asking him about it. I wanted Pat to solidify his greatness. I wanted to bring the trophy named after the Hunt family back where it belonged.

The KC fans wanted all that too. After six years there, I know that the loyalty and support and optimism of Chiefs fans runs deep. And with our run-up to the playoffs, we'd given them ample reason to hope. Still, based on the team's history, I doubt anyone was surprised that day when things against Houston got off to a rocky start.

The Texans jumped to a 24–0 lead in the playoff opener. Houston scored on a long pass and a blocked punt. These were uncharacteristic mistakes, the kind that can end even the most promising season.

ALL THAT WEEK leading up to that important game, amid sweaty practice sessions and endless hours studying film with my fellow offensive linemen, I tried to eliminate distractions. I created a bubble, in order to be able to focus solely on my opponent, because I understood that any energy I put toward anything other than doing my best on the next play, for the next quarter, over the next game, was ultimately energy that I had wasted. At the end of a long and physically torturous season, I needed to devote every ounce of focus I had left to process.

Hence my decision to meet regularly that week with Jean-François Ménard, my mental coach. Sports psychologists are just as important as strength and conditioning coaches in helping players reach their highest potential. Earlier in my football career, I had worked with a sports psychologist in Kansas City who'd been suggested by the team. At a certain point I'd decided it would be helpful to work with someone from home, someone who spoke French, my first language, whom I could communicate with more easily, and who also instinctively understood the subtle challenges of being a Canadian working in the US, including the differences between our cultures. In particular, I needed someone who understood that football was not my only passion, that my life was also dominated by medicine, and medical school, and that I didn't want to define myself as only one thing—as either a doctor or a football player. I always struggled with anyone saying I needed to focus on only one thing to maximize my success. Take football, for example. If I *only* played guard, how would I cope with the rising anxiety when I didn't perform well? Or in medicine, how would I handle the pressure of caring for my patients? Football helped me deal with medicine, and vice versa. I believed each occupation could make me better at the other.

Of course, pursuing two demanding things simultaneously is like walking a tightrope, and implies some paradox and sacrifice. When things are going well in both spheres, it's a success story that fans love to talk about; but when you underperform on the field, people (including myself) sometimes start questioning if your divided focus is the reason. They think there's a lack of commitment. *Maybe he should have been lifting more weights instead of working in a hospital during the off-season.*

For me, I tried to use my twin passions as a competitive advantage on the field, reducing the performance anxiety of playing in the NFL. But building that mental toughness and creating that bubble around me to protect myself from all the outside noise during times of adversity didn't happen by magic. You need to visualize it, break down your reasoning to the most fundamental and basic essence of *why* you are doing what you do, and then build up that mental toughness to give yourself a greater purpose. That's why I needed to work with somebody who wanted to get to know me as more than just an athlete. And that's why I needed a sport psychologist.

I'd met Ménard at the Winter Olympics in South Korea in 2018, while I was on-site moonlighting as a broadcaster, telling stories about Canadian athletes in connection with one of my favourite topics, the intersection of science and sports. I wanted to do a piece on Mikaël Kingsbury, the most accomplished mogul skier of all time. He would win the gold medal in men's free-style at those Games, but before officials could hang it around his neck, his PR team declined my interview request, saying he would not speak to the press until after his event's conclusion. Having turned down a few hundred similar asks myself, I understood his thought process (wishing, only half-jokingly, that we could make it an NFL policy).

I still wanted to find a way of doing the story, though, so I approached Ménard, who was Kingsbury's mental coach, and asked him for an interview. He accepted. We rode a chairlift up the same mountain where Kingsbury would compete, filming as I asked questions. He described teaching Kingsbury to use this ride up the mountain to analyze his competitors' performances. Even riding the chairlift offered an opportunity to shift his mindset into the "zone" that would help him win.

I liked Ménard. I called him after the Olympics and we began to work together. He tweaked the programs he used for Canadian Olympians to accommodate me, a right guard who played professional football across the border. At the start, there were commonalities to focus on, such as separating the environment around any huge event—an Olympic final, say, or an NFL playoff contest—from the game itself. Meaning: The atmosphere only makes some football games *feel* bigger, more chaotic. The game itself hasn't changed at all. The task at hand remains the same. The key is to not focus on the result, or the implications and consequences I will be forced to confront if the game goes poorly. When you're playing a sport as fragmented as football, the secret is to stay in the present, to view an average of 65 offensive snaps as 65 independent events with opportunities to execute successfully.

It's amazing, the simple tricks you can use to corral your mind. Ménard suggested that I tie a little ball of athletic tape on my shoelaces. Whenever I felt overwhelmed, whenever external forces threatened to break my focus, I would look down at that ball and centre myself. If the crowd's energy started to distract me, I'd look down. Same thing when fans screamed obscenities, or an opponent tried a dirty move. Look down. Breathe deeply. Remember what I'm doing. Remember why I'm here. Then, analyze the situation: the time on the clock, the alignment of the defence, my assignment for the next play. Whatever had happened on the last play, good or bad, amazing or terrible, did not and would not correlate to what might happen next—unless I let it.

There are keys to slowing down a game that moves rapidly, not just on the field but in your mind. What if you consider your opponents' fears rather than your own? How can you magnify their doubts? I could run to the line of scrimmage before a play starts, showing them exactly what kind of shape I'm in. I could, here and there, give a defender a little extra shove after the referee's whistle signals the end of a play, sending the message that I have the will to be more physical than him. I could celebrate with my teammates after successful plays to illustrate just how much fun I'm having, and to show, of course, that I'm coming right back for more. Just thinking about the game in those terms, with that perspective, gave me an edge.

I resolved to not succumb to downward spirals or negative non-verbal cues. I would, instead, hand them out. I would not lament the difficulty in any one assignment. I would, instead, seize the opportunity to shine, telling myself that a difficult block was a key opportunity to maximize my contribution to the team's success. In one of my courses in medical school we'd learned that human beings excel at reading non-verbal cues without even noticing. One study even found that 93 percent of communication between human beings is non-verbal. Approaching a high-stakes game this way, parading your upbeat mood and your might, was putting that principle into action.

I DREW ON those lessons going into that first game against Houston, and as we fell behind. As important, maybe even more so, was the way the Chiefs had established a culture of winning. If that sounds like a cliché, it also happens to be true. Since Kansas City had selected me in the NFL draft in 2014, I had watched Coach Reid build that very culture, day by day, brick by brick. So, when we fell behind against Houston, no one panicked. Instead, we pumped each other up. We kicked into gear. Pat was out there, slinging passes, scampering away from defenders, while *our* defence stopped our opponents from scoring again. And we roared back, scoring 51 of the last 58 points, as Pat threw five touchdowns.

That afternoon, we established a pattern for the 2019 post-season: Fall behind, overcome. Fall behind, overcome. We would even trail 17–7 in the conference title tilt against the Tennessee Titans before drawing on our mental fortitude to mount another comeback.

We were Super Bowl bound.

Momentum cannot be quantified, but I maintain that it's the *best feeling* in sports, when teammates look up at the scoreboard, see a seemingly insurmountable deficit and smile. That's a team that plans to win. They *know* they'll win. They can see their opponents slump, and argue, and hope to hold on—but they know they won't.

I watched the other teams throughout our comeback-heavy post-season. Their body language, collective and individual, told the story. Human brains record so many details that we don't pay much attention to. But when I'm cognizant and focused, I can be both on the field and watching what's happening from a distance, at once present and removed, as if I'm up above and outside myself, looking down.

This isn't something you learn in the flurry of a post-season run, or even over a single regular season. Like strength, technique, strategy, it takes years of practice to manage your mental approach to the game, and each player has to find the mindset in which they think they perform best.

For a long time, I have done visualization exercises in the lead-up to each game. (My first few seasons I'd even looked up some of the other stadiums where we would play, simply to familiarize myself with the environment.) I picture walking from the locker room to the field, running through our warm-up; I imagine the crowd, all the hip hop blaring, the jets zooming overhead, the pageantry and the nerves. Then, when I go through that exact experience on game day, everything feels muted, less overwhelming, more within my control. I've already seen it, already done it. I can then put my energy where I most need it: on the field. During the playoffs that season, I used the same process after plays, looking down at the ball of tape on my shoe whenever I needed focus or reassurance.

Mental toughness is harder to build than the physical kind. It's also a differentiator, a way to make good players into great ones, through the control and use of stress and anxiety in a sport with no shortage of both. Like a drug, stress is good as long as it stays within the optimal dosage. Mental toughness is what makes it possible to remember, when you're in the thick of it, how you want to play. It's how you project confidence, and not in a fake way. You *are* confident. You *are* ready. Even for Super Bowl–sized stakes.

But what about even higher stakes than a pro football title? Entirely different stakes? I was immersed in the unfolding of a particular history—an exciting, distinctly Kansas City storyline. I was immersed in my own opportunity to push myself to the height of my athletic abilities, to compete in the ultimate contest. The world had not yet changed in the way that 2020 would ultimately change everything. So even when, in the midst of the buildup to the grand spectacle, I was asked to confront the "novel coronavirus" that was popping up in the news, I had no idea that my mental toughness training, which at that moment was 100 percent geared toward the upcoming championship game, would soon be put to the test in ways I could never have anticipated—and that test would play out nowhere near a football, an offensive line, a circus-like press conference or a stadium bursting at the seams with raucous fans.

Indeed, stadiums filled with raucous fans would, for a time, and by necessity, be in very short supply.

CHAPTER 2

THE CHAMPIONSHIP

When I got my good friend and fellow med student Charles on the phone, he was between shifts at the emergency department in a Montreal hospital.

I asked how things were going. We talked over some of the cases he was seeing. Anything puzzling? Troubling? Fascinating? Had he seen any patients he felt he'd truly been able to help out? I'd done emergency room stints myself as part of my own medical school training—emergency medicine is the kind I'm most drawn to—so I had some sense of what Charles was in the midst of.

I was calling Charles from my hotel room in Miami during the days leading up to Super Bowl Sunday on February 2, 2020, when I would join my Kansas City teammates on the field to face the San Francisco 49ers. And even though I was set to play in the Super Bowl in a few days, I have to admit that it bothered me to realize I was falling behind my medical school colleagues. There was Charles, already finished his residency and working as a fully licensed doctor. And many of my friends were in the same position, whereas I had yet to get beyond clinical rotations.

Clinical rotations are intense enough. You're encountering situations you maybe haven't dealt with yet in real life, as opposed to studying them in a textbook or taking part in a role-play scenario. Your performance matters, not just to your future prospects as a doctor but to the person in front of you who needs medical care. It's not as if you're working solo; you are assisting full-fledged doctors with way more experience. Still, the pressure is on to put your "book" knowledge into practice, the pace demanding (especially in emerg), the learning curve sharp. I knew what it was like to be wholly immersed in this challenging, exhilarating experience—in exile, essentially, from ordinary life.

I was in exile now, too, in the these days leading up to the championship. A totally different kind of exile, in support of an entirely different pursuit, it also felt oddly familiar. I was away from my ordinary daily life, immersed in a life-changing experience. Exhilaration? Check. Pressure? Check.

Charles was beyond all that, but not so far that he didn't remember how it felt to be, in essence, on trial in a pressure cooker, away from home, on your own. We'd both been there. It was really good to hear his voice.

AFTER WINNING the AFC Championship, we had two full weeks to prep for the Super Bowl—one week in KC, the second week in Miami. During that first week, before flying out, we installed the offence we would deploy against San Francisco. Many of the plays that the coaches included in the game plan were familiar. They'd been used all season, to produce an offence the rest of the league was scared of, but even though the plays were nothing new, the coaching staff added motion, personnel changes and switches in formation in order to confuse the defence and make us more unpredictable.

Once we got to Miami, only the final preparation remained. We worked on goal-line runs, the kind that take place near the end zone, where space is tight but where points are available, ready to be scored. We studied what kinds of pressures—the defence's various strategies to rush our quarterback whenever we chose to throw—we might see, depending on how much yardage we needed for a first down. We knew that San Francisco's defensive line was generally considered the best unit at that position in the entire NFL. But we also knew that, if we could handle what we hoped to handle, the Chiefs would win. When analysts describe "key matchups," this is exactly what they mean.

By the 20th week of a grinding NFL season, my body and mind are set in the same routine: what to practise on Wednesday, what to review on Thursday, which clips of game film to watch on Friday to study the opponent's tendencies. The schedule becomes baked into my DNA, and that baking, and the rhythm that comes with it, is often the key to success, because you start to see the game as the result of a long week of prep. If you prep well, and build confidence in yourself, you tend to like the result on Sunday.

And yet, before the biggest contest of all, the league throws teams a curveball, adding this extra, paradoxically less demanding, week of prep. The extra week involves lighter practices, less physical contact to ward against potential injuries in practice, and an emphasis on the finer details. While all the elements that surround a championship game give it an "extra" feel for the fans and the public, as players, we actually face more leisure time than normal. Successfully navigating that downtime—with that Big Important Game looming over there on the other side of it—becomes a whole new challenge.

As I rested in my hotel room before and after meetings and practices, I immersed myself in Twitter, Instagram and Facebook feeds, along with various links to news articles. I normally don't spend that much time scrolling, let alone searching. But with the Super Bowl rapidly approaching, I couldn't resist. I allowed for a little reading into the virus that had broken out in Wuhan, China, the same one I'd been asked about by the reporter in one of our media sessions. But the disease that would eventually be known as COVID-19 didn't yet seem urgent enough to hold my attention. I veered back to the game.

I noticed social media posts from my hometown, and throughout Quebec, that showed locals supporting the Kansas City Chiefs. They hung banners from storefronts and slapped stickers on bumpers, until what seemed like half of Montreal displayed the same two words: *Go Chiefs*. I was amazed. Montreal is, to its core, a hockey town; as pro sports go, in the public consciousness, football's way down the list. All this hype was, crazy as it seemed, down to me, a Quebecker in the NFL, *their* Quebecker in the NFL, heading to the Super Bowl. I even watched clips from reporters as they visited my family's bakery.

But the more I read about the upcoming contest, the more I began to notice anxiety creeping in. It was all too much. Recalling Coach Reid's advice to avoid distractions, I turned away from the news feeds and social media.

I had a better idea. I ran myself a bath.

We were staying at a hotel in Fort Lauderdale, about 45 minutes north of Miami proper. We each had our own room, which doesn't always happen; sometimes, teammates are paired together. After checking in, I'd found my room, dropped my luggage and headed straight for the bathroom. That's always the first thing I do when we're on the road: check out the tub. To see, first of all, whether or not there is one; often, there's only a shower. But this time, this glorious time, I saw a bathtub big enough for a man my size—six feet five inches tall, and somewhere in the neighbourhood of 320 pounds—to climb into. This pumped me up way more than I want to admit, and I'll tell you why.

A football season requires a player to push his body to its limit. After flying back from a Sunday night game, for example, and landing at the airport in the middle of the night, you head home, sore, hyper and dehydrated. You're often so sore that you literally cannot sleep in your bed. On a night like that, dropping into a bath for an hour, maybe even two, helps me to heal and relax. Sometimes it's the only way I can fall asleep.

It's also not a bad place to be while catching up with a friend, or your girlfriend. That week, I placed lots of calls while soaking in that roomy, comfortable tub, just to ask friends, or Flo, how their day was going. I caught up with Charles in Montreal. I talked with my friend Étienne, an entrepreneur, about a project he was working on. I spoke with Flo about loads of things. When I'm on a call in the bath, I try not to move the water, to be discreet about it, so the person on the other end won't know where I am. But my friend Mary, a psychologist who was still working on her PhD back then, always knows, because I pull that trick so often. She called me on it. We laughed. Then we talked about a case she was using to make an argument in her thesis about managing anxiety in adolescent populations.

I couldn't have found a better way to spend my time. My friends are my barometer. They hold me accountable. They bring me back to earth. Because they knew me long before all this NFL hype, they understand that no matter how much I love football, no matter how much I appreciate the opportunity to play at the highest level the sport has to offer, the sport doesn't define me. It's a project. A project to which I've absolutely given my all, but still just one project among many in my life. Flo and my friends, they get that. They didn't ask me, "Are you excited to play?" but "How are you feeling?" We'd joke around. We'd laugh. Talking with them meant turning my own focus away from the looming championship game and onto the things they were experiencing, putting myself in the midst of *their* day. Listening.

Bottom line: I'm not a big fan of the jet-set lifestyle. I don't want to be flashy. I just want to stay true to who I am and the way my parents raised me. All those friends I met long before football are my barometer, they hold me accountable so I stay the Laurent they used to know, and that is precious to me. I won't lie: it's hard sometimes, because the reality I live in KC is so different, and pro athletes are often put on a pedestal. But those conversations remind me that the earth is still spinning, that people are still going about their business. When I get off the phone after one of those calls, I look around the hotel bathroom and smile to myself, knowing that this amazing reality I find myself in is just a blip in the bigger picture. It's not all about the Super Bowl.

FEBRUARY 2, 2020: Millions of football fans tuned their televisions to Fox to see if the Chiefs could upend their tortured history, or whether Coach Kyle Shanahan, and the 49ers, would add another Lombardi Trophy to an already crowded trophy case for one of the NFL's most storied franchises. Some 62,000 fans packed into the Hard Rock Stadium, everyone sitting next to each other, on top of each other, breathing the same air, sharing the same space. Nobody wore a mask. Why would they? The fast-spreading novel coronavirus was definitely in the headlines—in fact, the first death from the disease outside China was reported that day—but where we were, its threat remained distant, hypothetical. The need for masks or other public health measures was not yet on anyone's radar.

I mentally prepared for kickoff. I visualized how I wanted the game to go, starting with warm-ups and continuing into the second half. San Francisco featured that defensive line stocked with first-round picks in the NFL draft. I knew what I was facing. And I was confident in our ability to handle it.

I knew the layout of the stadium, so that I could maximize my efficiency, avoiding wrong turns, even for my walk onto the field. I knew that halftime would last longer, so I needed to stay warm. Potential distractions were all around. I spotted celebrities like DJ Khaled on the sideline. Pitbull was performing nearby in the parking lot during the warm-up. I looked down at that rubber ball of tape attached to my shoelaces. I tried to find my centre. *Focus. Focus.*

The game began. After our first offensive possession, despite the unfamiliar stakes, I settled into familiar rhythms. The hardest thing to do in football is to summon the manic energy, and precise technique, to move another large man wherever my coaches want me to shift him, then pause, catch my breath during a commercial break that's not even three minutes long, and not let the immensity seep in, whether we are playing well or poorly. In that game, as in all games, I needed to concentrate only on the next play. And then the next one. And the one after that. I needed to recall the potential strategies the 49ers might use, based on their defensive alignments. I needed to know when a blitz might be coming, when to double-team, or where to bulldoze open rushing lanes. That's partly why I love football. There's no other sport that combines this type of analytical, in-the-moment analysis with pure, unadulterated brute strength. Stress can lead to avoidable mistakes. If you focus too hard, you may get tunnel vision, which is not good. When you're nervous, you tend to focus only on the man in front of you and you miss a ton of information around you, from the position of the safeties to the structure of the defence, all of which helps you to anticipate the movement of your opponent. The goal is to stay in that zone, to see the defence in a holistic way, but to seize the adrenalin to aggressively move the defender in front of you off the ball. That's the amazing duality of this sport; it's what hooked me when I was young, and it hasn't let go yet.

We fell behind early on, 3–0. Nobody panicked. Later, we fell further: 20–10. Still we kept our cool. We'd lived this script before, and reworked two other playoff endings in our favour. Then, partway through the second quarter, injury struck. I got accidentally kicked by a defender. My right calf tightened up. As injuries go, it wasn't debilitating, it was even fairly minor, but in the midst of a championship game no affliction is insignificant. Now, not only did I need to block DeForest Buckner, Nick Bosa, Arik Armstead and Dee Ford—four of the league's best defensive linemen—I needed to summon my best effort on a bum leg. Physical injuries affect your game for sure, but I have found over the course of my career that the mental aspect of an injury often has more negative repercussions on your level of play than the actual limitation from the injury. Knowing that you have to block a defensive lineman who's operating at 100 percent when your right leg is working at 80 percent creates a lot of anxiety. That's where your mental preparation comes in. You don't want to second-guess yourself. Why would I assume he is 100 percent? Does he know that I am banged up? Despite the pain, does it really affect my ability to play?

*

AT HALFTIME, I needed the extra time to regroup both mentally and physically. But between our last drive late in the second quarter and the halftime extravaganza—which combined fireworks, dancers, and performances from Shakira and Jennifer Lopez—something like 45 minutes passed. My calf stiffened. I'd be lying if I said I didn't have any doubts about my status, or our odds, as I trudged gingerly back onto the field. I wasn't alone in my fears, either. Flo later told me that during the second half, she was mentally preparing to deal with my response to this disappointing ending to what had been such a special season. She felt as if she was grieving. My parents, meanwhile, were so anxious, they left their seats and paced around the stadium in an effort to calm down.

During the third quarter, we were trailing by 10 points when Coach Reid found me on the sideline. He looked into my eyes, and I could immediately sense the urgency he wanted to convey. "Doc," he told me, calling me by one of my nicknames, "you're the best option we got." That simple phrase had the effect of an adrenalin shot. It was a real confidence booster. Moments like that provide a window into why Coach Reid is one of the greatest leaders ever to coach a football team. He knew exactly what I needed to hear, and he drew on decades of experience to prod me in just the right way, at just the right time.

I actually felt less pressure after that brief huddle. I started to warm up and move better. Then our offence began to convert first downs. Momentum shifted. That fickle beast turned back our way, with both arms spread wide open.

Coach Reid also made a key adjustment in the fourth quarter, when he elected to go with our two-minute offence earlier than usual—a sped-up version of the usual one that's employed when scant time remains on the clock. He hoped to save the precious time we would need for our offensive revival. We run that particular offence like every other pro football team: at a faster pace, with few stoppages between plays and no huddles. Unlike our competitors, we also had Pat, whose ability to read pressure, scramble, evade sacks and open throwing lanes made him a savant, and transformed the Chiefs into one of the best teams in the NFL in those exact situations. We also often used fourth down late in games, when other teams would punt, giving up a possession, or attempt to make a field goal that's worth only three points. Using four downs instead of the typical three to convert first downs carried some additional risk. But it also gave the offence an additional play to work with.

In any two-minute drive, even when there's more than two minutes left, the first handful of plays are critical. An opposing defence will be at its most fresh then, and they know that we are working with a smaller playbook that is mostly centred around passes, which makes us more predictable. We want to establish dominance, wear down the defence and avoid drive-killing mistakes. That's exactly what happened late in the Super Bowl against the 49ers. Our comeback began with seven minutes and 57 seconds left on the game clock. Coach Reid mixed calls for short passes with timely runs, as the Niners' formidable defence began to tire. The bigger holes we opened led to longer runs and deeper passes—at least until this drive stalled before we reached midfield.

At that point, we faced a third and 15, a down (third) and distance (15 yards) with low odds for any offence, even ours. This marked the kind of play that would define seasons, and in this case, for us, a championship lost or won. Against a defence exhausted by our hurry-up approach, Pat scrambled away from the defenders who were chasing him and floated a long pass to receiver Tyreek Hill, who caught it. Instantly, the 44-yard bomb became part of Super Bowl lore. My job on that historic sequence: block and block and don't stop blocking. Don't hold on to the defender's jersey, either, incurring the kind of penalty that can portend disaster. I did my job successfully, and three plays later we crossed into the end zone, having trimmed the deficit to three points.

Next offensive drive, same thing, starting with five minutes and 10 seconds left on the clock. Pat completed three short passes, continuing to grind the Niners down. With almost no break between plays, that's all prelude, a set-up for another big play—in this case, a heave to Sammy Watkins down the right side of the field. It went for 38 yards. We scored again, and I could see the body language change for the defenders, who started sniping at each other and complaining to the referees. I could see how gassed they were, as they sucked in air, bent over, hands placed on hips. They had not been able to substitute freely, nor find brief pockets of rest. We would stop them again, and score again, for a 24–20 advantage with just 2:44 left on the clock. We had broken them. We'd secured our win.

IT'S HARD to describe the energy I felt in those moments leading up to the end of the game. It's like a drug. Like magic. I was so exhausted, and so happy, all at once. Look, every team in the NFL is good; many, elite. To win that game, in that way, with those stakes, with our offence marching down to score against one of the best defences in pro football—there's nothing better. That's what we work for, what we endure pain for, why I play a sport like football in the first place.

When the game clock hit triple zeroes, the final score read 31–20 in favour of the Chiefs. I remember Pat screaming so loud that it echoed off the tunnels beneath the stadium. I might have been yelling louder. I lifted tight end Travis Kelce—one of the funniest, best-baller, most loyal goofballs I know—off his feet. We'd scored three unanswered touchdowns in the second half. We had rushed for 129 yards, a direct result of elite offensive-line play. Pat had thrown for 286 yards. None of that mattered in the immediate aftermath, though, not as I thought back over my improbable journey, the path I had taken from Canada into the NFL, pushing the model of the student athlete to the highest level.

At that moment, I was both a medical school graduate and a Super Bowl champion, the combination as unlikely as the fact I had just become the first person from my province to win the biggest game in sports.

THE TIME that passed between the final play and my chance to lift the Lombardi Trophy remains vague. Was it an hour? Three hours? We ran onto the field, we were showered in confetti, we celebrated together, as teammates.

Amid the euphoria, hundreds of broadcasters rushed toward us with their camera crews. A familiar face emerged. It was Didier Orméjuste, a TV reporter from Montreal who had followed me since the beginning of my career at McGill, starting in 2010. The last time I had seen Didier was two weeks earlier, after our victory over Tennessee in the AFC Championship Game. I'd been so excited to see someone from home, I'd accidentally knocked him right out of the camera frame during a live interview. On the field in Miami Gardens, just as Didier began to interview me, the scene unspooling live on TVs back in Quebec, I yelled, "Don't worry! I'm not going to push you this time!"

As I stumbled through the interview, hardly knowing what I was saying, I spotted my father, François, my mother, Guylaine, and my girlfriend, Florence, out of the corner of my eye, making their way toward me through the pandemonium. I stopped mid-question and sprinted toward them. We formed a teary family huddle. The camera continued rolling, sending video footage of this emotional moment back to Canada, and to everyone I remained in contact with and loved. So many of the viewers, including those I did not know at all, understood my story and the improbable nature of that moment. I looked into the stands, at my more than 30 friends who'd travelled to south Florida. I pointed at them. I would not have been standing there without their enduring support.

I didn't know then that Flo and my parents had got lost on the maze route down to the field. Or that they had spent several anxious minutes scanning all over, trying to find me. Flo would later describe our embrace as an "intense moment of joy." She likes to say that she couldn't—that she *still can't*—process the series of events that had led us there. We both knew that if any one thing had happened differently, we might not have been there at all.

A few hours later, rather than head to the glittery nightclub where many of my teammates celebrated until sunrise, I went back to our hotel. After I showered, Flo and my agent, Sasha, picked me up. I had told them that if we won the Super Bowl, I wanted to do something with the people I was closest to; if we lost, I might instead sit in my hotel room and brood.

A world-class planner, Sasha had found an Italian restaurant in Miami, usually closed on Sundays, that he hoped we could rent out. It turned out that the owner was actually a transplant from Montreal. He'd moved to the US about 15 years earlier and opened a small spot on the second storey of a building near the beach. He told Sasha he would open for us that Sunday, win or lose.

By the time we got there, it was nearly 2 a.m. We took the elevator to the second floor, and when the door opened, I saw my family and close friends, the most important people in my life. Charles was there, and other friends from medical school, from McGill, from my old CEGEP football team. Even my grandmother was there. Everyone stood, cheered, whooped and hollered. My ears rung. Champagne corks popped, food was served, and we all marvelled. My God, I'd done it. I was a world champion. I actually was. For real. Nobody asked me, "Man, during that third down, what did you think about this?" We talked more about emotion than the specifics of the game. How my parents had walked around the stadium because they were so stressed. I'd never asked them before what it was like to watch me on TV, to see me get injured, how that felt. So when they told me, we talked about that, and how, during a game three years earlier, they'd done this, or how once when I got injured, they were watching from Montreal. We talked about high school memories, football memories, random stuff. It was just a normal dinner with the people I most cared about.

Except that we were in Miami, it was the middle of the night, and we had three generations of Duvernay-Tardifs in the same place because of a football game I had won in the United States. Oh, and just like the rest of us, my grandmother stayed up till 4 a.m.

TWO DAYS later, we went to the parade in Kansas City, the kind of event that, a few months later, would be totally inconceivable. Cramming a million-plus people into a handful of downtown streets? Drinking, and cheering, and hugging in sub-zero temperatures? It's likely that many fans unwittingly passed along the virus that day, infecting strangers and fellow revellers, who then went back into their communities, continuing the spread.

I arrived there nursing a hangover. In those post-triumph days, after I smudged the Lombardi with my lips, I loved the time I was able to spend with my teammates. Season over, cup in hand, our interactions were no longer hampered by time constraints or the competitive nature of our jobs. We no longer had the next NFL Sunday hanging like an anvil over our heads. We were free to just bask in the moment together—the aftermath of a historic season, playoff run and championship. No one else could really understand what it took to get where we were, how it felt.

We rode buses through downtown Kansas City. The streets were so packed that the crowds seemed less like a collection of individuals and more like walls of humanity painted over in our team colours. I love those fans and their devotion to the Chiefs. They had waited through all the missed kicks, the bad calls, the "buzzard's luck"—for exactly what we'd finally delivered. They had stood there, in the snow, the year before, when we'd lost at home to New England. They'd remained in the stands after we had beaten San Francisco, thousands of miles from home, and turned Hard Rock into Arrowhead Southeast. All they wanted at that parade was to say thank you, and I wanted to thank them back, because I understood what an advantage it was to play in a city driven by its football team, especially when you're from another country. The vibe helps. The home-field advantage is real. And they'd welcomed me, from my first day, like one of their own.

I could feel that history, the lifting of the burden, the future teeming with promise, on those buses. I could sense how much it meant. I could hear what seemed like every single person lose their mind when Pat caught a beer, chugged it and spiked the

35

can on national TV. The whole scene—and all the pivotal events that led to it—reminded me of why sports matter, of the emotion baked into the games we play, the way that teams connect communities, through the worst times and the best ones. I hardly sat in the bus that I was assigned to. I mostly jogged in front, forever playing my part: offensive lineman. I slapped hands, bumped chests, drank beers. At that point, still early February 2020, confirmed novel coronavirus cases around the world were ticking up, the tally rising each day.

After the celebrations ended, Flo and I packed up our KC apartment and got our things in order while Sasha acted as my PR firm, handling dozens of media requests by himself. Finally, we flew home to Montreal. There, I had my very own parade. There must have been 5,000 people, including Mayor Valérie Plante, in St. Helen's Island Park when I was honoured by the city. Police lined the perimeter, idling on bikes, sitting atop horses, cheering just like the fans. A projection screen flashed pictures of children who'd written me cards of encouragement for Super Bowl week. A video played of us celebrating the win. Even the reporters seemed excited, maybe also a touch proud. I was overcome. It was one thing for Chiefs diehards in Kansas City to show up en masse for a party, quite another for my fellow citizens in Montreal, thousands of miles away from Missouri, to do the same.

I dropped a ceremonial puck before a Montreal Canadiens game, standing near all my hockey heroes, the players on my favourite team. The ovation, delivered by a packed crowd, lasted for more than three minutes. I was stunned. I felt sheepish. It may have registered as the longest cheer ever given for an offensive lineman. I could see the players cheering for me too. After the din finally quieted, team officials directed me toward the red carpet I should follow to leave the rink. But I was so excited, I ran out onto the ice instead, made a beeline toward the Habs bench and high-fived everyone in sight.

Soon after that game, I visited Quebec's National Assembly and received a medal from the premier. Everyone I bumped into wanted pictures. I signed hundreds of autographs. In some ways I felt like an imposter, or someone who is living a life that's not his own. Maybe this resembled everyday life for, say, LeBron James. Or Drake.

To see the community of Chiefs fans in Missouri and then to experience the remarkable support back home touched me. I understood that winning the Super Bowl was a team accomplishment. In the game we won, I had not even touched the ball. I also knew that winning the Super Bowl would change my life. Every time you push the boundaries of what you're physically or mentally capable of, you change your world in a certain way. I changed my world when I got drafted. I changed my world when I graduated in medicine. Each time you accomplish something, your reality, your context, your horizon has shifted; life can't go back to the way it was before.

But on my return to Canada, I came across something I had not necessarily expected from my fellow citizens, even if perhaps I should have: pride. I'm sure many NFL champions feel similar emotions when they return to their hometowns after the ultimate triumph. The difference for me was that my hometown was actually more of a home country. The support I felt from people across Canada, the widespread excitement over our win, reminded me of the profound place sports can hold in people's lives, just how much, even to society as a whole, sports can mean.

*

AS THE DAYS passed, and the post-championship adrena-lin waned, the chaos of those initial post-championship weeks began to wear on me. My calendar had filled and filled until it overflowed with obligations. Montreal was simply too intense. Politicians asked for meetings with me; even the office of Prime Minister Justin Trudeau reached out.

If something like *too much celebrating* exists, that's where I was. Perhaps that became most clear after the hockey game. I dropped the puck, bathed in that standing O, accepted congratulations, briefly met with the team doctors (legends in the medical com-munity at my university, McGill) and departed immediately—not because I wanted to, but because I had another obligation to ful-fill. Rather than stay for the game, which I would have paid to attend under less frenetic circumstances, I went out to the park-ing lot. I had to change into dress pants and a suit for my next event. It was dark. There was snow on the ground. I didn't know where to put the honorary puck the Canadiens had given me. It had my name, and my team's title, engraved on one side. I sat it on the roof of the car.

I thought, jokingly, that I better not lose it.

I quickly changed, stowed my stuff in the car, started the igni-tion, and Sasha and I pulled away from the Bell Centre. Not far away, I stopped at a red light. That's when I heard the thud. And I saw a black disc shoot down right before my eyes. I'd left the puck on top of the car, and when I hit the brakes, it had tumbled down over the windshield.

I jumped out of the car to pick it up and heard someone yell, "LDT!"

When I got back in the car, Sasha said, "Can you imagine if somebody had found your puck in a snowbank? For sure that would have made the cover of the newspaper."

We were both so tired that we couldn't stop laughing.

This whole situation was unreal.

Yes, my life had changed. Now, more than ever, I needed time to process in what ways, and how dramatically.

CHAPTER 3

THE
SAILING TRIP

U sually, soon after the football season comes to a close, I
resume medical school—classes or clinical rotation. After a
certain date, because of my other obligations, I'm unavail-
able for media or public events. But that year, after our Super
Bowl win, when the attention and requests for interviews and
appearances reached a fever pitch, I had nothing, no definitive
reason to easily explain disappearing back into private life. Since
my conversation with Mitch after the AFC Championship,
about what I was going to do with my future—that old football-
versus-medicine conundrum—I hadn't had a moment to sit down
and digest any of the extraordinary events that had taken place.

Flo and I went through so much during that time (in a good
way), so many emotions. Some mornings we would wake up and
wonder if the last two months had really happened. The whole
situation was so intense for both of us. She had turned her
schedule around in order to attend the playoffs. We knew, at that
point, we needed time to reconnect and process everything we'd
been through. It might sound really elitist to say this (I know the

option isn't available at the drop of a hat to just anyone), but I felt the only way to find some much-needed quiet time was to leave. To get away from Montreal for a while.

Flo and I came up with a quick plan. We flew to Antigua. There, we spent a week at a hotel, letting all the hype, pomp and adrenalin seep away. Well, I did, anyway. Flo, an art curator and author with a master's degree in art history, had another deadline. She was writing an article for an international art magazine, and the mayhem around the Super Bowl had caused some interruption, to say the least, to her work life. So, for a week, while I relaxed, worked out, tried to have a little fun, Flo wrote.

A situation like that—me hanging around with zero obligations while Flo works—adds a bit of balance to our relationship. At times like these, she's the one with deadlines, the one who dictates our schedule, and I'm the one who has to be flexible. This creates an important, necessary balance in our life together. When Flo and I met, I was a medical student at McGill University, spending most of my days at my parents' bakery on the south shore of Montreal, listening to recordings of my lectures at slow speed. Having entered medical school at an English university with only the most basic CEGEP English course behind me—more on why I was doing med school in English instead of French later—I couldn't follow the professors in class. So I'd resorted to digital recordings, something that would be fairly normal now, especially after these years of COVID, during which so much education has gone virtual. Back then, Internet connections weren't as reliable; bandwidth was smaller, speeds slower. I was living in the basement of my grandmother's apartment and found it easier to do this "online" study at the bakery.

Every day around eleven thirty, Flo would come in and pick up some bread for the restaurant where she worked, just across from the bakery. Sometimes she'd take her breaks at the bakery, sipping coffee and reading the newspaper. I was drawn to her. Not only was she beautiful, but she was interested in what was going on in the world. She was curious. I began to notice that I was waiting for her to come in. Eventually, I spoke to her. At some point, I asked her to join me for lunch. It took six months of talking, being friendly and working close to each other before we finally got together.

By then, what might seem on the surface like a vast gulf between our worlds was clear. I was a medical student; she was an art history major. I was captain of the football team; she'd been a serious ballet dancer who'd had to give up dancing due to an injury. I was at McGill, an English university, an "old school" kind of school, sort of the pride of Canada; she was at UQAM, a French-speaking, more liberal institution. To us, though, the intersection between our two worlds was interesting, even exciting. And we had more in common than might first appear. We were both high-level athletes. We'd both grown up in situations that threw us into new places, contexts and cultures. In her case, her father's naval industry career meant she'd lived in Nova Scotia, Texas, Louisiana and the Bahamas. In fact, the year my family's second sailing trip had taken us to the Bahamas, Flo was living there. And though she's in a completely different industry than I am, in her realm she's unstoppable. She's a go-getter. She's ambitious. She's really project driven and looking to make changes: in the way art is exhibited and shared and experienced by people, and for artists themselves, and the conditions in which they work.

When our relationship began, nobody had any inkling that football would become, for a significant period of time, the focal point of my life, especially not in such a profound, all-encompassing way.

And because the demands of NFL football are so intense, and so incompatible with anything like an ordinary life, it's Flo, with her freelancer's schedule, who's wound up accommodating, for the past several years, my all-consuming commitments, my work-out regime, my appointments, my six months a year in Kansas City, my, ahem, playoff runs and championship games. It goes on and on, even sometimes in the off-season. Because Flo's the private contractor, and because, like the balanced person she is, she consciously builds her schedule so she can enjoy life beyond her work, there's that intrinsic conflict: she's the one who is expected to be flexible, to move her commitments around, so that we can have a life together. I hope one day I will be able to help her with one of her projects in the same way she has always helped me.

That week in Antigua, with me waiting for her to finish and submit her article, the shoe was on the other foot. It was good for us both.

No longer operating in survival mode, back to what felt like our ordinary selves—especially me—we then flew to St. Lucia and drove into the jungle. We went far enough that we lost cell service. We kept going. We were in the middle of nowhere, a phrase that's kind of a long-standing joke between us. Way back when Flo and I had finally got together after all those months of polite chit-chat in the bakery, the timing pretty much stank. The very next day I was leaving for Gaspé, a city in a remote part of eastern Quebec, to teach sailing for the summer. Flo said, "Oh, that's OK. I'm planning a road trip. I might stop and see you, because it's on my way."

Actually, Gaspé is like the end of the world. It isn't on the way to anywhere. But that was Flo's way of maintaining her independence, which she's still really good at doing after 12 years together, including eight of me being in the NFL, and I love that about her. She drove to the Gaspé Peninsula and we laughed about it and spent a week together—our first great week of so, so many.

This time, we'd gone into the middle of nowhere together. We found our destination at the end of a dirt road: a marina where we rented a 40-foot sailboat.

Sailing can seem like a calm pursuit, especially when you're standing onshore watching a boat, sails up, drift along the water—a tranquil leisure activity. It's not. There are maps to read, sails to tie, winds to gauge, weather forecasts to study, radars to monitor, docks to find, tides to manage and maritime rules to follow.

Because Flo and I were not using our own boat, we had to stay on top of all this while becoming acquainted with an unfamiliar, fairly large vessel. That's the work side. On the exploration side, a sailing trip couldn't be more different from a beach holiday. You're always on the move. There are towns to visit, coves to explore. We had a loose, fluid schedule, and moved through the Caribbean without too much planning beyond what was required for safety. Sometimes we'd climb off the boat after stopping near one picturesque oceanfront town or another. We'd walk in, find a restaurant and order some local lobster, conch fritters or any available fresh fish. At night, I would grab my phone, check the weather report for the next day and find a place to dock the next night. We'd take in the night sky, the stars, the vastness of the sea.

I was so glad that Flo, who had done some sailing with her family in childhood, had agreed to this kind of holiday adventure. After the intensity and excitement of that football season, this completely unrelated but wholly absorbing "holiday" was exactly what I needed.

*

FOR THE DUVERNAY-TARDIFS, our collective happy place is the open water. Sun beaming down from above. Shades on. Endless blue and turquoise, light and dark, cavernous and shallow, spreading forever in every direction. Beaches. Islands. Palm trees. We first discovered our sailing spirit with our initial year-long trip, in 2000, when I was nine years old and in grade five.

Neither of my parents had any background in sailing. Still, my father had promised a voyage to my mother on their very first date, when they'd met for coffee. He couldn't make a full-fledged sailing excursion possible right away, so instead, he took a series of calculated steps—the same way I did with both medicine and football—to inch an improbable, fantastical dream closer toward reality.

First, my parents bought a boat. Then, for four years straight, they put aside 25 percent of their salaries. Both my parents, at that point, worked in agriculture—my dad as a teacher, my mom as an inspector for the government. In their spare time, they learned how to sail, taking increasingly longer jaunts and learning everything from weather to storm patterns to the fickle nature of the ocean. Eventually, they had enough experience and enough money put aside for our whole family to embark on a year-long voyage: myself, my parents, my older sister, Delphine, and my younger sister, Marilou.

My parents' plans were ambitious, but also frugal and practical. They stockpiled bags of rice, collected cans of vegetables and hunted for any fishing gear they could find on discount racks at sporting goods stores. Supplies gathered, we set sail, travelling from Montreal to Boston to New York, from Delaware Bay, to Chesapeake Bay, then on to Miami, and farther south. We shot through the Gulf Stream, then made stops at various islands all over the Bahamas and the Exumas.

Marilou learned how to walk on that boat. On that first trip, both my sisters slept on the dinner table, which could be folded into a bed. My bed was a thin mattress jammed underneath a bench. We mostly ate rice with canned vegetables. My dad and I would also spear fish, asking between dives what my mom and sisters wanted to eat for dinner. We'd drop anchor just off a beach and cook onshore, sparking a fire next to a palm tree. We'd make our own bread by turning flour and water into dough then digging a hole, shoving a pan inside and putting charcoal in for a makeshift oven. We learned to drill a hole into the shell of a conch and drag it behind the boat as we travelled; the salt water kept the protein fresh. We picked up many tips like that from other travellers along the way.

We had gallons of soft water hanging on the side of the boat, and wind turbines and solar panels. We hung bananas and bags of coconuts over the side. It was not your typical Caribbean holiday sailboat. It was not a luxurious trip. But for that year, it was our home. And we were so freaking happy.

That year on the boat was one striking example of the way I was raised, in a family that encouraged all its members to adopt a curious, resourceful and innovative approach to life. It was a way of living exemplified by my paternal grandfather, Guy Tardif, and my grandmother, Ghislaine. A long-time politician, he served as Quebec's minister of transport and consumer protections for nearly a decade, helping to protect our French language and culture. Like the rest of our family, my grandfather possessed a fierce independent streak and cared little for convention. In the mid-1980s, after losing in his bid for re-election, he retired from his distinguished public service career and founded a vineyard in Saint-Denis-sur-Richelieu. He came to produce wine, cider and unending joy from what was once a field of corn.

In 2001, after our first sailing trip, my parents joined the enterprise as full partners. My family became a team. My grandfather handled all the licences, permits and paperwork, both nearby and as far away as Europe and Japan, where we exported the ice cider wine. My grandmother ran the marketing, the boutique and the reception area, and my parents steered the operation, from the grapes and how we grew them to the fermentation process. That venture, our first family business, demanded countless hours of sweat equity from the whole family. My dad never went back to teaching. My mom never returned to her inspector gig. And we three children became full-time pupils of life and all the directions it spun in. That vineyard became our new classroom.

I learned how to bottle wine and affix labels like a pro. At age eight, I would suggest bottles of wine for guests and lead group tastings. I didn't drink yet, obviously, but I could describe our ingredients, blends and flavour profiles in great detail. I must have sounded like the youngest wannabe sommelier in the world.

Over the years, we added thousands of grapevines, until more than 10,000 intertwined across the property. Each spring, when the temperature dropped below freezing, something that would damage the grapes, my family would spend nights lighting hundreds of small fires near the vineyard in order to protect that year's harvest. If we failed to spark those flames, we could lose everything in the fall.

I would sometimes miss school after staying up all night manning the fires. Other times I would stagger in, bone-tired. While it was exhausting, I think I learned more important lessons working on the vineyard than I would have in, say, another math class.

Eventually, my grandpa realized that it's hard to make great wine in Quebec, because the relatively small number of warm days prevents the fruit from fully maturing and reduces the sugar and flavour content. The property was also home to a small apple orchard of about 2,000 trees. And so we adapted, pivoting into cider production. Our whole family tended the apple trees. Before I was old enough to get a driver's licence, I was driving the truck to collect the fallen apples. At first, we made regular cider. Then we realized that if we left the apples on the trees at the beginning of the winter, those apples, once pressed and extracted, made for a far sweeter juice. It also could be fermented and made into liquor, in the same way vineyards in Ontario manufacture ice wine. With this realization, and its implementation, business exploded. When we ran out of space to plant orchard trees, we leased land all over Quebec and rooted trees wherever we could plant them, using dozens of new orchards to meet the ballooning demand.

By following my grandparents into this life of entrepreneurship, of creating, maintaining and expanding businesses, my parents imparted important lessons to me: find comfort and wisdom in new undertakings; don't just consider the directions your life might take, but pursue them with everything you have. My hopes didn't have to be realistic, or viewed that way. You can have so many dreams, but they don't mean anything if you don't go after them, my parents would say. The sailing trip, the vineyard, the orchard—the proof of that maxim was all around me.

Growing up in Mont Saint-Hilaire, a small community an hour outside Montreal, I went to alternative school. The school's approach to education meshed with my family's approach to life. There was a focus on arts such as dancing and painting, but mostly on learning *how* to learn. I took that principle, and my family's entrepreneurial spirit, to heart.

One year, when I was 13, after watching some videos about how to raise chickens, rather than find a summer job, I decided to go into the poultry business—for myself. I built a coop and bought a hundred one-day-old chicks. They had just hatched from their eggs, and they were small, yellow and beautiful, almost angelic. When I would beg my mother for extra money to feed my brood, she helped, but only for so long. I started mowing lawns to purchase bags of grain. But one chick would die from a broken leg, another would die after being stepped on. I could see my profit evaporating with every mishap in the coop. By the time they were ready to sell, only 70 had survived. I added up the pounds of meat I expected to yield, and figured how much I could store in our new oversized chicken-specific freezer. I calculated my margins, so that I knew I needed to peddle my birds for six dollars a pound to make a profit, which is how I learned the hard way that the chicken business, at such a small scale, offers a less than ideal cash-flow situation.

My projects were not limited to poultry. Or to money-making. I played the violin. I learned piano. I taught myself woodworking. I also learned how to manufacture maple syrup from tree sap. At 13, I opened a business with two of my best friends, and we named it, naturally, The Sailors. I planted basil in our garden to make pesto, and we sold the finished product to nearby agricultural farms or at food fairs. One summer, my "partners" and I made $3,000.

I can't help but smile when I think of that period of my life. It was one project after another. What was the secret to such productivity? I guess the secret was a barely functional Internet connection, no cellphone (before I went to college), plus a strict, limited and enforced policy for watching our family television. (My parents never sprung for cable.)

It wasn't just parental influence, though. I was a kid with energy to spare. And that meant that sports were part of the mix.

I played badminton and hockey. I cross-country skied. To be honest, my foray into those pursuits didn't exactly scream *future professional athlete*. I tried soccer too, but I was not good at soccer, not at all.

I also spent a lot of time with one of my best friends. We were adventurers at heart, teenagers who desired to build fortresses and survive in forests, but when we took those pursuits inside, we wreaked havoc, destroying everything in sight. My friend's mom decided we needed to harness our excess energy. She suggested this wild game called football.

It's not as though the sport is unknown in Canada. But it was to me. It sounds crazy, with the Canadian Football League growing its audience every year and with the NFL splashed all over our televisions, but because of our snail-like Internet connection, our limited TV time, and both my family's and my own litany of creative endeavours, I knew nothing—literally, *nothing*—about the sport that would become such a huge part of my life.

When I learned the basics, the game appealed to me. Especially, at that age, the physical aspect of it. You line up against somebody. It's your strength, your speed, your willpower against theirs. I went to spring tryouts for a youth league but weighed in over the limit. I wasn't obese, I've just always been big for my age. The only option I had was to play with older kids, but that possibility, which might increase my risk of injury, concerned my parents. We agreed that I should wait a year then try again, hoping that the gap in size between me and my peers would close.

"If you really love football," my dad told me, "you can get back into it."

In the meantime, I played badminton (I'd become a mixed doubles specialist) and the Duvernay-Tardif clan set sail once again. My parents bought a new sailboat, this time a full 40 feet in length, and planned a second year-long excursion for the family. We left Canada the fall when I would have begun my junior year of high school. My parents stowed textbooks on board. My father would teach us science; my mother, humanities, social sciences and French. The trip itself would be a geography class, albeit outside, in classrooms that resembled scenic paintings.

This time, I wasn't simply along for the ride. At 16, I was old enough to help navigate the vessel, alternating shifts with my mom and dad, along with interpreting tide charts and monitoring our radar devices. Sometimes I caught dinner, which meant I had to master spearfishing—and avoid the sharks that often circled whenever blood spilled from the prey I pierced. I discovered that inlets were good places to probe for fish. I learned to operate the metal spear like a slingshot. If I missed my bull's eye, the top third of the head, the fish often just kept going, our dinner swimming away. When we spotted other boats with Canadian flags, I asked them for fishing tips and discussed techniques. I would then apply the lessons I learned to my next hunt. We also sometimes dropped fishing lines behind our boat, which netted the occasional large mahi mahi that would feed all five of us for days.

One week some friends flew to meet us and travel with us, so for a little while we had seven people on the boat. It was pretty cool. The night before they left, we were spearfishing and we had our usual fire on the beach. We were grilling fish, having fun, not noticing that the tide was coming in and that our inflatable dinghy, which we hadn't anchored properly, was drifting away. We would have to swim back to the boat, which was anchored in the bay a hundred metres offshore. We were all a little nervous about this, for understandable reasons: we'd seen sharks swimming nearby while we were prepping our fish.

The island we were on was deserted. The night was pitch-black. There were no other boats. So we lit some palm leaves on fire, put them in the water and used them to see where we were going. We all got onto the boat—*phew*—but we were still anxious to find the indispensable dinghy. While I was brushing the horizon with a big spotlight, one of our guests, at the tip of the boat, looked back, got blinded by the beam of light and fell into the hatch. She broke two vertebrae. We had to have her medevaced out. Sailing is a dream vacation until stuff starts to go wrong. Due to the close quarters and unpredictable elements, when things go bad, they can quickly escalate.

Another time, we were sailing straight for a couple of days to make up some ground. Those were busy days: you're focused on preparing food, sleeping and driving the boat. My dad, my mom and I rotated shifts at the helm. There was no school those days, which was awesome, but Delphine and Marilou had to find games to play to fill the time. They can be long days on a boat, with not much going on. Delphine came up into the cockpit at one point just as the wind suddenly changed direction. The boom for the mainsail flipped around and she got hit so hard by the rope on the end of the sail that she got ejected down into the main cabin and broke her clavicle. We didn't know the extent of the damage right away, and sailed to a nearby island in search of a clinic for an X-ray. The only thing there was a small private port for yachts, a port so luxurious that, though the island itself had no health services for its few hundred inhabitants, it boasted a veterinary clinic for yacht owners' dogs. Delphine got her X-ray there.

On that family trip, it felt as if we stopped at every one of the 700-odd islands in the Bahamas. Some remain unoccupied, too small even to be dots on a map. Others featured only family huts that had rarely been visited. But whenever we stopped at an island that had a schoolhouse, I knew my parents would be dropping me off to spend the day there. I would be surrounded by unfamiliar faces and forced to communicate any way I could think of, while my parents searched for groceries. All three of the Duvernay-Tardif siblings are shy to some degree, but back then I was probably the most outgoing; and so, whenever we entered a new school, my sisters would hang back and I would step in front. Back then, I was already an offensive lineman.

While my parents wanted to immerse us as much as possible in other cultures, they also wanted to show us that *how* we learned mattered more than reciting facts or attaining high test scores and grades. They told us we would carry that learning process with us for the rest of our lives, as long as we remained curious. These experiences led to the development of our family ethos: adapt, learn, thrive. Those school visits are what I remember most from that time—not the scenic geography classroom, not even the great shark escape. I became more open-minded, increasingly aware of so many lives that were nothing like my own.

My life as I would come to know it started on that trip, because it taught me to pursue what I wanted without conventional expectations. Make it work. Find a way. Light the damn palm trees on fire! Whatever it takes. I could be, I could do, anything I wanted.

IN 2003, a few years before that voyage, my grandpa—the man who had always taught me, through both his words and his actions, to never try to be "normal"—died. After a while, with him gone, my family decided to exit the cider business. When we returned from our second year of sailing, my parents opted to open a bakery. They travelled to France for an informal apprenticeship—by air this time, not boat—studying techniques and learning their new craft. This came naturally to them, because both had agricultural backgrounds, and agriculture is central to making bread. The French traditionally use sourdough, but my parents came up with their own recipe twists. They used a slower fermentation process, which added a unique flavour profile. In partnership with local farmers they researched different varieties of grain, eventually finding an ideal mix that would yield a divine flour. Those ingredients, combined with their *savoir faire*, made for an agreeable texture and taste.

We named our bakery Le Pain dans les Voiles. That's French for "Bread in the Sails," a nod to our sailboat escapades. And it turned out there were similarities between making wine and baking bread. Both involve yeast and fermentation, exact measurements, and time elements that must be followed. The biggest difference is that with wine, operators have to start over every year; with bread, they restart every morning. The pace and the challenge suited my parents. By 2011, they'd captured second place in the baguette competition at the World Cup of Baking. (Yes, such a thing exists.)

Meanwhile, I took another run at football. There was no football team at my small high school, so I played on a team in the nearest city. I was still into badminton too. I was clearly hyperactive, and looking back, it's still hard for me to process how much exercise I would do in a day. I'd get up early and ride 15 kilometres to school, where I practised badminton, showered, studied all day, played hockey over lunch, then rode 10 kilometres to the city for football practice. Sometimes I'd forget to bring enough changes of clothes, so I'd put my shoulder pads on over my white school shirt. My mom didn't like that. She'd come to pick me up after practice and we'd drive home with my bike lashed to a rack on the car.

I still knew next to nothing about football at the highest levels—nothing about CFL franchises, college powers in the States or NFL stars, and almost nothing about how this strange sport actually worked. And I'll be honest: on the field, I wasn't very good. But I liked the game, loved the physical contact and dug the camaraderie I developed with my teammates. Plus, I was big, and I was athletic for my size. And I knew from experience that I could learn to do pretty much anything. In Quebec, you finish high school in grade 11 and then attend CEGEP for two years, a program that combines what would be, elsewhere, the last year of high school with a first year of post-secondary. It allows for more independence for 17- and 18-year-olds. They can specialize in their studies, and they often move away from home. It's kind of like junior college. And it has football.

I decided I would go for CEGEP football. Who knew if I would make it. But I had the bug. I couldn't not try.

TWENTY YEARS LATER, as Flo and I travelled through the warm southern Caribbean, February turned into March. The NFL championship and the heady, hectic days that had followed gradually faded. I started to feel lighter. We sometimes encountered massive yachts that reminded me of the first times I'd seen boats like that, back on that second trip, when I was 16 years old and completely awed. They'd seemed to me then like floating mansions. When we spied their owners struggling to anchor, my father and I would climb into our small motorized dinghy and drive over and help, lifting the anchor to lessen the tension in the ropes they needed to affix to nearby hooks. If we had extra fish, we would offer them a freshly caught dinner. They would often give us something in return. One captain handed me a $20 bill. Another offered us potato chips. Whether a person is wealthy or pinching pennies, kindness, humanity and empathy can go both ways.

Whenever our spotty Internet allowed, I would check CNN or *La Presse*, a major daily newspaper in Quebec, for updates. The news was concerning. The novel coronavirus I had first been asked about at that Super Bowl podium, now officially known as COVID-19, was ramping up. Infected patients had begun to pop up all over, from Hong Kong through Asia, to Iran, then Europe, and now the United States.

Every time I picked up my phone to check on the state of the world, there was some new and unsettling COVID-19 development. It was beginning to overwhelm health care systems. It was threatening professional sports. And it was starting to close borders, like the one we needed to cross to get back into Canada.

When I read that, I thought, *Holy shit*.

We needed to hustle back home. We docked in St. Lucia and changed our departure date so we wouldn't get stranded. Then we sped to the airport. We boarded the plane, but before takeoff my phone pinged with an alert. Starting at midnight, any traveller coming into Canada from another country, including Canadian citizens, would need to self-quarantine for two weeks.

Our arrival time meant we would fall on the quarantine side of the line. My initial reaction was one of shock. I had plans and obligations I didn't want to delay. And to have to stay home for 14 days? The very notion was difficult to process. I could hardly imagine staying put for that long. Who would have thought, then, that we'd be at this for two years and more? Who'd have thought we'd still find ways to experience joy even while under curfew? That's my biggest take-away from the past two years: our ability to adapt.

But I didn't know that then. Not yet. By the time we landed, the vibe felt different, more critical and intense. I grabbed my backpack from the airport carousel. I tried to reconcile what I'd heard and read with what I saw in that airport, at that baggage claim. I thought: *There's just no way all these people are going to stay home for 14 days. People have jobs, obligations, meetings.* It was impossible to conceive that all the people in the airport were just going to, impromptu, go straight home and into isolation. Then I extended the logic: Say there were thousands of people in the world doing the same thing, ignoring the same out-of-the-blue rules, downplaying the same threat. Imagine how many of *them* would catch COVID-19, and how many others they would pass the virus onto, and how many lives could potentially be lost. At that level—what in medicine we call a population level—the scenario was horrific. But I won't lie, from an individual stand-point, the idea of losing personal liberty in order to protect our society collectively was not super-appealing to me at first.

When the world first went into lockdown, we still didn't know that much about the virus and there was a lot of anxiety due to the uncertainty. Even though health officials initially told us the lockdown would only last a few weeks, it quickly became clear that with no vaccine in sight, those isolation measures—which were the only way we had to fight the virus—were there to stay.

Flo and I went home and into isolation. By the time our quarantine was over, almost every country had enacted protocols meant to slow the spread of the virus. People were dying; hospitals were overwhelmed. I no longer knew when I might be able to return to Kansas City. I only knew that I wanted to find some way to help.

CHAPTER 4

THE TRAINING

Montreal in mid-April offers glimmers of spring, some mild days, enticing hints of the melt to come—but winter has yet to fully retreat. Luckily, hockey season's still in full swing, especially if, as they were in 2010, the Canadiens are stirring things up in the playoffs. I remember I went to a sports bar with some friends to watch Game Two of the Habs–Caps playoff series. The party stretched long past the final whistle; so long, in fact, that I slept at a buddy's house, on a couch in his basement.

In the morning, I peeled myself off the couch to answer my phone. An official at the Université du Québec was on the line. He asked where I was. My interview was starting in 10 minutes. What?! That woke me up, and fast. He meant my medical school interview, a single event that would decide my fate, determining whether I was eligible to study medicine at any of the top three French-language medical schools in the province to which I'd applied: Université de Montréal, Université de Sherbrooke and Université Laval.

No, no, I said to the voice on the phone. He must be mistaken. My interview was the following week.

It wasn't. I had written down the wrong date. I panicked. I asked, I pleaded: Could I reschedule? No, that wasn't an option.

I paced my friend's kitchen, half-dressed and chugging an oversized Gatorade. I considered jumping in a taxicab, knowing I would arrive more than an hour late, with dishevelled hair, wrinkled clothes and half my usual brainpower.

That wouldn't do.

I accepted defeat. It wasn't going to happen. Right there, in that kitchen, I thought my dream of studying medicine had evaporated. I'd worked for years just to land that interview; in one morning, due to one massive, and entirely avoidable, mistake, all my carefully laid-out plans collapsed. The following week I called all the football coaches at those schools and asked if they could help me schedule another interview. It quickly became clear that they could not. I was crushed.

But the truth is, I didn't deserve a shortcut. And now, I'm grateful. It was a twist of fate, a moment of carelessness that completely and utterly changed my life.

GROWING UP, I didn't want to become a doctor. I wanted to be an engineer.

I loved projects, and I loved to build things. I would pester my parents with endless questions. Why, for example, did our car's engine run that way?

"Well," my dad would explain, "there's a cylinder, and a piston, and an explosion that drives power."

"Why is there an explosion?"

"Well, because there's gas."

"Why gas?"

"Well, gas is made up of molecules, a bunch of carbon and a

couple hydrogen," my dad would respond, with his infinite patience. "If you inflate a balloon with hydrogen, it's going to deflate, because the hydrogen is so small it's going to leak through the balloon."

I was the same way at school, question after question. For a long time this didn't go so well for me. Imagine trying to teach a class of 30 kids, to get through a lesson, when one of them just won't stop asking questions. I wasn't throwing paper planes or doing stupid stuff like that, I never tried to be mean, but I can understand why my teachers wanted to strangle me. They really did want to. At one point I came close to being expelled. The situation was so bad that my parents repeatedly had to show up at the school to meet with my teachers.

Luckily, I went to a secondary school that was really big on teaching you how to learn. They recognized that my questions were constant because I was so curious, because I desperately wanted to understand how everything worked. But they also had to make it possible for my teachers to teach, for the class to function. I played badminton, so the director of the school placed three badminton birds on my desk. They represented the three questions I was allowed to ask for the day. If I asked one more, I'd be out of badminton for a week. Eventually, I came across a teacher who understood that I wasn't deliberately trying to cause trouble. He'd hand me his chalk and say, OK, Laurent, if you're so smart, go and explain to us how such-and-such equation works in physics. I would walk up to the board and go through the steps, explaining the whole thing so everyone had a recap of what we'd just learned. He'd found a way to use my annoying attitude, to put it into some sort of framework that made sense. I don't know if it was me who changed or if my teachers got used to me, but it worked so well that when I graduated from high school, I wound up being named the top student of the cohort.

By CEGEP, I'd figured out how to be a functional, and even very successful, student. I understood that if I wanted to open doors, I had to at least try to be good at everything. But I was happiest, and got my best marks, in the sciences: biology, chemistry, physics, math. I see science everywhere, in fact. If I walk outside and see frost on a leaf, my mind instantly begins to work through how it got there, and why: there was a sudden temperature change before the sun came out, the humidity in the air froze, then crystallized, and here's the result on the leaf. That's pretty cool. Same thing if I see, say, a deer jump over a fence. I'm thinking: the vector force in his knee is really backwards; it's crazy he's able to propel himself so high.

Given this way of looking at the world around me, engineering seemed an obvious choice for me. At least until I sat through too many programming classes and realized how much of my future life I would spend behind computer screens. I'd barely been able to handle that in school, so why would I want to do it in my working life? Engineering became less appealing as a career.

There were no physicians in my family, no one with a history in medicine or even an obsession with *Grey's Anatomy*. But medicine is science: intricate, fascinating processes all wrapped up inside the human body. So I began to think in that direction, and I quickly realized that, unlike engineering, medicine can't be practised at a computer screen. It's practised with people. I love interacting and connecting with people. And the thing about people is that they're vastly different from each other; people are infinitely complex, with no two, not even twins, exactly alike.

As a doctor, I would be able to use both sides of my everbusy brain. I'd have to. It would be my responsibility to understand patients' socio-economic circumstances, their lives, beliefs, family histories and exercise routines. I'd also need to understand the human body, how it works, what diseases infiltrate it and how to fix them. Art and science—bingo!—together in the same job. In a medical career, I would be actively solving complex problems, putting my incessant curiosity to work to help improve people's lives. And, essentially for me, every day would be different. With people in the mix—patients, that is—and their vast range of personalities, circumstances, illnesses and ailments, every part of every day would be different from every other.

I'D MISSED my one interview and thereby lost my chance to study medicine at a French-language university. However, one option remained. I'd had a fourth school on my application: McGill University, the first university in North America to start a medical school, and a highly revered institution seen as a key member of the "Ivy League of the North." For me, though, McGill wasn't all that appealing. Problem number one: it was an English-language school. I'd grown up speaking French and still struggled in my second language. English was one of the courses I hadn't excelled at in CEGEP. The thought of studying medicine in English was daunting, to say the least.

But language wasn't the only reason I hesitated over McGill. By the time I was considering medicine as a career, I'd also got into football in a pretty big way. My first year playing, back in high school, I was a running back. My friends were all playing football video games, watching football with their parents on Sundays. In my family, we watched a Québécois science show on Sunday evenings. We didn't even have cable. My love of football had nothing to do with the hype around pro sports. I didn't really know anything about football. It was more like, finally, I could battle with someone in a legal way without breaking a window at my parents' place. It was an outlet. A very welcome one.

During one game that year, I remember making 10 yards on a 1st and 10, and going to my coach hugely disappointed. All my friends were scoring touchdowns, and I'd only made 10 yards. I had no idea at the time that, in the NFL, if you're able to make 10 yards on the first play of your drive—well, it doesn't happen often, let me put it that way. It's a really good play. But when you're a kid, all you want to do is score. My coach was like, "Bro, you made first down on the first down. That's unbelievable. That's great." And I remember thinking at that moment, OK, maybe I *am* good at this.

Because I played on a team in the nearby city during high school, I wasn't going to school with any of my teammates. I'd arrive a half-hour before the game, play the game and go home after. I was also playing other sports: badminton, soccer, cross-country skiing. It wasn't until I got to CEGEP and was able to play football with my classmates that things changed. Because I had played on a city team rather than a high school team, nobody in the school football system knew who I was. Nobody had come to scout me. I literally turned up at the first training camp practice and asked, "Can I play here?" I remember seeing the disbelief in the coaches' eyes, staring at this six-foot-five player they'd never heard of. They were like, *Who the hell is this guy?* It was pretty much: here's your helmet, here's some shoulder pads, we'll take you. And boom, I started to live in a more football-oriented world. It was good for me. I had a bunch of teammates who also wanted to get good grades. So, on a Thursday night, I'd go with my buddies from the football field to the library to study for a couple of hours. Then, sometimes, we'd move from the library to the bars for a couple of drinks.

It was a really cool balance during those three years, from an academic perspective and a sports perspective. We were like living models of the student-athlete, exactly how you hope to see that combo work. Also, by then, I knew my way around the field. I could play. I'd even won awards, including best defensive lineman in the league. That's not a misprint: in my early football career, I played on the other side of the ball. Looking back, I'd evaluate my D-lineman skill set as somewhere between minimal and mildly promising. I gave maximum effort, I had some power, and, because of my size, I could occupy space that running backs might otherwise have wiggled through.

In short, by the time I applied to medical school, football had come to matter to me, and I wasn't half-bad at it. In fact, I had promise. I was a strong enough player to be considered an asset on a college team. McGill, however, was not known for its football team. That is, not in a good way.

It's not as though the school had no gridiron history whatsoever. Many of the sport's historians believe that when McGill played Harvard on May 14, 1874, the players on that field took part in one of the first-ever intercollegiate games in college football history, if not *the very first*. McGill won its first championship in 1902, and captured six more titles through 1960. After Canadian colleges created the Vanier Cup in 1965, McGill made three appearances in the championship, finally winning the cup in 1987 for its first—and only—time. It was now 2010, and the team had yet to make it back to the final.

At McGill, I would be studying in English, which would mean working twice as hard and at a huge disadvantage relative to my peers. I would also be at a school where the football team was widely considered the worst in the province.

Now, though, I had to accept a dose of reality: if I wanted to study medicine, McGill was my only hope. So I sure as hell didn't miss *that* interview. On the contrary, I was desperate to make a good impression. I tried to emphasize my humanity, as a way to distinguish myself from other applicants, describing our family business ventures and sailboat trips, and my experience as a young entrepreneur. I presented Laurent the person rather than Laurent the football player. I knew that how well I might do on the gridiron would hold little sway.

I also needed to excel in the medical school–specific portions of the interview. Rather than simply answer questions, aspiring doctors are tasked with responding to different scenarios, sometimes with real-life actors, to see how they respond to the chaotic environments they will encounter while in school, or afterward, in hospitals. In these settings, applicants have eight to 10 minutes to react before a whistle sounds to signal that they should move from this room to the next, where they will be given another conundrum to solve.

The scenarios aren't necessarily medical in nature. After all, aspiring doctors will attend years of school to learn that stuff. The circumstances are designed, instead, to gauge how prospective students interact when placed under intentional duress; to see how they solve problems, with a time limit, under pressure. An actor might play the role of an older, confused customer anxious to get into a bank where there's a long line of impatient customers waiting to withdraw money from an ATM. The actor will pantomime panic, shaking their walker, insisting they need to cut in front or they'll miss their bus. If I let them go ahead, everyone else in that line will be angry; if I don't let them pass, they'll call me out for my lack of humanity. In each scenario, I'd be judged on my response throughout the unfolding situation, rather than on the basis of one clear-cut decision.

Interviewers also pose random questions, such as: How many piano repair specialists work in Montreal? You can't prepare for a question like that, and the actual answer doesn't really matter. It's the thought process you undertake to arrive at a possible figure that is important. I considered elements such as the city's population, the total number of families, how many might own a piano, how often a piano should be tuned, and of course how many pianos a capable specialist could tune in a normal workday. I still don't know how well I did with any of my answers. The interview is designed that way, a blitz from one station to the next with zero feedback, lest it inform the approach you take in the next room.

In the end, I felt good about my performance, but I still wasn't certain I would get in. But I did believe I had one advantage, born from my life experiences to that point: I had learned *how to learn*, applying rational thought and critical thinking to everything from chicken coops to spearfishing.

I wasn't quite accepted. I made the wait-list. And so, I waited. Eventually, my acceptance came through, fortunately on the day before I departed for a four-week backpack journey through Europe. I had saved the profits from every pot of jam and bag of caramels I'd sold, and it was a relief to know my plan for the next fall before I left.

After receiving my acceptance, I called Sonny Wolfe, the university's football coach, from the patio in the backyard of my parents' house. A native of the greater Montreal area, Wolfe had long ago played defensive back at McGill. In 2007, after 19 years in charge at Acadia University in Nova Scotia, he'd returned to Montreal to take over the program at his alma mater. His task was immense but doable: return a once-proud program to its rightful perch of prominence.

I wasn't like one of those elite recruits in the US who are splashed across the covers of sports magazines while receiving hundreds of scholarship offers from fawning coaches who visit their high schools and eat dinner at their homes, which is all part of the multi-billion-dollar enterprise known as college football in the States. (Those scholarships, by the way—the privilege of being able to study while pushing to excel at the top level of sport—are such an incredible opportunity. We have to embrace this practice in Canada; it's so important for athletes' future lives. Pro football careers are short, injuries happen, and education offers the possibility for a strong second plan.) I was an athletic kid who'd proved himself on the field at the CEGEP level. I was big. I also truly loved playing football by then. These were assets I suspected Coach Wolfe could use.

He began laying out defensive formations and how I might fit into various alignments. Training camp would begin in less than two weeks.

To hear him talk about it, the prospect was almost irresistible. But I had been waffling for weeks, facing a conundrum that even now, years later, I have yet to fully resolve. My advisers had already told me that I would not be able to keep up in my academic work and also play football. I knew their concerns had merit. Medical school would be a pressure cooker. It would be hard for any med student to make time for a demanding varsity-league sport, but it would be that much more of a challenge for me, because I wasn't yet fluent in English. I knew that becoming a doctor would prove the greatest challenge of my life to that point.

I finally had to tell Coach Wolfe it would be too much. I wouldn't be in the right mindset. I quit football that July, before a single practice had commenced in my first college season, before I even sat down for my first university class. I wanted to play, but not badly enough that I would jeopardize my chance to become a doctor.

Coach Wolfe told me he respected my decision. He also left the door ajar. "If you change your mind," he said, "call me."

WHEN I'D MOVED away from home to study at CEGEP, we'd done some work on my grandmother's basement in Montreal to turn it into a makeshift living space for me. The ceiling was six feet high, which would be perfectly fine for most people. But I was six foot five. I had to duck when I entered. Now that I was in university, my grandma's place remained my student pad. I would take the train home from McGill and study in that basement, bent over my notes.

On the first day of medical school, the dean, the associate dean, the doctors and the professors spoke to our class. They emphasized the importance of our chosen field, the lives we would hopefully save and how we would become societal leaders one day. I think they meant to inspire us, but my instinct was to call bullshit. Like: *Really? This group of teenagers will have that kind of influence? Why are we being put on a pedestal before we've accomplished anything?* It felt like an ego trip. I told my parents about that meeting. "Who do they think they are?" was the response. Consider starting school with that kind of elevated pressure. In what world do 19-year-olds deserve that kind of power and attention?

That fall, as I began the gruelling job of studying medicine in my second language, I learned that my love for football did not extend to spectating. At least, not in the circumstances I found myself in, having given up a spot on my school's roster. I couldn't sit in the stands at Percival Molson Memorial Stadium and enjoy watching McGill play. Those guys on the field should have been my teammates. That should have been my game. I started to long for football. The feeling of missing out, of not being complete, nagged at me.

I spent most of the time I would have been practising at home. I grew bored, then unhappy. My grades dropped below my capabilities. It didn't take long for a terrible realization to sink in: deciding not to play football had left me feeling unmoored. By caving in to my fears, and to that well-meaning torrent of advice to avoid taking on too much, I had made a major mistake.

Part of my yearning, I came to realize, stemmed from the focus that football provided me. When I was playing, I wasn't thinking about my girlfriend, or my classes, or anything other than my next play, series and quarter. Whether in games or practice, the grid-iron gave me a framework. I absorbed the lessons in, say, my biology class better after two hours spent in pads at practice. I drew from the camaraderie and friendships, the energy and atmosphere. Games helped me to reset. They provided a familiar rhythm that propelled me into the next week.

When I chose to shut down that part of me, other parts shut down too, which was surprising but maybe, in hindsight, should have been expected. I'd watch television in the evenings after classes rather than complete all my homework assignments. I called my family less often and became more withdrawn.

What I learned in that basement, hunched over my studies, textbooks balanced in my meaty hands, is that not only did I love football, but I *needed* it. I needed balance, but not the kind of balance you achieve by reducing your workload and commitments. The kind of balance I needed would come from doing *more* rather than doing less. I didn't need more time for medical school, and I didn't need to spend any more time stuck at home.

Football? . . . Or medicine?

Lineman? . . . Or doctor?

My answer: Yes. To both. Sports and medicine were my twin turbo engines.

I didn't know this at the time, but I'm not alone in the need to feel busy, to have a combination of passions on the go, in order to be able to focus and reach my potential. In the book *Range: Why Generalists Triumph in a Specialized World*, author David Epstein explores how many notable high achievers, from artists to writers to business executives, have successfully undertaken a variety of pursuits with the same level of passion. Epstein cites Van Gogh as one example, noting that before he became an artist of world renown, Van Gogh "had been a student, an art dealer, a teacher, a tutor, a bookstore clerk, a pastor-in-training, a preacher-in-training, and an itinerant catechist. He had an immense work ethic; his minister father preached of the sower, who must put in work now so he can reap later: 'Think of all the fields that were turned down by shortsighted people.'"

That sounds just like my dad talking.

Or perhaps my grandmother, who was smart, who handled the marketing for our family business and who knew how to enjoy life. I admired her, and I loved her. Living with her was a privilege I had been granted for four years. But that September of my first year at McGill, I hardly made for an ideal roommate. My general malaise aside, I didn't excel at, say, cleaning my room or washing my clothes. I lost my keys on more than one occasion and had to climb in through the basement window. I often arrived home to find notes on my desk.

Don't put the eggshells back in the carton.

Don't mix colours and whites when you do the laundry.

Don't take my bottle of gin.

Meanwhile, she showed me by example the real makings of an ideal roomie. She encouraged me to invite friends over. She'd down martinis with us, then dominate our poker games. At that low point in my life, she was very supportive and helpful to me.

Fortunately, the fix became obvious. It started with returning to the sport I had just quit. It had felt like an eternity, but it was really only a month into the fall term when I called Coach Wolfe, gulped and asked for my spot back.

Winning over a coach who needed players was the easy part. It would be more difficult to integrate into the locker room in the middle of the season, having already missed every practice and all of training camp. Convincing my new teammates that I had not abandoned them, that I did not think I was better than them, would require a skilful effort—not to mention time. And I needed to do that while keeping up with medical school.

Whether in college or the NFL, the best way to gain your teammates' respect is to put the team first, to make sure, every time you're on the field, that you sacrifice a little more for the benefit of the greater whole. Finishing a pancake block, or straining to shove my guy past the quarterback, might not seem like a lot in the grand scheme of things. But the little details, they matter, and they add up. When I first arrived, partway through the season, my teammates were respectful, yet I felt they remained understandably wary of me. I still needed to prove not only my value to the team, but my loyalty to them. If anyone looked at me and thought, *Who does he think he is?*, well, I thought that too. I had to become part of the ecosystem that is a locker room, and I did that gradually, by being myself.

Meanwhile, upon my return to the field, I made a promise to myself that would reverberate 10 years later, in 2020, when an improbable sequence of events forced me to choose between medicine and football once again: I would not be afraid to buck convention, to go against well-meaning, even seemingly reasonable advice, to do what felt right for me.

AT McGILL, students happen to play football the way their classmates happen to run for student council seats. I played not for the glory—there wasn't any—but because I loved the sport, same as my teammates. We took bus trips to away games rather than flying on chartered planes. We stayed at budget hotels. We didn't don seven different uniform combinations emblazoned with logos from apparel sponsorships designed to attract the latest batch of big-name recruits. We bought our own gloves, and other forms of less essential equipment. We wore the same cleats all season. We didn't receive any special treatment in our classes. Non-athlete students didn't flock to our university because of football, or join the team for all the pageantry and tradition, things that drive the sport in the US.

Even the specifics of the game in Canada are different than in the US: 12 players on the field, not 11; three downs, not four; longer fields; unlimited motion before the snap; greater room to operate.

At an early October practice that first year, not long after my return to the game, one of my coaches, Matthieu Quiviger, shook my hand for the first time, then jumped back, exclaiming that it resembled a catcher's mitt. He declared that you don't usually find players my size at a university with the rigorous academic standards of McGill. He would call me *cadeau des dieux*, a gift from the gods. But since he coached the offensive line unit, I didn't play for him that fall. I remained a defensive lineman, lined up directly across from the players he cajoled into improving with every practice.

73

Before my second season, in 2011, the coaches and I both noticed the same thing: the Redmen roster was imbalanced, with more capable defensive linemen than offensive ones. (McGill's sports teams are now known as Redbirds, due to the racist connotations of that earlier name.) At one practice, there weren't enough O-linemen to field a full offence, so Coach Wolfe and Coach Quiviger asked my position group if anyone would switch for the day. I raised my hand. "Hell yeah," I said, "I want to try it."

I was curious. I wanted to know: What was it like to make blocks rather than shed them? I thought that trying out offence, gaining that perspective, might improve my game on defence.

One day became a week, then two weeks. I began to believe I was better suited for the other side of the ball. Offensive linemen need to rely less on instinct and more on thinking, processing information based on how the defence is aligned, making instant adjustments between plays, only to have to adjust again before each snap, based on what we see as we approach the line. I loved how O-line play was like a game of physically demanding chess, with moves, counters, and counters to those counters. Once the play started, we'd brace for impact from men who were similar in size but generally better athletes, while we shuffled backwards, often while crouched down. This was art combined with science, my wheelhouse. Apparently, my coaches agreed with my assessment of where I belonged, because I never did switch back. I became a full-fledged offensive tackle.

It was no cakewalk, though, reconfiguring my role on the field. Coach Quiviger likes to tell the story of my first practice after the position swap. He noticed both my natural physical prowess and my total lack of technique. I could run. I could kick-slide. I could shuffle. I would be able to take other large men and move them where my coaches wanted me to move them. I could get where I needed to go, usually, and more often than not I could figure out a way to block a guy. But I didn't yet know how I was *supposed* to block him. I struggled with the more technical aspects of offensive line play, specifically my hand placement, which was often all over the place, and rarely where it should be. Everything in football is a question of vector of force and leverage. On the line of scrimmage, a strike with upward force and low hips will always win over brute force, and I needed to learn that as the competition became more fierce.

Playing on the O-line, I discovered, is all about consistency. I could make a good block with bad technique, but I knew that wasn't a sustainable way to excel. I could be an above-average athlete for someone my size, but I would rarely be more athletic than the person I'm blocking. I had to rely on technique, footwork and proper hand placement to maximize my consistency. I had to position myself to drive my opponents, no matter what approach they had chosen, whether trying to cross my face, jump upfield or rush down the middle. That's where consistency came in, especially as I played at higher levels, against better athletes. Every little piece of technique, and anticipation, helped.

Even as I learned and was energized by the challenges of my new position, I found it more difficult to gauge my progress. On defence, my improvement was measurable, in objective ways, not to mention obvious to even the most casual fans. They could see the sacks recorded, plays disrupted and passes batted down. On offence, I opened paths for running backs or kept defenders from knocking down my quarterback. But fans focus on whoever touches the ball, which I never did. Like a plumber, or a dam inspector, I was most noticeable when I made mistakes, because of the calamities that resulted from them. And because I was used to gauging my growth based on statistics, I felt like only an average player, as though I was just holding my own. I had no other way to assess myself.

One day, my new position coach, Quiviger, asked me to stay after practice.

"You know, I was a pretty good player when I was here," he said. I nodded. I didn't really know, but I didn't want to leave the wrong impression. "You and I are not part of the same team."

I felt embarrassed. I wanted to run home. "Yeah," I finally stammered. "I really suck."

His response nearly knocked me down. "No. You are so much better. You are going places that you won't believe."

I was surprised. "The CFL?" I wondered.

"No. Beyond that. When the hockey coach saw Gretzky on the ice for the first time, I'm sure he knew he had something special."

It's a little much to be compared to the greatest hockey player who has ever lived. Coach Quiviger, at that point, believed in me more than I believed in myself. But he still needed to guide me so I could maximize the talent he saw in me. He started by helping me to understand the quiet nature of my new position. I would not be judged by individual stats, except for the amount of sacks I yielded. He taught me that offensive linemen are judged by how they work together, as one unit, moving forwards or backwards in unison, and how they fail when they cannot coalesce.

He worked with me to build on traits I already possessed, such as flexibility and speed. I listened, and I worked. Because I listened, and because I worked, I improved. Quickly. Steadily. Until I could plow through, seal off and knock actual defensive linemen, in real games.

Gradually, I uncovered the power of playing together, as one unit, as five men who care little about individual statistics and define their success by how many yards a running back gains, or how clean the quarterback's jersey looks when the final whistle sounds. If football is the ultimate team sport, then the O-line is the ultimate team within the ultimate team sport. We can only be as good as the players who stand next to us. And when we communicate effectively, we play in harmony, we look out for each other, and we sacrifice for our linemates because we know they do the same for us. Once I discovered that collective nature, I embraced it, and when I embraced it, I loved football even more.

I grew into a solid player, then a serviceable starter. I also "grew" in the literal sense, at the urging of my coaches. I added muscle mass through workouts and alterations to my diet, which was the opposite of a *diet*. Instead, I ate everything in sight. But don't think for a moment that my quest for football improvement was focused on a future professional career. Not then. I was too consumed with medical school to realize how my football prospects were shifting, and just where they might lead.

Coach Quiviger began to call me the "big engine that never quits."

Eventually, he asked me to wear his old number, 66, which hadn't been donned since his senior season in 1994. Then he went to the other coaches, the same ones I had quit in front of roughly 16 months earlier, and declared, "Laurent is going to the NFL."

And, he would later admit, everybody laughed.

FOR MOST medical students at McGill, there's a standard program. I elected, instead, to fast-track my curriculum, opting for the version of pre-med—basic science such as anatomy, biology and chemistry—that's condensed into a single year. This choice ultimately saved me two years of schooling.

Given that I had always struggled to learn English, an infinitely complicated language, this decision to fast-track was maybe a little ambitious. I was the guy who, back in high school, had answered "zero" when my English teachers asked how many friends I had. (I thought *friend* meant brother.) Such embarrassing English-language moments weren't rare for me. Fortunately, most of my lectures were recorded, so instead of attending them in person, I'd usually access them through the department's website while seated at a table at one of our bakeries. I'd listen at half speed, taking notes and using my English dictionary to look up whatever words I didn't understand.

Halfway through my first semester at McGill, I was able to speed up the recording—not all the way, but it was a start. By the end of that first year, I could sit in class and take notes without a dictionary. My English had improved that much, even if teammates continued to joke that I spoke only one and a half languages.

Eventually, I could take apart a cadaver and tell a story in English about what I'd discovered inside. Those classes, with up to 50 dead bodies spread across various tables, were a little creepy. At least at first. But we spent a whole year with our own cadaver, getting to know it, learning what nerve goes through which muscle and how all the musculature connects.

In my second year, we transitioned into actual medical school, and I continued to learn the basics in medicine, football and English all at once. Every month, we took exams that covered subjects ranging from the cardiovascular system and immunology to dissection, muscle anatomy and the nervous system. Rather than embrace all the newer forms of social media, I stayed away from Facebook and Twitter in favour of developing real, actual relationships with people, if only for 30 minutes at a time. Usually, I'd meet my friends after school, or after I finished lifting weights, for a beer or, yes, a *glass of water* before bed. That was the full extent of my shrinking social life, but the discipline paid dividends when I managed a 3.9 grade point average.

In the fall of 2012, my third year at McGill, we started clinical rotations, shifting from classrooms into hospitals or other facilities, such as nursing homes or rehabilitation centres. At first, we didn't hold what we call "patient-care responsibilities." We learned in small-group settings, alongside doctors, in a series of apprenticeships that generally lasted for eight weeks. Eventually, we would care for patients directly. But it was clear, immediately, just how time-intensive the rotations were, in part because they're so wide-ranging, covering every facet of the medical field, but also because, as we found out, being a doctor is hard work, with high stakes.

I absorbed sessions at the simulation centre on how to intubate patients in order to protect their airways. Once we mastered the technique on a mannequin, I would sometimes get to perform the same procedure on a real patient in a controlled environment, such as an operating room. Later on, I would do the same procedure on an unstable patient in the ER, under supervision. I loved that type of learning, the procedures involved, the steps. It was physical manoeuvring combined with careful planning combined with analytical thinking and adrenalin born from how much was at stake. It was a different kind of stress, but it was similar, in its level, to playing football.

We sometimes did rotations in the evening, or late at night, or overnight. The beginning of each shift, as we transitioned through hospital departments, from the psychiatric rotation to geriatric to ophthalmology, was intense. Each new situation was complex and nuanced, with a steeper learning curve than walking into a strange school while on a year-long sailing excursion. We had to fight the feeling of being overwhelmed, to better deploy our focus toward figuring out our co-workers, their personalities and how everybody fit together on the medical team, all while trying to absorb information and make a good first impression.

I would only later realize how these continual resets prepared me for pro football, for dropping into locker rooms, being the new guy and trying to ingratiate myself with an existing team. Similarly, McGill's vast alumni network of doctors who met regularly with me and other students became necessary mentors as I navigated the byzantine nature of university medical school—just as my coaches and trainers would later do for me on the gridiron.

For my internal medicine block, I showed up each morning and performed what we call rounds, meeting with patients to assist the only doctor on a floor with 30 full beds. The doctor supervises the floor, with the aid of one senior resident. They're typically on call 24 hours a day for a week straight. They also have junior residents, who are in charge of, let's say, 10 patients. Medical students like me would handle four of a junior resident's 10 cases, including reviews and supervision. I would look over patient charts—*Mr. X, 75-year-old smoker, admitted for pneumonia, on Day 3 of antibiotics*—and talk through any spikes in fever, blood pressure or heart rate. Mr. X might tell me that he's feeling better but can't shake a little cough, or about his shortness of breath. I could suggest to my supervisors that they change his medications or increase their levels, or recommend an appointment with a respiratory therapist. Even then, several years from becoming an actual doctor, I could see the impact of my work with the patients, and that impact became fuel, reinforcing my sense of the value of my chosen field, the empathy and humanity that define medicine.

For one particularly enjoyable rotation, I did sports medicine, apprenticing under our team physician, Dr. Scott Delaney.

I did my shifts at our stadium, helping to tend to players on all of McGill's sports teams through evaluations, rehabilitation and suggested training techniques. Dr. Delaney sympathized with the tricky balance I was maintaining between my studies and my sport; he would always dismiss me in time for practice. As an added bonus, Dr. Delaney worked as the team doctor for the Montreal Canadiens. Sometimes he took me to their training camp, where I helped him do the players' pre-season medical examinations.

I was amazed back then just to be around professional athletes. I never expected I would become one. In fact, Dr. Delaney and his colleague, Dr. Vincent Lacroix, would introduce me to my hockey heroes as a McGill football standout who *might* one day play in the CFL. They, too, laughed! I didn't blame them.

Due to the staggering demands on my time, I missed more than a few practices. The surgery rotation required up to 70 hours a week and as much as 14 hours for a single procedure, making football, and all the gruelling training, seem easy by comparison. Many of my medical rotations took place at the century-old Royal Victoria Hospital, which overlooked our practice field, meaning that most of my life at that time unfolded on the same Rue University block. I undertook anaesthesia, trauma ward and postpartum care rotations there. Sometimes, whether inside a patient's room or on break in a space designated for employees to relax, I would gaze out the window and right down at my teammates toiling away on our practice field. Then I might return to my duties, helping with the intubation and prep of a patient about to undergo brain surgery for the removal of a glioblastoma.

The process was tough but instructive, and it made me more creative and self-sufficient. I learned to pour protein powder directly from a zip-lock bag into my mouth, or crack and down a hard-boiled egg during a short elevator ride or, later, in the library, where I would study after my shifts. I learned to adapt, a skill I would later need, and put to critical use, in the harrowing fight against COVID-19. My classmates would sometimes marvel at my memory, my ability to juggle all this information at once and retain what I needed. I didn't see it that way, necessarily. For me, it resulted from the simplest of combinations: time, effort and the balance I had found.

CHAPTER 5

THE NFL

(NO, *REALLY*, THE NFL)

A typical day during my medical rotation began around 5:30 or 6 a.m., about 90 minutes before the first procedure started. My medical school surgery rotation took place in the late summer of 2012, butting right up against the start of McGill's football season. My shifts were at St. Mary's Hospital, which is close to the University of Montreal's stadium, where we would play our home opener on the last Friday of my surgery block. I did rounds that morning with junior and senior residents, then went to the operating room, where we observed four or five procedures.

I wouldn't have time to rush back to campus after my shift, so I'd grabbed my pads at McGill the night before, arrived at the hospital before dawn and crushed a huge bowl of pasta between cases. Once my supervisor delivered my final evaluation, I sped off in my trusty old gold Toyota Yaris. An incredibly small car for a person of my size, it had logged more than 200,000 kilometres. The back seat was strewn with laundry and textbooks that bounced and jostled at every sharp turn. In the winters, I would sometimes forget about half-eaten food containers I had left in the passenger seat. They would freeze, and then they would thaw when I used the heating vents. The defrosted leftovers smelled so bad I would have to roll down my window just to drive.

I arrived at the University of Montreal's stadium not long before kickoff, grabbed my helmet from amid the mess in the back seat and jogged into our locker room. My teammates were already dressed, getting ready to sprint out onto the field. I hadn't even practised in the previous days. In fact, due to my hospital obligations, I'd missed training camp entirely. I tugged on all my necessary equipment while they warmed up.

I played miserably, and we got our butts kicked.

I had done my best to schedule my medical training rotations before football season to avoid just this kind of scenario. But in a schedule like mine, it wasn't possible to avoid conflict entirely. I walked the finest of lines, fitting everything in. As I advanced further into my curriculum, I had to constantly consider and reconsider my balance, making continuous tweaks. This required creativity, adaptation and a lot of help from others, especially everyone in my inner circle.

When family medicine rotation came up in 2013, I began driving an hour or more outside Montreal for shifts in rural communities. Because of the commute, I missed more practices. It's safe to say that my schedule was unusual, if not unprecedented. During those weeks when I couldn't practise, another offensive lineman would take all the reps. But when the game kicked off, that same lineman wouldn't play: I would step in. The whole situation, unavoidable though it was, made me uncomfortable. I wouldn't have been surprised if some players considered the time I missed unfair. But no one griped to me about it. And what I actually missed most, absent all week then parachuting in for games, was the camaraderie, the post-practice lunches, the locker room vibe, and the jokes.

I tried to multi-task. I came up with strategies. For a while, I slept in an apartment near the rural hospital to save time commuting. I organized virtual meetings with coaches to learn the game plan each week. This was years before COVID, when Zoom became standard practice for everyone. Back then, a multi-person online call was a sizable technological undertaking. We'd go over the different names for calls we'd use, in order to switch certain plays at the line of scrimmage, along with tweaks for the plan specific to our next opponent, or new designs that had been added to the playbook. At least, that way, I would know the basics of the playbook and focus any extra time I had on training and staying in shape, so I could still be useful on the field. As the season went along, I did manage to attend some practices, just not as many as anyone wanted me to, myself included. I averaged about one a week. In fact, one time a scout came to one of our practices, in part to evaluate me. I, of course, was two hours away, working at the rural hospital.

Sometimes I would lament this existential tug-of-war to Sasha, like on the weeks I worried I would not arrive in time for a Saturday kickoff at McGill. "I'm stuck in the middle of nowhere, doing this rural medicine rotation," I would complain. "I'm just going to try and be on time for Saturday. That's all I can do." And somehow he'd get me laughing. That helped, but it didn't do away with the stress.

I guess it would have been easier to drop medical school for a year, enrol in less demanding courses and focus primarily on the gridiron. But back then—and still now, really—my Plan A was medicine. With so many things that can go wrong in any football season, it wasn't worth delaying a year of classes I needed for my degree. Plus, by then, I had already promised myself that I would fight for both passions, rather than one or the other. Whatever it took. If doing both school and football meant sleeping on a pile of towels in our locker room so I could arrive on time for some morning meetings, so be it. My teammates would nudge me awake for meetings. They also bestowed upon me the nickname "Dr. Kill," because I would show up just before practice, still wearing my scrubs, then change, before levelling my opponents on the field. I'm not sure I really liked that name, but I liked the idea of having a nickname.

So even though balancing proved chaotic, I'd found peace in my decision. I even—except for the times when I felt desperate—relished the challenge of doing both. After all, I figured my final season at McGill would be either my last in football or at least the last time I would have to do both at the same time. If I did manage to play at the professional level, I wouldn't be able to study during seasons. That thinking informed my mindset: putting everything I had into the game I loved meant I wouldn't have regrets, and it also helped me forget about the scouts sitting in the stands and the pressure I could faintly feel building with regards to my pro prospects.

Whatever Coach Quiviger had said about my future prospects, by the time I started my fourth year at McGill, my mindset was still more in sync with the people who'd laughed when he'd mentioned my name and the NFL in the same sentence. Never mind how much focus and energy I was putting into my studies instead of into football, it was incredibly rare for any players from Canadian universities, even those from powerhouse teams, to reach the NFL. We didn't pass the eye test; in some ways this was true of all college programs in Canada, but especially McGill. Of the 36 football games I'd played for McGill, we'd logged just six wins. Meanwhile, Université Laval in Quebec City, the team I had most wanted to play for before I missed that med school interview, went 48–3 during that span, winning three Vanier Cups. And yet playing for McGill had served me better than I could have anticipated or guessed. Our mediocre standing had minimized playoff commitments, allowing for the flexibility I needed to finish med school. Playing for McGill had also led to the position switch that better suited my skill set. Meanwhile, studying and playing at McGill meant I'd had no choice but to learn English, which is useful, naturally, for someone playing in the US. In retrospect, if I had gone to one of the French-speaking schools, or played on the defensive line, there's no way I'd have made the NFL.

The first inklings that American football might be a real possibility for me came in 2013, after the East-West Bowl in London, Ontario, where the best Canadian college prospects undergo a variety of speed, strength and agility tests. My scores alerted talent evaluators to my potential. Before one contest for McGill that fall, I heard that a Chicago Bears scout would be in attendance, and he would be tasked, in part, with evaluating me. I couldn't believe someone from the NFL wanted to watch us— watch *me*—play. But that started to change the prism through which I saw my football career. "Make sure you're ready," Sasha reminded me. We already had a long-standing joke between us that he would become my future agent. Like Coach Quiviger, he could see my improbable future before I came to realize just how much it had changed.

Even then, I believed many pro coaches would perceive my doctoral aims as a negative, because of the time and focus that they required—time and focus that would inevitably be stolen from the game. In the event I actually got myself in front of them, I was sure they'd advise me to halt medical school, just as most of my mentors in medicine continued to suggest I didn't have time for football. Mostly, though, I wasn't entirely convinced I was good enough to play pro football. Was I wasting my time even thinking about trying to pursue it?

Sasha believed I was good enough, that I wasn't wasting my time, and that, basically, he knew better, because while I had been sailing and making jam and pesto as a teenager, he had stoked his sports obsession, focusing on the NFL above all others. He would, as much as anyone, open my path into the most lucrative—and popular—league in North American sports. And it started with him convincing me it was possible.

THERE'S NO ONE like Sasha. He's smart, meticulous, loyal, rare. A kid with an Egyptian mother and an Iranian father, both immigrants to Canada. In youth, Sasha was the biggest sports geek alive. We met at CEGEP. I didn't know anyone. He was part of a group of friends from another high school with whom I connected through my teammates. He'd invite everyone over to his place to watch football on Sundays. I went once or twice, but I found it so boring, spending the whole day sitting on the couch. But I liked him. We got along. We became a study in contrasts. I was big; Sasha, not so much. While I loved to play sports, I remained indifferent to the industry side of things; Sasha was an encyclopedia of pro sports stats—baseball, hockey, basketball and especially football. (He was a Chargers fan, which later led to some friendly animosity between us, since the Chiefs and Chargers are division rivals in the AFC West.) He listened to sports-talk radio in preparation for, first, his desired career as a commentator and, later, his desired career as a sports agent. That latter goal became a running joke between us: he'd be an agent one day, and he'd represent me as I pursued my football career. When I started medical school, he went to study law at the Université de Montréal. The law makes for a pretty solid foundation for anyone who wants a career as an agent in professional sports.

I never took Sasha's joke about representing me seriously until agents started calling me in 2013. Many were, like me, from Canada, and some of them had NFL connections. They all, without exception, told me that if I wanted to have a real chance at a lasting career in a league like the NFL—where the average player doesn't last three seasons—I needed to put medical school on hold and focus on football. I wasn't willing to make that sacrifice, and I wasn't convinced they were right.

I was skeptical of agents in general because of the inherent bias of money. If, as a player, all you want is the biggest contract, then the incentive of a typical agent (who gets a percentage of what you make) is in line with your career as a player. But if you're a player like me, who sees football as an adventure and wants to keep their other passions alive, it's hard to find an agent who understands that kind of mindset. Professional sports agents are only motivated by money.

I began to think about Sasha and those old jokes. Was he, the one guy who knew me *and* the sport, actually the ideal option? He was in Australia, living in Perth and finishing law school at the University of Western Australia. He'd stayed in touch, occasionally nudging me about my football career, sending relevant draft rankings he found online, like the one that listed me as the—*gasp*—top CFL prospect. That article was more evidence that led me to believe maybe I *could* play in the pros after all.

Sasha wasn't due back in Canada until late June, and I was scheduled to leave for a trip through Europe before he arrived home. I called him in mid-May, over Facebook Messenger. Due to the time difference, he answered in the middle of the night. When he was awake enough, I said, "Do you still want to do this thing?" I told him I'd been meeting agents, not getting a good vibe, nobody understood my medical career, they just wanted me to sign, to make money. Should we, I asked, could we, turn our old joke into a reality?

He said yes.

He also said he didn't want to be chosen simply because we were friends. He wanted me to pick the best person for the job, and he insisted that he would present his plan to me before I left. He even changed his departure date from Australia to return two days before I took off, and we met for lunch the next day at the pub Benelux. Sasha did have a plan. He did present it. He didn't need to.

We cemented our partnership by signing, of all things, a napkin.

It was a nice moment. But we had no earthly idea of all that was to come.

THE VERY NEXT day, before we'd even signed an official contract, Sasha sent me a document that he had filled out like those equations in the movie *A Beautiful Mind*. It laid out, in detail, how we would realize the dream that we now shared. At that point, Sasha had no licence, no training, nothing beyond his law school classes. He didn't know a soul in pro football, not a coach, not a scout, not a single personnel executive. He began studying for the CFL agent exam while searching for a certified NFL agency that fit the criteria we were looking for, since he couldn't take the NFL's exam until 2015, after, and if, he passed the bar. When we'd agreed on our partnership at *the* bar, the drinking kind, Sasha had also showed me the boilerplate contract for CFL agents. He had not yet filled in the box for the percentage fee he would garner from my salary and other earnings. I wrote down "at the player's discretion," and that was that. We sent it to the CFL. (They rejected the whole "discretion" bit, but he became my representative anyway, acing the exam just before the NFL draft in 2015. Sasha now represents over 25 players in the CFL and three or four players in the NFL. He knows the scouts and executives of all 32 teams, and is a respected agent in the same way I'm a respected player. And we did it together.)

Sasha would later say that my face told him I did not truly believe this effort would come to anything, that he didn't think I believed I had a "shot in hell" at the NFL. There was some truth in that, but I resolved to take what shot I had. I started calling my college coaches, asking them where I could improve, asking what they thought of my chances. They offered to call pro teams and sing my praises. Their confidence boosted my own.

My first off-the-field football team began to form. Sasha made plans, took tests, dug into research. Flo was right there alongside us, offering support. She still wasn't a football fan, but she understood me, and the power of my dreams. She knew the window was small, that I needed to be at my very best in the time period between my final season and the drafts, that I probably had one chance—and only one. We had no clue what we were doing, no idea just how big a gated community the NFL really was. Every step from there became part of a new experiment.

When we reached out to the NFL to secure a spot at its annual Scouting Combine, the crucial showcase held each spring for franchise decision makers to test highly touted, mostly American prospects, the league didn't respond. This was a huge setback, the kind that could end my run at the NFL before it had really begun.

But not yet, not entirely. My non-Combine prospects were multiplying, starting with that first visit from the Bears scout. Other talent evaluators, from both leagues, began to ask for my film. Meanwhile, Sasha realized I had never seen an actual NFL game live. He wondered if that lack of basic understanding had driven some of my skepticism, and so he scheduled a road trip to Philadelphia for an Eagles game in November 2013.

The spectacle around the game, the pageantry, the vociferous Philly fans, left me awestruck. At McGill, I was used to crowds of a few hundred, a few thousand at most. Here, more than 65,000 fans crammed inside a noisy stadium. And that was after tailgating for hours before kickoff. The fans cheered so loudly, so lustily, that every play felt like the most important sequence in the world. I honestly got goosebumps. As I watched Fletcher Cox, a mammoth Eagles defensive tackle who still wrecks entire afternoons for his opponents, I thought, there's no way on earth I could block a human being of that size, who also happens to move that fast.

Remember, I had grown up on an orchard, with parents who banned video games and limited our television exposure. We played outside all week, until Sunday night, when millions across the world tuned into an NFL showcase game, the one contest held in that time slot, with two teams placed squarely under the spotlight. Only then were we allowed to settle in front of the small screen in their bedroom closet. But it was not for football. Heavens, no. We watched a program on Radio-Canada called *Découverte*, which aired stories on science and technology.

Before Sasha and I settled into our seats at Lincoln Financial Field, I had three options for my future: the CFL, where talent evaluators expected I would be a high draft choice and where, due to a shorter season, I'd have more time to devote to medical school;

the NFL, where splitting time between football and medicine might be a big issue; or forgoing both to concentrate solely on my future as Dr. Duvernay-Tardif. I preferred, in order, the NFL, the CFL and then neither. But I remained unsure. That day in Philadelphia, the crowd's energy, its intensity, worked on me. Maybe inspired me. My options whittled down to one, to the shot I had to take, whether I could partake in the Combine or not. I would take aim at the moon.

I turned to Sasha and told him that I had eliminated all lingering doubt. I agreed with him, with the agents and with my parents. I imagine many people in that situation would tell their kid to finish medical school, especially with only 16 months remaining, rather than map out a complex schedule and push back their graduation date for a one-in-a-hundred chance of being drafted by an NFL team. My parents had even less of an idea than Sasha and I did about what I might be getting myself into. But if there was one thing they'd taught me, it was to seize opportunities. They told me to see the NFL as another adventure, but they didn't push me in either direction. Instead, they served as my safety net, telling me I'd be fine no matter what. I can't express how powerful that was.

"This is what I want to do," I said to Sasha. I could see my future, in high definition; what I wanted was suddenly crystal clear.

But first, I needed to find enough time to make that vision possible.

I DECIDED to meet with Dr. Robert Primavesi, a respected emergency physician at various local hospitals who doubled as a beloved professor and assistant dean at McGill's Faculty of Medicine. With important, but time-sucking, rotations coming up, I worried I might be overextended as my final season ended and my preparation for two pro drafts began. Some of the rotations were split into smaller blocks that lasted one, two or four weeks, and if I had to fly to the US to meet with NFL teams, or train in order to show the most athletic version of me to the scout, or play in other showcase games for draft hopefuls, I might miss some of those rotations entirely.

I laid out my dilemma for Dr. Primavesi, along with an important caveat. Despite what I had decided in that stadium, I said that if football threatened my degree, I would choose school. Please understand how absurd, and remarkable, this conversation was. It's not like I played for a major power like Alabama or Georgia. It's not like NFL teams were banging down doors to enlist my services; I had, maybe, a small chance to become a pro football player across the border. It's not like I even played a high-profile position. It's not like the Combine organizers had changed their collective mind and invited me to participate. I wondered if the dean might burst out laughing.

Instead, he listened, then pulled out a calendar. "When does the Super Bowl take place every year?" he asked.

The first week of February, I told him, as we began working out an unanticipated, but welcome, compromise. Assuming I could resume my schooling at the conclusion of each NFL season, I could start each year around February 15. Next, we looked at what NFL teams called Organized Team Activities, or OTAs, the lighter spring workout sessions that I could potentially skip each off-season, depending on my class load. Worst case, I could partially attend them, come back to school, then leave again for training camp in late July.

I almost couldn't believe the tenor of that meeting. We were able to hash out an unprecedented schedule where I could put months every year, when not in the thick of a demanding season, toward becoming a doctor. It meant few, if any, vacations for the foreseeable future so that I could graduate by the time limit in May 2018. That meant interning and studying when my (still theoretical!) teammates were relaxing. But for me, the plan also created balance—a glorious opportunity to do both, to *be* both. By planning my schedule in that way, I was assuming I would play four years before even stepping onto an NFL field. It was crazy, but it was the only way to ensure I could do both things. Otherwise, what would be the point?

This new plan allowed me to take a leave of absence starting that December. That way, I could train for the draft. If I made an NFL or CFL roster, we would extend the leave, and I would return to McGill each off-season for four years, so that I could make up for all I would miss, which amounted to 16 months of medical school that we broke up into equal chunks. That plan would also give me enough time to chase both dreams with all I had, without losing either one, simply by delaying my graduation.

I'm especially proud of the difference that schedule made for other students at McGill. Dr. Primavesi says many students, including dancers and Olympians, received similar waivers because of the leave I took. He believes that helped several students who aspire to work in a field where depression, anxiety and suicide run rampant to remain in school, rather than be forced to quit due to unexpected or unavoidable circumstances. That matters more than someone who's unfamiliar with the grind of medical school might think. Most understand that it's difficult and hard to keep in balance. But every year, it gets harder to obtain the grades necessary to continue. The pressure rises in lockstep with the competition.

I believe it's important to give opportunities to students who have another passion so that they can explore it, learn from it and be better for it. At the end of the day, it's these experiences outside the medical world that help you to develop empathy and understand your patients better. When I look back at my curriculum, if I could have done anything differently (except attending my interview, lol!) it would have been to complete a full-on undergrad before applying to med school. By always trying to take a straight line toward my medical goal, I feel I missed opportunities to explore other fields of interest that might have been connected to medicine and eventually helped me better understand my patients. You can know all the science you want, but if you don't have experience that helps you relate to your patients, it's hard to communicate, it's hard to show empathy, it's hard to understand the challenges of life. Especially when you are a white man with academic talents and a childhood full of privileges.

That the McGill faculty allowed these kinds of approved absences, both mine and others', is huge. Because it reinforces to us, and all the medical school students, that empathy matters, and so does the way you treat people. I am convinced that more extracurricular activities yield more tools, a better grasp on the real world and a greater ability to cope with various situations as a doctor. There's no doubt in my mind that I will be a better physician because of all I experienced in the NFL. And I'm grateful that Dr. Primavesi saw that, encouraged that and approved that.

After he granted me both a longer timeline and his unconditional support, we built one exception into my new schedule. In order to graduate in 2018—because, at McGill, every medical student must complete the curriculum within eight years of starting it—I would need to complete my pediatrics rotation. So we agreed that for one month in the spring of 2014, I would return to medical school while training for the NFL draft. That meant I had to come back to McGill for a month before the draft, regardless of how that might affect my training, just *in case* I outlived the average NFL career span and still wanted to graduate.

If we stuck to the new schedule exactly, without deviating, I could graduate on time and continue to chase the NFL. But that remained a sizable *if*. I also needed to be realistic. The chances that I would make an NFL roster, in a league that has historically signed few players from my home country, were slim at best. So slim, in fact, that if I made it, I would be only the 15th player from a Canadian school ever to get that far. Given that, Dr. Primavesi and I also built in a contingency plan. If I failed, whether right away or after any of my first four seasons, we would adjust the timeline, speeding it back up. At least then I would be content, knowing I had no regrets or excuses. I had everything I needed. Which meant one thing: it was time to buckle down, focus and get to work.

THE EAST-WEST Shrine Bowl is an annual big-stage game for top US college prospects to impress draft-day decision makers that also raises money for Shriners Hospitals for Children, benefiting a network of non-profit medical facilities spread all over North America. Organizers invite two Canadians every year, one from the universities in the west and one from the universities in the east, with both selected by a vote of coaches across the country. It's usually held in January, and it marked my best chance to get noticed by NFL scouts.

In hopes of landing one of those two coveted spots, once my leave from school was granted, I moved down to Tennessee to train with other prospects. Part of our preparation meant zoning in on the tests everyone takes at the NFL Scouting Combine, making sure I could run (the 40-yard dash) and lift (225 pounds on the bench press, as many times as I could), and zip around cones fast enough to impress my future employers. Fortunately, I had the whole test thing down, from my sports medicine experience in medical school. That became my advantage, or what I hoped would be my advantage: I learned quickly and retained information well.

I worked, and worked, and worked some more. I lived with prospects from Vanderbilt, Baylor, Notre Dame—more traditional football programs, all of them certainly several levels above McGill. But my trainer later told me that my maturity stood out to him. He noticed how I did my dishes, cleaned my living spaces, pushed my roommates to act like grown-ups and treated everyone with respect. He said I reminded him of a "grown-ass man" rather than a 21-year-old guy.

I had no idea what I was walking into. It's probably a good thing I never watched the college version of the sport growing up. I didn't know there would be well over 100 schools in Division I, and that each graduated dozens of players every year. In other words, I didn't know I was one of thousands of prospects—and one of the only hopefuls who was still learning the game and still mastering technique. Had I known, I might have been discouraged. I guess sometimes ignorance really is bliss.

While I toiled, Sasha put together a DVD of my less than ideal college highlights. The problem wasn't so much that the package we presented was less than ideal. It was more that my best plays looked really great; actually, maybe too great. Because I played in a league unfamiliar to most scouts, it was difficult for them to compare me with other prospects, or place an objective value on the DVD. They had no idea of my level of competition, which often led to assumptions and variance. Still, we mailed copies to NFL scouts, general managers and personnel executives, hoping to hook just one.

Sasha also put together a list of factors to consider in choosing an agency that specialized in NFL representation. After contacting those that fit the criteria and would complement our team, we decided to hire A3 Athletics. A3 helped me hook up with a second trainer who focused specifically on technique. The crash course helped me set a tone, learn a ton of additional techniques, and discover small nuances with regards to the rules in American football compared with the Canadian version. The timing aligned perfectly, once again, as I received the invite to participate in the East-West Shrine Bowl—our version of a golden ticket from Willy Wonka.

I flew down to Tampa Bay for the game itself, and to participate in all the events that led up to it. Some of the prospects discussed their memories of travelling by charter with their college teams, fearsome opponents they'd toppled on national television, their connections with East-West teammates from other schools. I kept McGill's football standing to myself. There was no need to get into those bus trips or lay out all the losses. My roommate had a PS3 video game console that he had been gifted at a bowl game, one of dozens of post-season matchups that feature college teams in the US. I didn't know what bowl games were, let alone that they gave out gifts. Even when I went to the orientation, where players meet their short-term teammates and officials go over the schedule for the week, I worried that we might have made a mistake, that I hadn't *really* been invited. I practically leapt out of my seat when I heard my name called.

Sasha had come with me, to help soothe my fraying nerves, along with Chad Speck, a founding partner at A3 and the organization's president. Even now, I can see Sasha at my first practice, clad in this flashy orange polo, shorter than everyone else, scampering around the field in search of the best vantage points. It seemed as if he celebrated every good block I made, while introducing himself—and me, plus our story—to NFL scouts and executives. He emphasized the truth, that I was big, strong and athletic, and that I loved football and could learn pretty much anything. He framed what I did not yet possess—technical proficiency—as part of my potential. I don't consider myself a shy person, but there is just no way on earth I would have been able to present myself to NFL GMs the way Sasha did that week.

I ran up to Sasha and Chad at the end of my first practice, removed my helmet and told them, "You know, I can play with these guys." By the end of that week, we figured I would at least be signed by a team and given the chance to try out.

I still worried that I would continue to face doubt over the lack of competition I'd faced while playing at a Canadian university. In my DVD highlight reel, there were no Georgia defensive tackles getting pancake-blocked. We didn't even play the same version of football, which would make it even harder to evaluate me.

But not only did I hold my own in practice, I also crushed my opposition after kickoff. Suddenly, representatives from several franchises were a lot more interested in speaking with either me, Sasha or Chad. I began seeing my name pop up on different draft lists, too—*NFL* ones.

I went back to Tennessee. Kept practising. Kept training. Kept learning. My football ability grew by leaps and bounds. Sometimes, Sasha was forced into the role of defensive end, so I could work on my angles from a three-point stance. Other times, he stood near me as I went over my hand placement. One time, when we were practising my technique in a hotel room, I accidentally punched him in the face.

Eventually, word of my improvement reached J.P. Darche, the long snapper from McGill who had fought his way into the NFL, playing for the Seattle Seahawks and the Chiefs for nine seasons, despite entering the league as an undrafted free agent. J.P. also studied medicine, so he could relate to my twin passions. At first he couldn't fathom that a lineman from our school would exhibit real, actual, pro football promise. But when he saw my highlight tape, he told me, "You're mowing guys down like I've never seen in college."

That April, I returned to McGill as scheduled, to complete my pediatric rotation before the draft. I flew home and went back to my little apartment. In a strange twist, I watched one surgery at the Shriners Hospital in Montreal only a few weeks after I played in the game the Shriners organization had sponsored. There are more than 20 different Shriners hospitals in North America, and the specialized, cutting-edge treatments they provide for kids are truly amazing. The Shriners Hospital staffs care for the patients and take care of the families too. My brief time there reminded me how medicine, as a field, should work.

Meanwhile, off-shift, in my little apartment, I remained bummed about the Combine but buoyed by the fact that team reps were starting to watch my game film. I was also excited to see Flo, after our first experience with a long-distance relationship. We were back together, in person. We were a team. That same small, dumpy apartment is also where we planned everything with Sasha, the three of us holding long conversations deep into the night. Next steps included Sasha trying to create some buzz around my name before the draft. One night, he kept detailing his myriad plans while standing at the door frame in our room, delaying a good night's rest. At that moment, he earned another nickname: the Third Wheel.

Sasha also called the CFL league office to request a slot in their version of the Combine. But officials there told him that NFL scouts neither attended it nor paid attention to any of the results. Since it appeared I would be taken early in the CFL draft, I didn't need a slot that would be better used by someone else. That's when we came up with our craziest idea yet. We noticed that the NFL rules stated that players could undergo Combine-like testing at a university within 80 miles of their hometown. But McGill did not put on a Pro Day, nor did any other nearby Canadian college football programs.

No Pro Day? No problem. We decided to create our own.

SASHA KNEW NOTHING about a Pro Day, let alone how to put one together. Nor did he know how to convince important, and busy, NFL scouts and executives to fly to another country just to watch one player. As if that wasn't a difficult enough starting point, the task of organizing the whole thing fell entirely on him, because I was busy with that pediatrics rotation.

As I patrolled the same floor every day at the Montreal Children's Hospital, working shifts, caring for children, it seemed as though everyone I came in contact with was sick with some type of cold or flu. I lived in so much fear of catching an illness before my Pro Day that even my medical colleagues laughed at me, knowing my body was not used to germs from children. I must have washed my hands 20 times each day. I went to see my supervisor and asked for five days without shifts in the emergency room before the big day—a wish she granted.

While I tended to my patients, Sasha fleshed out a script that featured various drills, tests and measurements intended to showcase me in the best light. At least, that was the hope. A3 Athletics helped us reach out to teams. Then Sasha rented out a huge facility, the Soccerplexe in Lachine, Quebec. He invited any reporter who wanted to chronicle our little slice of Canadian football history to join us. He catered a lunch of sandwiches and salads. He made booklets with my info for the scouts who planned to visit, and gave *me* booklets with their information, which I studied. Years later, in KC, scouts who attended that Pro Day still talked about how perfect its organization was! I guess Sasha did something right.

Even so, I worried no one would come. Years had passed since the last player from a Canadian university program had been drafted into the NFL. This led to a new, dreaded twist on an age-old question: If a Pro Day doesn't take place in front of a single scout, did it really happen? But nine teams eventually confirmed their plans to send a representative, despite a date we shared with Johnny Manziel and his highly anticipated Pro Day at Texas A&M. Four CFL teams said they would dispatch their own decision makers too.

Sasha made the event into a family affair. My parents came with pastries, hot chocolate and coffee. Around 20 of my best friends showed up to form our version of a crowd. The whole day warmed my heart.

Looking back at that day, we always laugh at how little we knew, at our own hubris. I don't know how the day went so perfectly, only that Sasha made it so. Sasha, my close friend who had listened to my doubts for years. He's the one who talked me onto that field, the one who changed everything for both of us. I knew then that I would be working with Sasha until the end of my playing career. As friends, I knew we'd remain close for as long as we lived.

Yes, our Pro Day wasn't a typical showcase. Sure, it featured a middling NFL prospect who continued to doubt himself. (One who also had a stressful pediatric medical exam coming up in less than a week.) Between the official weigh-in at the Shiners game and the morning of the Pro Day, I had dropped 23 pounds. That stemmed from the pediatrics rotation, working too much and stuffing my face too little. I weighed in below 300 pounds, which would count against a prospective NFL guard. "Don't worry," Sasha told me, "just run faster." A snowstorm even hit the day before, delaying flights. *Really?* What are the chances? I wondered if we had been cursed.

I reminded myself to control what I actually could: my results. I also wanted to relax, stay cool and have some fun. I called Sasha the morning of our event and told him I was sick, a joke he laughs at much harder now, in hindsight. Despite the snowstorm, all nine teams showed up. I ran a 4.94-second 40-yard dash and a 4.59-second shuttle, where I sprinted around, and between, cones; broad-jumped nine feet six inches, good for a personal best; bench-pressed 225 pounds a full 34 times; and recorded a 31.5-inch vertical leap. These were elite numbers. For comparison, the first guard chosen in the 2014 NFL draft, Zack Martin, ran a slower, 5.22-second 40-yard dash, posted an identical 4.59-second shuttle, didn't surpass nine feet on the broad jump, registered 29 reps on the bench press and a 28-inch vertical leap. I'm not saying I was a better prospect than Martin, a seven-time Pro Bowler with the Dallas Cowboys and one of the NFL's best linemen. But the numbers showed objectively that we weren't playing football in different universes. After my dash, one scout turned to Sasha and said, "What the hell did he just run?"

I was giddy afterward, drunk on promise. Maybe I wouldn't be drafted. But I had done my best, and now had a much better chance.

CHAPTER 6

THE DRAFT

I went back to the hospital the day after the Pro Day, hoping throughout my shift that I had impressed someone with, say, Arizona, Buffalo, Chicago, Oakland, Philadelphia, San Francisco, Green Bay or the New York Jets. Despite my physical performance, I had my doubts.

At lunch on Pro Day, one of the scouts in attendance had asked whether I could snap a football for them, meaning spiral it between my legs in their direction. "Absolutely," I said. "No problem." But there *was*, in fact, a problem. I hadn't snapped a football in all my four years at McGill. I could *not* snap. I asked Sasha if he had a minute, and we left the room together. Once we were out of earshot, I told him to make sure this scout never found a football for me to snap with. I knew it was a bad idea—and it was more proof of just how much I had to learn.

Despite my worries, Sasha sprang into action and found a local company to sponsor a website for me. Scouts and team representatives could find game film there, along with biographical information and my Pro Day results. When the Pro Day had ended, I'd figured my performing for draft experts had concluded as well. I had no idea that teams were allowed to invite players in for visits, to meet with coaches and continue with evaluations. These visits would not lead directly to offers; the teams were just doing their research on prospects in advance of the NFL draft. Only *that* day, draft day, would I learn my fate. Meanwhile, I needed to make the best impression I could on all the coaches and execs who showed the slightest interest in me as a player.

To my relief and surprise, the invitations came—and kept coming. I ended up visiting nine teams, while finishing my final three hectic weeks in the pediatric rotation. Talk about balancing acts. On one visit, a coach asked what I knew about the franchise. He threw in a *be honest*, opening a door I probably should have closed immediately. Instead, I was honest—brutally so. "Listen," I said, "I don't know anything about the Raiders, except that you guys play on a shitty field." (Maybe, in the moment, that sentiment was a little too frank. But it was true. The Raiders shared their field with a major-league baseball team, the Oakland A's, meaning part of the football field was also an unlined baseball diamond. I ended up playing there six times, and each proved my assessment even more correct.)

The truth was, in many ways, even though my prospects had changed, I was still the same guy who, when reporters who covered McGill asked me to name my favourite NFL franchise, had to admit I did not have one. When they asked for my favourite player, I often gave a different answer, based on whatever name I could come up with at that moment. When Sasha mentioned NFL stars like J.J. Watt or Vince Wilfork, defensive juggernauts I might end up blocking, I often responded, "Who?" I still needed to learn who the Bills were (a football team in western New York) and where they played (Buffalo). Same—seriously— for the Kansas City Chiefs.

Don't take this to mean I flunked my interviews. When coaches asked me to grab a marker and diagram plays they had only just taught me onto a whiteboard, I flew through it with ease. When they asked about my football experience at McGill, I told them that I'd started 26 games in three seasons, gained 65 pounds along the way and played through a torn labrum (cartilage in the rim of my shoulder socket) my senior season.

Sasha helped me prep for these visits, compiling documents stuffed full of information for me to study in advance. They included the names and pictures of head coaches and their assistants, so that I would recognize them. Same for high-level executives, on the off chance they would meet with me. Sasha laid out summaries of offensive schemes and offensive line depth. One time, he explained the West Coast offence to me, which is mostly short passes built on timing and precision. Before I went to Green Bay, Sasha gave me the scoop on the Packers: they play at historic Lambeau Field, have a rich history and won the first-ever Super Bowl. I took those files he compiled as seriously as my medical school curriculum. I would read and memorize each one on my journey to whatever city I was visiting next.

As for stars, I really only knew of New England Patriots quarterback Tom Brady and Arizona Cardinals wide receiver Larry Fitzgerald. They became the "players I looked to emulate" during my interviews.

While Sasha prepped me, he was also juggling his own studies for the bar exam. He told me he didn't want to be the reason we failed. Neither did I. So every morning, when I went to work at the hospital, I took my passport and my suitcase, just in case I had a flight to catch on short notice, to visit another team. One time, when I couldn't get to Philly, I did the interviews over videoconference while wearing hospital scrubs—again, long before the pandemic popularized this thing called Zoom. I think my stethoscope even hung around my neck as I went into the nearest bathroom, locked the stall and talked to the O-line coach for an hour.

Some of my hospital colleagues knew little or nothing about the NFL, but all seemed to understand the unique opportunity I had—if only I could realize it.

During my visits, several franchises sounded roughly the same alarm. They asked pointed questions. *Do you really want to finish medical school while playing in the NFL? How do you know you can be committed 100 percent to learning the playbook, with med school on the side?* Having already decided I would no longer compromise—I was going to do both, be both—I mustered the strength to sit in front of famous head coaches and tell them that if they drafted me, I would, for sure, continue my studies. But I started to worry again that I might not have a choice.

Then I met with Kansas City and the team's coach, Andy Reid. I laid out, with full transparency, how I needed to make progress toward my degree or I would never become a doctor, wasting the schooling I had already completed. Other coaches in similar positions had asked, *Will you still have time for camp?* Or: *How much time will you spend studying the playbook vs. your textbooks?* But not him. Coach Reid said he admired my drive, that I straddled the line between confidence and arrogance well.

"You must be smart," he said, offering one of those all-knowing Coach Reid winks. "And if you're here, even though you love medicine, that must mean you really love football too."

He saw no reason I could not do both.

Finally! I'd found someone who understood me. I later learned that his mother, Elizabeth, had been one of the first female doctors to graduate from McGill; she was, in fact, a part of my medical tribe. Had this been a factor in his response to my commitment to my medical training—his mom's McGill history, or simply that he'd been raised by a doctor? I couldn't say, but it was a nice connection to discover.

Coach Reid will never fully know how much his affirmation helped, steeling me for the immense task ahead. He saw me less as a football player and more as a human who happened to play football, which is how I had come to see myself.

One question, though, lingered: Would I make it into the NFL?

THE 2014 NFL draft started on a Thursday night, May 8, when each team—at least those that had not traded away a pick—would make their first-round selection. I did not expect to be drafted that first day. By that point, the league had stretched the event out over three days, broadening its audience, making something as simple as pairing prospects with their new employers into more of a spectacle. The show would be beamed all over the world, and moved to different cities, where crowds of upwards of 100,000 people gathered to watch players walk across the stage to shake the hand of Commissioner Roger Goodell. Anyone attending in person couldn't even hear the endless analysis of each pick, from all the pundits on all the networks who spent weeks offering their opinions.

On Day 2, the second and third rounds would take place, and I believed I had a small chance of being chosen later in round 3. Or, if not, perhaps I would realize my NFL aspirations on Day 3, when rounds 4 through 7 would complete this particular draft. After speaking with interested teams, Sasha and Chad believed my realistic range extended from the third round to the last pick, the variance due to my unusual pedigree. I didn't believe I would start a bidding war, the surefire way to be taken earlier. It was one thing for a team to express interest in drafting you, quite another for that team to fear someone else drafting you. Since my prospects had risen late in the draft process, I didn't see much of a chance of that happening. It remained possible that I would go undrafted, and several franchises had floated the possibility of signing me as a free agent if that happened.

I went to work that Friday, in the neonatal intensive care unit no less. Of course, just when round 2 started, my unit received a page about an emergency C-section, for twins who would be born prematurely that afternoon. This marked a prime opportunity to learn from, and be exposed to, a rare case, and perhaps even scrub in and help with the procedure. I didn't need time to think about my options or the draft; I elected to view the surgery.

I told Sasha I would meet him at his place around 6 p.m. for a party he had planned to host with family and friends. But as the procedure stretched on longer than anticipated, it became clear that the festivities would start without me. It also became clear that I wasn't going to be available to talk if any offers actually came through. I handed my phone to one of the nurses and told her, "If somebody calls from a random area code and asks for Laurent Duvernay-Tardif, just answer the phone and say *yes*." I figured that any random number would likely be from an NFL team.

While I studied the complex procedure, Sasha heard from a source that the Jets had called to ask how I spelled my name. He left several voice mails on my phone. But no team called with the news we wanted.

I didn't make it to Sasha's place that night until after eight thirty. Day 2 had all but concluded and I had missed most of the shindig. Most of the guests were gone. I had not been selected. I stayed over that night, and we both went to bed early. I was exhausted from my week, and Sasha was tired from studying the bar exam. Maybe it was better that I didn't know what to expect. I wasn't too stressed about whether I would be taken or not, because I could still, and likely would, be signed as a free agent. Not being drafted would lower my chances of making the roster, yet plenty of free agent hopefuls do just that every season. At that point, all I wanted was one chance to go to an NFL training camp and show one team what I had learned and what I could do.

We hosted another draft party the next day, one I was actually able to attend. The fourth round flew by. The fifth round went more slowly, but it also passed without my name being called. When round 6 began, I was neither nervous nor certain I would be selected. Most of my crew, numbering around 60 people, crowded in around me as I plopped down on the couch in front of the TV. Sasha would later say he never doubted I would be drafted, even as teams continued to call to position themselves for the free agent frenzy that begins the very second the draft ends. I wish I had shared his optimism. But the truth is, I had no idea how things would play out.

Finally, during the sixth round, an 816 area code flashed across my phone. Everyone in the room went quiet. I yelled out, "Oh, M-O!" seeing those letters on my screen. I figured they stood for Missouri, home to the team in Kansas City. Sasha glanced at the television screen. The Chiefs were on the clock. Was this it? Our moment?

I stood up to take the call. Sasha pulled out his own cellphone and began to film. The video still exists. That's me, in a grey T-shirt, standing behind a couch with various diamond-like patterns, the room silent, people taking pictures, hanging on my every word.

I answered the call. It was indeed the Chiefs. Coach Reid and then general manager John Dorsey were both on the line. They wanted me to fly to Kansas City the next morning. Shortly after we hung up, the pick was announced on live television. My name and my new team were drowned out by a roomful of screaming family and friends.

The funny part is that Flo wasn't there. She was in New York taking a seminar as part of her master's degree in art history, and her absence spoke to the core of our relationship and our respect for one another's passions. We push each other to excel in completely different worlds, and if that meant she missed the moment I was drafted, good. I know she would've loved to be there, but there was no way she should miss an opportunity of her own just to hear my name called on TV. That's not how we roll.

For so long, all I'd wanted was to get drafted, and when I was, I knew: there's nothing like it. But after I spoke with Coach Reid, I fully realized what I was about to do. I had never gone to bed before thinking about hopping on a flight to the US to play pro football. The flight could have been to the home of any of the 32 franchises, but it ended up being the one in Kansas City. Within minutes, my life had changed, and I was leaving behind the places—and the people—I knew best, for a new city, a new team and a new career. I would have to learn the playbook and integrate into the locker room—*and* I would need to find a place to live, obtain a driver's licence, get a car and insurance, and on and on. It was dizzying to consider, so I decided to set all that aside for a few hours, and just celebrate with my friends and family instead.

I did try calling Dr. Primavesi, because I had a major exam scheduled for the following week. I assumed he had not been watching the draft. When I couldn't reach anyone from the school, I left for Kansas City, as my new team had instructed, taking only a backpack, a toothbrush and some clothes in a suitcase I hastily packed. (Fortunately, hospital officials would eventually see the news and congratulate me. Alas, I did have to make up the exam.)

As the 200th selection in the 2014 NFL draft, I became the 15th player from a Canadian university to be drafted by an NFL team, and only the second in the previous 15 years, ending a drought that started when the Jacksonville Jaguars took long-snapper Randy Chevrier in the seventh in 2001. A lineman from north of the border hadn't been selected since Mike Schad in 1986 (Rams, 23rd overall). This was downright historic. And lucrative, in a relative sense. If I made the 53-man roster that summer, the minimum salary would be $420,000, plus my signing bonus. Now the opportunity to make an NFL team, to be part of an NFL roster, was right there, close enough to smell and touch.

CHAPTER 7

THE CHIEFS

Being drafted wasn't like the climax of a sports movie, with an end point, the quest over, the happiness frozen, everyone celebrating my new job as an NFL right guard. It was one thing to hear my name called during the sixth round. It would be another thing entirely to become a true Kansas City Chief.

I arrived at my first training camp that August along with 89 other hopefuls—a number that would be cut down by nearly half to shape the actual roster, which consists of exactly 53 slots. In the NFL, there's also an eight-man practice squad for every team, where younger prospects could be stashed; they could practise but would not dress, travel or play in games. (Practice squad members can be signed at any time by another team.) Even if I managed to secure my standing on the active roster or the practice squad, my job would not be safe, not for a while, if ever. I would continuously compete against potential replacements of similar size and ability, with, in all likelihood, more experience. I could be released. I could be traded. I could get injured. The NFL offers a tenuous existence, unlike the NBA or MLB, where 100 percent of contracts are guaranteed.

Coaches remind players of that all the time. After a poor performance, one coach told our position group, "Guys, you know, on the third floor of the building there is a whole army of scouts who are looking for better, and cheaper, players to replace you. And trust me—they're looking hard."

On the football team at McGill, we were fuelled by camaraderie, loyalty and shared purpose. I heard from some with pro football experience that I should not look at the NFL the same way. They reminded me that I was entering a business, where loyalty was a fluid concept, dependent, always, on performance (mine, my teammates'), needs (of my new team) and how many games we won or lost.

To integrate into this new ecosystem, I had to create my own internal playbook. A lot of guys have some kind of touchstone when they first enter an NFL locker room: they played against one of their teammates in college, they had a brother who played in the league, they shared a coach with another player, etc. Meanwhile, I could still not even name all 32 teams, let alone the big NCAA colleges that all the other recruits had attended. The more seasoned players were another ball game entirely. Some of them were highly paid, with growing families, an army of representatives, no time, their own goals, and a bevy of endorsements to manage. They were used to travelling to other cities on private planes, riding to games behind police escorts and playing in front of tens of thousands of adoring fans.

These were my new teammates, and I would need to bond with them, find common ground. It wasn't going to happen overnight. As far as first impressions went, I saw what looked like question marks on many faces when they learned my background. Med school? Canadian? Speaks French? I had to shake how out of place I felt, and I did that by immersing myself in every aspect of my new existence—my technique, my workouts and my aptitude for offence.

Externally, all the necessary tools were provided—and then some. Our headquarters resembled a country club. I couldn't believe the gear we had access to: new cleats every week; top-of-the-line workout equipment; various jerseys with different colour combinations; a closet filled with hats, sweatshirts, T-shirts and jackets, everything red and gold. We had access to whirlpool baths, cryotherapy chambers, yoga instructors, nutritionists and some of the best doctors in the area.

It was hard moving to a new city without knowing how long I'd be there. It would have been easier simply to stay in a hotel. At the same time, I wanted freedom, and to personalize where I lived. Should I be investing time in things outside football, when I had to show my ability to learn, play and excel? There was a balance to be found, putting effort and energy into creating an environment outside football where I felt comfortable, because I knew that feeling comfortable could strengthen my bid to make the team roster.

I decided to rent a small one-bedroom apartment and buy a car. Otherwise, I tried to save as much as possible. And speaking of my wheels, I should note: I *hate* shopping for cars, because I'm always torn between opting for high performance or considering the brutal reality that they're not really assets, and their value depreciates quickly, starting the second they're driven off the lot. Many of my teammates cruised around in luxury vehicles, and I felt I had to show up for work in something other than my gold Yaris.

One day, on my drive home from team headquarters, I spied an awesome ride for sale on the side of the road. It was a 1984 Jeep Scrambler, an iconic, and distinctly American, classic. It didn't have doors. Or a roof. But it only cost $12,000, making it a cheap car with a lot of cachet. The Scrambler hit big in the locker room, which, as a bonus, helped with my integration. Teammates would stop by my locker to say things like, "Nice toy you got there, Frenchie."

Then winter hit. The temperature plummeted. Snow fell. Not only did I not have doors or a roof, I didn't have a heater. Forever adaptable—or maybe just stubborn—I drove that beast around all year. Sometimes that meant throwing on two winter jackets and a toque. I became known as the Canadian bear that season.

Everyone in my family adjusted too, whether it was my parents splurging for a cable package so they could view NFL games rather than science and technology programs, or Flo realizing she would need earplugs after a single trip to Arrowhead Stadium. Chiefs Kingdom was—*is*—that loud.

Some nights—most, even—I would call home, complaining to my parents or my girlfriend about how far behind I was compared with the majority of my teammates. Most of them had played football all their lives. Sometimes I compared this submersion to when I first entered medical school: the NFL was that nuanced, that idiosyncratic, that different of a universe from any I had ever known. "I'm not close to their level," I would say.

I *was* making progress. But it felt as if it wasn't fast enough, not for an environment as competitive as the NFL. After one particularly rough practice early on, Coach Reid asked loudly, "Hey, Frenchie, have you ever played football before?" Ouch. But I could see his point. I knew I needed to improve. It was discouraging, especially after shifting all my focus and energy toward football. Deep down, I felt that Coach Reid appreciated both me and my efforts, but I still had to meet his baseline expectations. Gradually, as I started to inch closer, he'd call out, "Good job, Doc." He also started calling me Larry, until eventually the whole team referred to me that way.

It didn't take long before I felt more comfortable in the locker room, more like one of the guys. But my future would hinge on far more than my personal relationships. I needed to improve at football, to approach the game more like a craft, in order to register immediate, and dramatic, progress.

IT WAS TIME to create a new plan, one aimed at snagging a roster slot. To start with, I needed to put the weight back on that I had lost during the pediatric rotation before the draft, lest I be pushed around, or bowled over, by defensive tackles. But I couldn't just add weight in a vacuum, because I didn't want to lose one of my strengths—the ability to sprint into space and block, or occupy, would-be tacklers. So I put the weight on slowly, through a healthy diet of high-calorie meals packed with protein.

I spent months honing my technique: learning different sets, or how I would best position myself to pass block, so that I could vary my approach to rushers based on their strength/weakness profile or to confound their expectations. I view this part of football, all the adjustments and the counters to them, as the game within the game. Like when a defence lines up in a way that indicates they plan to be aggressive, and we line up to make it *look* like we want to call an inside zone run play, which an aggressive defence would typically obliterate. But we're really going to throw the ball, and by using the defence's alignment against them, sending the running back in motion before the snap, and understanding our own scheme, we can make individual adjustments, and collective ones. I can gauge how much room I have to set up in my stance based on the available information, along with my splits—how far I set up between the linemen on either side of me—which way to lean and how far. It took me a year at least to begin to integrate that level of nuance into my game, and I am far from done learning. I am a perfectionist, and this is the kind of stuff I love paying attention to instead of just relying on brute force.

To work on that game within, Coach Heck gave me a list of elite guards to study, plus instructions for how to watch their film, learn from their technique and apply it to my own skill set. "Look closely," Heck told me, referring to David DeCastro of the Pittsburgh Steelers, a six-time Pro Bowler. "You'll see: he makes everything look easy." Coach Heck was right. DeCastro did make it look easy. And I still had a lot to learn.

Teammates like Mitch Morse described me as "athletic" and "explosive," and they complimented my desire to never let up, to finish every play. But that also made me, as Mitch pointed out, "like a caged beast." Meaning: I couldn't make use of those traits in full until I understood how to truly put them to work. It was the difference between being a bull in a china shop and being a bull inside a bullfighting ring.

I worked on how to deploy different types of blocks without giving my plan away to defenders, whether by pointing my toes in the same direction for run plays or leaning the same way on passing downs. I mixed up my hand pressure on the same play at different points in the game, sometimes using all my force to move a defender, other times softening so that, the next time I went full go, I might catch the element of surprise. When you can do that, you start playing with it to give false cues to your opponents. The game within the game resembles poker.

I asked a million questions. My position coach, Andy Heck, affably answered all of them. He even spent extra time and energy schooling me on the language of pro football, because he wanted me to stick around. Sometimes he would say that "we're in a backed-up situation," and I would need to ask the most rudimentary questions. What did he mean by backed-up? (Answer: within roughly five yards of our own end zone.) Or he would go on about a draw play—a run that looks at first like a pass—and I wondered if he wanted me to physically draw something. Or he would mention EMOL, which stands for End Man On the Line of scrimmage. "Who is EMOL?" I asked.

I started to diagram our playbook in my spare time, in the same way that toddlers trace the alphabet. The extra study helped me differentiate any defence's base looks (how they normally lined up, whether they preferred bigger sets, with a fullback and a tight end, or favoured a wide-open passing game that meant more wideouts) vs. sub ones (where we tweaked our tendencies to add confusion, often against lighter personnel, like in three-wide-receiver sets). Diagramming helped me figure out the different approaches to defences that sent out three defensive linemen, or four, or five. I gleaned how NFL teams adjusted for four downs rather than the three we play in Canada, and understood how that one extra play per series added another layer of complexity, because teams could make more adjustments, with three chances to gain 10 yards before they were forced to punt the ball to the other team. Up north, the game was more symmetrical, with offensive schemes built out based on angles and space. Down south, they viewed defences differently, attacking specific defenders, or targeting weaknesses in schemes, or messing with safety rotations to confuse quarterbacks into throwing passes into the wrong windows, where defenders waited.

The more I practised, the more I could identify everything that a pro football lineman needs to identify for any given play.

I needed to know who I was blocking, how to adjust and how to work together to ward off blitzes. Learning to play as a unit was crucial, because all five linemen needed to drop to the right depth, at the exact width our coaches desired, or we would expose our hips and wouldn't be able to protect our teammates. In other words, the O-line puzzle needed to fit, and if it did, we created a bubble around our quarterback, so that defenders would slide by when they tried to speed around the bubble, or ricochet off us when they tried to find a crease to power through. Whether we were passing the ball or running it, the technique was distinct, even the angle I needed to take to block a defender, as well as the spot I needed to reach before them to engage at the right angle—along with my hand leverage, hand speed and whatever adjustments my quarterback might make at the line.

After my first few months, I called home and updated my parents on my progress. I wasn't *that guy* anymore, meaning perpetually behind my teammates. My footwork had improved, which meant my balance had become steadier, which meant I could adeptly pass block and run block—a prerequisite not only to making the team but to getting on the field. I took fewer long and heavy steps, now jabbing my way toward defenders instead of lunging at them, which made it easier for me to turn upfield.

That August, while strolling around an art gallery with Flo, I took a call from the front office. I'd done it. I had made the team. It was, honestly, a huge relief. I had worried I might be released like so many later-round draft picks. I turned to Flo, who of course knew from my face that something big had just occurred.

All I could muster was, "I made it."

Now it was time to play my way onto the field.

That would still take some doing. I wasn't a practice squad player, so I could not be claimed by another franchise. But I didn't play my entire first year, which I spent on the active roster. I wasn't dressed for any games, because NFL teams can only dress 45 of their 53 players. I was on the team but still apart from it, more like an apprentice. I'd be lying if I said I wasn't frustrated sometimes, that I didn't long for the McGill days, when my team needed me and I raced from the field to my textbooks to the hospital and back, again and again.

AT THE END of my first year, Coach Heck called me into his office. It was time for my end-of-season exit interview. As much as he had helped during my first season, he wanted to ensure that I understood the stakes. "We gave you that year to learn," he said plainly, looking me directly in the eyes. "But next year, when you show up, you have to have the mentality that you're fighting for a starting position."

A realization dawned on me. I was privileged to have this opportunity to play pro football at the highest level—more privileged, even, than I'd grasped. I had learned a new language, a new offence, a new locker room and a new city. Now I needed to continue my football transformation with a new, more cutthroat mindset, because I knew that if I failed to show results, the NFL machine would spit me back out. I knew that year I had been given to learn was a big vote of confidence on the part of the Chiefs, and now I needed to start contributing to the team.

But within a few days of the season's end, I had to carry that mindset with me right back to medical school. That off-season, early 2015, I trained as I never had before, in between hospital shifts, of course. I told everyone that I planned to fight my way into the starting lineup. This time, nobody laughed.

I reported back to Kansas City for training camp that August. My path to the starting lineup seemed clear, if not certain. I would compete with Zach Fulton for the slot at right guard. The Chiefs had drafted Zach the same year as me, in the same sixth round. But he had started all 16 games in the previous season, marking the biggest difference between us, and perhaps giving him a slight advantage.

For players on the fringe of the roster, competing for jobs, the pre-season always induces stress, raising the stakes for every snap in games that don't actually count. Most years, a team would start with something like 15 offensive linemen on the camp roster. But as coaches cut players, trimming the tally to the 53 they're allowed to keep (or guys were injured, opening slots), they'd whittle the number of O-linemen down to eight. Sometimes they kept one more, or one fewer, depending on how the rest of the roster was shaped. Out of the eight O-linemen who make the team, there are veterans with big contracts (like Eric Fisher) who are difficult to release without screwing up the salary cap and paying guaranteed cash to someone who isn't playing. So there aren't really eight spots available. There might be four, or one, and how many depends on a million other factors, such as the depth on the team at every other position, how that team wants to play and where it chooses to spend its money.

Before NFL seasons start, the intensity for more than half the players who arrive for training camp is already high, and it only gets higher. If they make the roster, their spot isn't guaranteed beyond that day. Scouts perpetually identify potential replacements, and bring them in for visits that sometimes end with new signings. The next season, the cycle begins anew, only there are more applicants for every job, many of them younger, and cheaper, than the players who managed to complete the previous year. That aspect of survival in the NFL can be hard to watch, let alone live through. I always thought about my teammates' families when the Chiefs released them. Despite that context—the NFL is, and always will be, a business first—I saw the fight for roster spots as a fair competition.

There was even still room for camaraderie between teammates engaged in zero-sum competitions. Just how much camaraderie surprised me at first, especially in my first two seasons, when veterans I competed with took extra time to help me acclimate, even if that assistance might ultimately cost them. One veteran in particular showed me the importance of competing as hard as possible to make the team, while also helping competitors improve, because the franchise's success hinged on the collective strength of all 53 players. That veteran was Jeff Allen, and he became a valuable mentor. I found him hilarious, huge, jolly and charismatic, but also smart on the field, and crafty. It would have been way harder to last in the NFL without his advice.

I didn't play in the fourth pre-season contest that year, and I didn't know that not playing in that particular game was actually a good thing. I know now that it's common for a coach to rest his starter before the beginning of a long season. So, not playing meant I had made the team again. It also meant I would start at right guard when the Chiefs kicked off for the first game of the 2015 season.

ONCE I SLID into the starting lineup, the realization, the magnitude of the opportunity, began to sink in. Not only would I run onto the field for the first offensive play of the season opener, but

I would block the Houston Texans and their ridiculously talented defensive line, led by a perennial All-Pro in J.J. Watt—a player I had not been aware of, despite his superstar status, only two years earlier. I had never even donned my uniform for a regular-season NFL game before! On top of that, we had lost Eric Fisher, our right tackle, the man I worked in sync with, to an ankle injury he suffered in practice the Thursday before the game kicked off. The Chiefs signed a backup, last-minute, four days before kick-off. In the twist of all twists, I helped *him* learn the playbook.

In another unexpected development, teaching the newcomer sharpened my focus, helping to distract me so I could push down my growing nerves. I reminded myself: I had nothing to lose, and a steady job as an NFL starter to gain. On the first in-season offensive snap of my pro football career, Vince Wilfork—a defensive tackle who's roughly the size of a single-wide trailer—lined up across from me. We had called an outside zone run to the left, and since I was the right guard, I was responsible for sprinting to my left and helping to open the gap that Wilfork desired to close, the one between the centre and myself. I was late, and he ran right by me, and my instinct was to lament a missed opportunity. Like, *Oh my God, I'm never going to be able to block this guy.* Fortunately, Wilfork had jumped offside. Whew. Crisis averted. In recalling that afternoon, Mitch insists that we shoved Wilfork even after one play, just two young, dumb O-linemen mixing it up while making our first start. Mitch remembers Wilfork laughing, and telling us, "You guys have a lot of football left ahead of you. You're going to have to conserve your energy, and pick the fights that are worth picking." Good advice.

I also drew confidence that afternoon from Alex Smith, our starting quarterback. Alex exuded an unshakable vibe. The San Francisco 49ers had selected him first overall in the 2005 NFL draft. But after a series of injuries, and a revolving door of coaches, many pundits had labelled him a bust. But rather than retire, or agree with them, Alex fought for his place in the NFL. He had transformed into one of the steadiest signal callers in the league. He was also decisive, and liked to throw the ball quickly. I liked that style of QB play, because his fast release meant less time I needed to hold my blocks—which helped me sign my lucrative contract extension.

After the season opener, I understood for certain what I already, on some level, knew: I belonged.

MY FIRST YEAR playing, I started 13 games. I also endured my first benching, after a brutal *Monday Night Football* loss to the Green Bay Packers that Mitch described as a "Biblical stomping" all across the line. I continued to work hard to improve, and got myself back off the bench.

Meanwhile, that season, the Chiefs were winning a lot of games. We were 1–5 when I got back into the lineup, and we went 10 for 10 for the rest of the season. When the victory tally ballooned, so did the attention. It was obvious whenever I went home. Strangers recognized me in restaurants or on the street. Television producers asked me to appear on their shows. Suddenly, the interest in our football team meant a whole lot of people knew me—way more than I'd ever expected. But the increasing notoriety also meant more journalists, some of whom would explore established angles (like how Coach Reid had yet to win a Super Bowl as a head coach) while others went after fresh ones (like the guard from Canada who spent his off-seasons in medical school).

As the spotlight found me, and the glare from it intensified, everyone from reporters to my teammates began to consider my unique relationship to a hot-button issue, that of concussions in sports, particularly the NFL. The question on most people's minds was whether my two passions existed in conflict—whether I felt it, whether it affected me. I caught their drift. At medical school, I was studying how to care for people. In the NFL, I was routinely, strategically, crashing into them.

For almost a decade, since 2008, news accounts had been homing in on concussions in pro football. Researchers were exploring links between traumatic brain injuries, or TBIs, and the degenerative brain disease chronic traumatic encephalopathy, widely known as CTE, which is believed to be caused by repeated blows to the head but can only be diagnosed posthumously. The scientific studies were piling up and putting great emphasis on the issue. Some studies were good, others were flawed because they included too many biases or lacked a control group. One study that got a lot of attention studied the brains of retired professional football and hockey players. Post-mortem examination of their brains revealed signs of CTE in the vast majority of retired players who had reported memory loss, dementia and a host of other issues. While the link has not yet been proven, it certainly seems as though it might exist. The issue even became the premise of a movie, *Concussion*, starring Will Smith, released in 2015.

Given my background, I became something of an unwilling participant in the public debate around all this. The questions from journalists were pointed. Did my passions present a paradox? Was I sending the wrong message by partaking in a sport where violence is part of the DNA? Was I taking unnecessary risk by playing? Would it damage my ability to excel as a doctor years later, down the road?

I had long ago asked myself the same questions. I had considered all of this, and decided that I would continue playing.

Don't mistake that to mean I didn't take the issue seriously. I did. But my calculus had to be focused on questions relevant to my career: What were those potential hazards and negative impacts of playing a contact sport like football versus my love of the game and the positive ways I knew the game would change my life? My thought process was deep and internal, and it was difficult to explain my reasoning to the world, over and over, while I tried to make peace with my decision.

I took steps to mitigate what risk I could, both from a personal standpoint and from a league-wide one. The NFL was altering rules every year—banning defenders from leading with the crown of their helmets when tackling, for example—to better protect its players, particularly its quarterbacks. Commissioner Goodell levied heavy fines on violators. Teams were told to limit contact in practice, cutting down on collisions. Doctors worked to improve concussion protocols, including testing for symptoms such as headache, nausea and tunnel vision, then comparing those scores after an injury to a baseline a player establishes in those same tests before the season starts. We are required to return to that baseline before we can return to practice.

Protocols are important, of course, because they provide an objective assessment of a player and put in place a set of rules to protect us. But I believe the most important factor in addressing the concussion issue is education and awareness. We must not ignore TBIs, but we also need to realize that the available data remains subjective; there isn't a known marker for when a player has had a concussion, especially when the symptoms exhibited are mild. Players need to trust the medical staff, so they can be honest about signs and symptoms and receive the right treatment and rest that will help them heal. To do that, players need to feel they *can* be honest, that they won't lose their job because they've told the truth. Professional athletes are competitive by nature and want to contribute on the field to the team's success. It's hard to put up your hand and say, "Coach, I can't play." Throughout pro football history, it has been common for athletes to hide brain fog from their doctors. But there is no reason to treat a concussion any differently from a torn ligament, even if they're less obvious.

Yes, the injury risks in a contact sport like football are real, but on a continent where childhood obesity rates are increasing every year, people often use this argument as a reason not to be physically active. Of course, you can pick a safer sport, but team contact sports such as hockey, football, lacrosse and rugby offer kids a way to stay active, and they learn a lot from the experience, too. In North America, there are many more people who suffer from obesity, hypertension and diabetes than there are who suffer injuries related to physical activity. To only consider the drawbacks while ignoring the benefits is somewhat close-minded. I don't fault parents who refuse to let their kids play football, but I don't fault those who let them play, either. I am not sure I would let my kids play if the environment was like the one I played in as a kid. But I think the benefits of playing team sports are important to the development of our youth. We need to start seeing the contact part of the game as a secondary element in what you are trying to accomplish as a team, rather than the primary focus. When I was playing as a kid, I saw too many coaches congratulate players on a big hit that had no consequence to the game itself. To me, that is stupid. It shouldn't matter how loud a hit was or how impressive it looked. All that should matter is: Did you tackle your guy and stop the progression of the football? If we change that culture in football, hockey and other contact sports, I believe the benefits of playing would definitely win out.

If you play a contact sport, there are numerous ways to decrease the long-term risks and complications of brain injuries. Awareness and understanding are key. My hope is that we're on the right track. But I'm not relying on hope alone. After finding myself, as a pro footballer and doctor-in-training, in the spotlight on this issue, I promised myself I would do everything I could to make the sport safer and use my unique approach to advance the field of research. I accepted a role on the NFL Players Association's committee for health and safety, along with roughly 40 physicians, researchers and experts from all over the US. We examined new studies, new technology and further rule changes, and our work reminded me of the distinctive position I now occupied, the result of the dual life I was building.

I also met with team-affiliated doctors and asked pointed questions, particularly about long-term side effects of brain injuries. I reached out to helmet makers to better understand new, emerging safety technologies. Their answers reassured me. I sat in locker rooms while teammates discussed concussions, and I believed that the committee could help inform them with real facts, and the right emphasis on the right developments: safer helmets, better tackling techniques, improved communication between players and those who care for them.

I sent my teammates the latest research papers, and those findings would spark more debates between meetings and practices. I believe that all the responsibility should not fall on players. Coaches should also be reprimanded for the malicious hits that lead to concussions, and they need to make sure those behaviours are not reinforced in the film room, behind closed doors. We should teach proper tackling technique, and talk about the risks to players who don't tackle correctly. Only then will the likelihood of serious, long-term brain injuries be reduced. Even though there's a long way to go, I have noticed steps in the right direction since I was drafted in 2014.

There was also a ripple effect to consider—would youth teams follow the pros' lead?—and a culture that needed to change. As NFL players, we have the potential to positively change our sport by becoming models to kids who play football. We need to make sure that coaches at the youth level have that same philosophy and teach how to play with contact in a safer way. No more hamburger drills, no more circle of death. We need to teach kids to play smart football. That's where education and awareness can become the primary driver for transformation.

Perhaps my own experience is instructive here. Because I didn't start playing football until age 16, and because I played in the Canadian university system, and because I didn't play in any games my first year, I had not absorbed the same number of blows as the vast majority of my NFL counterparts. In theory, based on data showing that brain injuries tend to result from cumulative events, enduring fewer blows could serve as a protective measure. Starting tackle football at later ages could reduce the number of concussions, and the associated side effects, for all players.

Sometimes teammates asked for my opinion, or inquired if I might speak with their loved ones, in order to provide context on one injury or another. I tried never to comment on a diagnosis or treatment plan—it was not my role to do so—but many times I was able to explain an injury to a teammate. I could tell someone who had fractured a fibula—the bone that runs the length of the back half of the leg—that it wasn't the end of the world. The fibula is responsible for only about 15 percent of weight-bearing capacity. Once the bone healed, a player would, in all likelihood, return to the field with no increased risk of long-term side effects.

I liked to remind my wounded teammates that when writers call a football player "injury prone," they are either oversimplifying or exaggerating, or both. All injuries are not created equal. Some linger. Some heal quickly. Some lead to complications that keep players out for extended periods beyond the timelines they're first given. Some result from poor decisions, others from thudding collisions, pile-ups of bodies, or dumb luck, like when supersized opponents accidentally fall into someone's legs at full speed. The NFL is basically a thousand different car wrecks every week.

I do not feel that football is in a state of crisis with regard to concussions. But I also won't plant my head in the turf and pretend the game is not dangerous. I know that every time I step onto a football field, I am taking risks. That's the baseline, the starting point for my self-health evaluation. I constantly ask myself the most important question: Is it worth it? And every time I'm injured, I reassess. Was football worth it? *Really?*

During the 2015 season, my first playing at the professional level, I suffered my first concussion, against Houston in the playoffs. I didn't play against New England in the next round, and we lost. Of course, I was heartbroken not to play in our final game that season. But I was reassured that I didn't need to put any extra pressure on myself *to play*, particularly at the expense of my future. I had six months to recover in the off-season, and a two-month rotation of internal medicine where I experienced no symptoms, which was a good test of my mental capacity and concentration.

A few years later, in 2018, during practice before a pre-season game, I got whacked in the head by a linebacker up the field. I didn't lose consciousness, but when I popped up, I could tell that something wasn't right. I erred on the side of extreme caution. I went to the bench and told my coaches I needed to come out.

I was asymptomatic, but we decided I would not play in the last pre-season game in order to give myself an extra week of rest. Two weeks later I was back, and I was not scared.

In both cases, I took the combination of sitting out and experiencing minimal symptoms as the best possible signs. But one thing is for sure, it's easier to discuss concussions when you're not the one who's suffered them. If my soul ever returned a different answer to those is-it-worth-it searches, I long ago decided that I would stop playing.

In the end, I did not see the conflict between my medical and football careers as a real conflict. Not a serious one. Not for me, anyway. But it's important to note that while I have graduated from medical school, I don't have all the answers. I'm still searching, still learning, like everyone else. I continue to consider my equipment, my technique and my lifestyle, and to ask myself whether changing any of those factors—or my nutrition, or my exercise routine—will help me further mitigate the hazards inherent in my football career. I believe I am doing, and have done, everything I can to keep my brain as healthy as possible. But I have to be honest with myself: there's so much about head injuries that we don't know.

In an ideal world, the NFL, with its platform and the resources it has poured into research, would be a leader on the concussion issue. But when it comes to changing the culture of our sport and inspiring kids and coaches at the youth level, the biggest platform in our sport does not belong to the league; it belongs to the players. If we collectively assume a bigger role, in raising awareness, in educating, in emphasizing just how serious this is, we can do more. All of us. Myself included.

Chapter 8

THE TEST

One night, during a rotation in the ER at Montreal General, two police officers led a handcuffed suspect into the lobby. One of the cops had suffered a bad gash on his arm while making the arrest. He needed stitches. The staff asked me if I was comfortable suturing the wound. I was, and I introduced myself.

"Aren't you the football player?" he asked.

Yes, I sheepishly admitted. It was a strange exchange to have with someone when you're trying to close a bleeding laceration in their arm.

The officer looked down. "Now I'm going to have your autograph for the rest of my life," he said, meaning the scar.

There were moments like that, when my worlds would collide or intertwine, despite my efforts to separate sports and school as much as possible. At the end of every season, I traded physical contact for human contact. Flo and I would drive straight home, listening to podcasts as we slogged through the 24-hour trip. The trip gave me time for the necessary mental transition, from Kansas City to Montreal, football to medicine—the kind of transition that defined my life.

The hardest thing was not the physical transition but the mental one. I was going from a locker room where I was the centre of attention and had a whole team of professionals there to optimize my performance, to the hospital floor, where, as a medical student, I was at the bottom of the medical hierarchy, part of a team that was there to optimize the care of patients. This meant moving from a place where I needed to be tough and intimidating to a place where I had to show empathy and listen. Truly, this transition could be very difficult.

Meanwhile, many of my teammates would have flown off on vacations to Hawaii or the Caribbean while I returned to McGill and my studies. I still lived in my cramped old apartment, and often started my rounds before sunrise. I bounced from hospital to hospital, rotation to rotation.

I was only reminded of football when I trained. I still had to keep in shape—proof that a clean separation between the two halves of my life wasn't really possible. During an off-season in the NFL, you're never really off. It wasn't easy. After a long shift at the hospital, all the standing, all the walking, all the lunch breaks that never happened, I found that summoning the energy to train was hard. All I really wanted was to sit and chill out. I came to really respect people who exercise regularly after a full day at the office. I had to find ways to motivate myself; if I wanted to play football, I had no other choice. I had to find the energy to lift with the same purpose and intention as my teammates, who were able to train in fancy facilities and made training the centre of their schedule. I had to push my limits, running faster, lifting heavier weights and jumping farther. So, kudos to all those cubicle workout warriors. I can relate.

Doing the reverse—fitting my education in around football— was likewise challenging. I learned a particularly painful lesson in

2015, while attempting to ace a medical school exam in orthopaedic surgery during our in-season bye week. Every NFL team is granted one week off each season, and that year ours was in November. But first we had to fly to London to play the Detroit Lions in one of the games the league schedules overseas each year, in an effort to extend its reach into emerging markets.

We did not beat the Lions so much as we trounced them, winning 45–10. I had planned to cram for my exam on the nine-hour return flight. But because of *how* we triumphed, and because this victory followed a stretch of five losses in six games, a party broke out, which is understandable, and reasonable, unless you're trying to study for a major—and majorly complicated—test. Hip hop blared from portable speakers as my teammates danced, whooped, hollered, drank and played cards. Several Chiefs with leftover British pounds had used them on booze at the duty-free shop. A dice game broke out in the back, with any leftover foreign currency used to make wagers. Mitch remembers other teammates asking, "Where's Larry?"

I was wearing noise-cancelling headphones and reading a textbook, trying to study but not really able to concentrate. Mitch never stopped joking about the size of that book: *so big*, he joked, *it could be used as a weapon*. Eventually, I gave up. They coaxed me to the back for a few rolls of the dice.

When we landed, the bye week began in earnest, and I chose reading over sleeping. I flew back to Montreal, cramming on *that* plane, and two days later, after 48 hours of prep, I took the exam. Fortunately, I passed, although I did not by any means ace the test. The whole scenario reinforced the discipline required to keep up with all the demands and commitments I'd taken on. And the more I could separate football and medicine during the season, the better.

We lost in the first round of the playoffs after the 2016 season, but as I sped back toward Montreal, I believed that we'd begun to build something—the kind of team that had a legitimate shot at winning it all. I wanted to remain in Kansas City, to continue playing for the Chiefs, but my rookie contract was about to expire, and if it did, I would become a free agent after the next season.

Rather than wait, the Chiefs began negotiations with us on an extension. While the negotiations were ongoing, I worked through my geriatrics rotation, and we tried to hop on phone calls multiple times each day. One night, Sasha phoned and said the Chiefs were offering something like $30 million. I responded with glee, "Hell yeah, let's sign!" But he said we should wait and ask for more. I trusted Sasha, but that time I pushed back, telling him we could lose the deal through greed. My response spoke to my nerves. But we did counter, and the Chiefs did agree to raise the compensation. Turns out, once again, Sasha was right. I signed the extension in February 2017.

As I affixed my signature, it was hard to believe how far we'd come. There we were, seriously wondering whether the five years—and up to $42 million—that Kansas City had offered was *enough*. I became one of the highest-paid players at my position in the entire NFL. Mitch, my offensive linemate, sent me a text saying I was the only Canadian who was actually living the American Dream. I laughed. It wasn't true, but I accepted the compliment nonetheless.

I called my parents and told them about the deal, and the numbers. I began to cry from excitement and joy. My mom paused.

"Great," she said calmly. "If that's what you wanted, I'm happy for you."

"Mom, do you realize . . ." I asked.

She put my dad on the line. He said, "That's nice for you. You are a man of many projects, and you will be able to accomplish a lot with that money."

Then: *Good night.*

Then: click.

I hung up, and glanced at Flo. Had that exchange just happened?

About 10 minutes later, they called back, super-excited, saying that they hadn't fully grasped what I'd meant. They told me how proud they were. They hopped in their car and drove to my apartment with a case of beer. We sat on the kitchen floor—a family tradition—and celebrated. For me, that call highlighted my parents' core values. They don't consider money, past a certain amount, all that important, certainly not as a defining element of their lives. "Money is a tool to realize projects you believe in," they always said. But they had come to see what the contract represented to me, and that's when they understood why I was so excited.

At the end of the night, my mom told me I should go to bed because I had a long day at the hospital in the morning. She said, "You should go to work tomorrow, otherwise you might never go back."

It was true, what my parents felt about money and what it means. Money has never driven me either. But in the NFL, money talks, and this sum said that the Chiefs were willing to make me the fourth-highest-paid guard in the league, while devoting a higher percentage of their salary cap space to keep me in the fold. The money was nice—don't get me wrong. It was life-changing. But it was also simply a by-product of their appreciation—for my skill, my work ethic, what I added to the locker room—which meant far more.

Also of note that spring: we used our first-round pick on a young, gunslinging quarterback from Texas Tech. Coach Reid had even traded two additional draft selections—including our first-rounder the next year—to move into position to take him. That April, Patrick Mahomes arrived in Kansas City. He was not yet a superstar, and there were doubts surrounding his style of play. No one knew how soon he would obliterate those doubts, after a year of apprenticing under Alex.

In Week 2 of the 2017 season, I handed the franchise another reminder of my own progress. We were hosting the Eagles that afternoon, and directly across from me at the line was Fletcher Cox, the menacing defensive tackle I had watched from the stands at that first NFL game I'd attended in person. Thing is, he no longer made me consider another profession. That day, in our 27–20 victory, I played my best game as a professional, limiting Cox to half a tackle for the entire game.

Again, we advanced to the post-season. And again, we stumbled in our playoff opener. I began to sympathize with Chiefs fans, the diehards who understood the history, who didn't root for a team that never made the playoffs but rather a team that never made the Super Bowl. That was almost worse, getting that close but never all the way. As competitors, it was easy to feel the sting of another disappointment. But we also had to remind ourselves of all the progress the franchise had made since hiring Coach Reid four years earlier. The reality of the NFL is that 31 of 32 teams feel that sting every year, and the reality then in Kansas City was that we were advancing ever closer toward becoming the one team that did not end the season disappointed. There's a fine line there—between acknowledging progress and becoming complacent. We wanted more. But we knew, too, what we were building.

In our despondent locker room, we vowed to become the team we knew we could be the following season, in 2018. That year, though, I would sit for my biggest medical exam yet. This particular test would determine whether I managed to graduate in the eight years that McGill allotted. It would also lead to my next step toward becoming a doctor: picking a specialty and beginning a residency. In order to do my part—for my degree, and for the Chiefs—I elected to take the exam in May rather than earlier, in March, to give myself extra time to study. I'd learned my lesson from that London flight.

The Chiefs in general, and Coach Reid specifically, were understanding and flexible. They didn't have to be. The date of the exam meant I would arrive three weeks late for spring camp. Some of those OTA workouts are voluntary, but most players show up anyway so that everyone can improve together. Coach Reid told me not to bother, which meant the world to me. That he told me to finish my doctorate at home in Montreal, excusing me from practice and all the attendant stress, was huge for my chances of passing the exam. I also saw that it meant he had faith in me, that I would hold myself accountable, remain in tip-top shape and strike the right balance once more.

The test would cover everything we had learned in medical school. I spent four months studying after the season ended, knowing that if I didn't pass, one of my dreams would be put on hold indefinitely, if not lost entirely. The pressure could not have been greater for all students, including me. The difference for me was that the broader public knew I was taking this exam. For four years I'd done interviews about my med school endeavours, while promising myself I would become the first active NFL player to graduate with a medical degree. At the moment of truth, it hit me, the flip side: What if I was the first doctor hopeful that legions of fans saw fail his board exam? Some legacy.

After the playoff defeat, I was engulfed by interview requests and marketing opportunities. I tried to fix a schedule that balanced it all with exam prep, including time for family, to visit friends I hadn't seen in forever, and to work on projects for the foundation Flo and I were setting up to support youth and kids in athletics and the arts. But it was too much, I couldn't focus; there was always something to pull me away from my textbooks.

Finally, in desperation, Flo and I moved to a friend's cabin for a few weeks. There, about a 90-minute drive from Montreal, I was near enough to dash home if need be but far enough away to hunker down in solitude. I transformed the cabin into a *Rocky*-like training ground, and created some favourite reading nooks where I could pore over my notes and thousand-page textbooks.

Every morning, I woke up at 7 a.m. to study. After a few hours without looking up from my textbooks, and a short meal, I worked out with kettle bells and elastic bands. When it snowed, I went outside dressed like a lumberjack, throwing medicine balls and jab-stepping through ladder drills. Afterward, exhausted, I'd study in the bathtub, my good luck charm. I studied while the sun dropped, and studied every second I wasn't training.

I worked through more than 1,100 pages of notes in those weeks. I took practice tests online, answering multiple-choice questions like: A 55-year-old man known to have diabetes, hypertension and coronary artery disease comes to the emergency room with abdominal pain. He is afebrile (doesn't have a fever) and there's no change in bowel movement. What's the next best step in the management of this patient?

I also prepped for the second part of the exam, which involved writing longer answers. I had not undertaken anything more challenging in my life. After being absent from school for six months, it was harder to focus for long periods of time, and I knew I would require that kind of focus for an exam that stretched over seven or eight hours. At that point, I only needed to do one thing: pass.

THE EXAM was scheduled for 9 a.m. Instead of running through a final review that morning, I decided to work out with my trainer. I wanted to burn off some of my hyperactivity. That, I knew, would help me focus. I promised myself to go easy with the workout, but, of course, once I got under the squat bar, I couldn't stop adding weights. I breezed through most of the 210 multiple-choice questions. But when I noticed that 12 minutes remained on the exam clock, I still had 10 questions left. I guessed at those, quickly, in order to keep up my pace. We had an hour-long break before the three-and-a-half-hour long-format part of the exam. I answered those questions with more ease.

For a passing grade, I had to score 246 out of 400. I managed that, and then some: I scored two points below the average, lower than I'd hoped but still high enough to open up my options. Aspiring doctors in Montreal cannot move forward in their training without that qualifying score. Now I could move into my residency training, which would lead to the title I coveted—Dr.—before my name. Even better, I planned to wait until after I retired from the NFL to begin that last leg of on-the-job training. I'd be able to make football my primary focus for the rest of my pro career. And, with the pressure of graduating now removed from the equation—plus a master's in surgery now completed—I could concentrate more on football than ever before.

Or so I thought.

The morning after taking my exam, I hopped back on an airplane and flew to Kansas City. All the science I had learned in the previous four months was pushed aside and stored in my memory. It was time to get back to football, to learn new algorithms, the kind that involved pass protections and run-play installs. Thirty-six hours after the test, I was back on the field, practising with my teammates. And despite the quick turn-around, I was happy to be there.

One month later, I flew back home for 24 hours in order to attend the graduation. Once again, Coach Reid agreed to let me miss practice. Stepping on that stage and getting my diploma was the biggest personal accomplishment of my life so far. That same day, after a lunch at the bakery, I once again flew back to KC.

Our team doctor made me personalized scrubs with the franchise's arrowhead logo stamped on the front. The team dentist stitched together something similar. My teammates surprised me with a cake after my first practice back, and Coach Reid announced my graduation in a team meeting, while all these players I had come to love cheered. Coach Reid also asked me to lead my teammates in the huddle after a practice, saying, "OK, Doctor, break us down."

WE WON five games to start the 2018 season, portending the run of three successful seasons in a row. But in a Week 5 blowout over Jacksonville, I got twisted around on one play. My feet were planted and a defender rolled into my right leg. As I was falling down in slow motion, I heard a crack. This was a freak accident, the kind that is impossible to avoid. Basic physics all but dictates that people of our size, who move at our speed, will inevitably apply so much force, to themselves or to each other, that injuries will result. In most cases, like for me that Sunday, what breaks is bones. The force of the defender falling into me acted like a lightning bolt.

When you get injured, it's a weird feeling. You really hope that everything is OK and you try to convince yourself that the pain is just a bad bruise or something minor.

You can feel the 80,000 people in the stands looking at you. You think about the rest of the season, your backup, your chance of coming back in time. It's weird how you can think about all that stuff in the seconds between getting injured and the training staff showing up on the field.

I tried to stand but could not. As the trainer raced onto the field, along with the team doctor, I considered all the potential diagnoses: patellar injury, tibial plateau fracture, fibula fracture, high-ankle sprain, ACL tear, MCL tear. This was a broad range, and would have constituted a poor answer to a question on an exam in medical school. I felt pain throughout my left leg, but the weird combination of pain and adrenalin made it really hard to pinpoint the source. Turns out I had a Maisonneuve fracture, which is a fibula fracture, with an added bonus thrown in—ankle instability, which explained why the pain had spread so far.

We found the best ankle surgeon in the country, Dr. Robert Anderson, and headed to Green Bay to see him. Flo and I flew to Chicago, where we met Sasha, and then we drove four hours north together. I told both of them I would be fine alone, but the truth was, I was comforted by their presence. Dr. Anderson performed the surgery, and the next day I flew back to Missouri to begin the long and torturous process known as rehabilitation. My goal: to beat, by two weeks, the average recovery time from my injury so I'd be back on the field for the playoffs.

The challenge was more mental than physical. It was difficult to square what I'd been a week earlier—a professional football player—with what I was now, an injured afterthought who needed an orthopaedic scooter and was barely able to care for himself. My recovery took longer than I'd hoped. I missed the rest of the season, including the run to the conference championship, a game we lost.

The really difficult moment for me was when I removed the cast and realized the atrophy and the limitation in my left leg. I had to learn to walk again, and run again, before I could even think about playing again. I was up against the clock if I wanted to come back in time.

Being injured sucks. You feel useless, but you have to find a way to show up to the training facility every day with one thing you want to get better at. Sometimes you plateau, but you cannot let that bring you down because there is always something you can work on. For 10 weeks I spent my days between the training room, the weight room (working on my upper-body lift and cardio) and the pool (for exercise and, of course, because I love bathing).

Two weeks before the AFC Championship, I was back on the field with my shoulder pads. I thought I was good to play, but my coach didn't want to risk sending me back in the game after being away for so long. Besides, the backup guard was doing well.

But I was frustrated.

So many things started going through my mind. If the backup is playing well, and he is younger and cheaper than me, will the Chiefs release me during the off-season? It was frustrating to fight so hard to come back and then be denied that opportunity. I'd have to wait seven more months before I made it back on the field. But I used that experience as a source of motivation in the off-season.

The Chiefs began the 2019 season on a somewhat optimistic note. We'd won two playoff games and were returning with most of our core players, as well as, now, the reigning MVP at quarterback after trading Alex Smith and replacing him with Pat, who was rocketing toward superstardom.

After a first off-season without medicine, I was in great shape and showed up to training camp with the firm intention of taking my spot back. I mounted my own comeback while our team rebounded and made the playoffs, roaring back from behind in every playoff game and eventually winning the Super Bowl.

Everything came together at exactly the right time. Yet it almost seemed too perfect. And I'd soon realize it *was* too perfect—for reasons no one could ever have anticipated.

CHAPTER 9

THE PANDEMIC

Before the 2018 season, a *Sports Illustrated* reporter named Ben Baskin came to write a profile on me. He asked if I would ever take a year off from football to do my medical residency.

I looked at Ben and said, "Are you crazy?"

The thought had never crossed my mind. Why would I take a year off, when average careers in the NFL are so short and not guaranteed? With steep competition for every roster spot, and the pressure that comes with that, I couldn't imagine leaving, coming back and feeling secure about starting again. What good could a sabbatical possibly do me?

Yet I was keenly aware of how quickly circumstances could change and turn my perspective upside down. I told Baskin, "It's fairly impossible to plan ahead. We have goals, things we're certain of. But life in the NFL is hard; it's so uncertain. It's hard to find time to make decisions, to really reflect on my life, because things are moving so fast."

I had no clue how prescient his question, and my response, would soon prove.

*

BY NOW WE knew that COVID-19 was already spreading across the world, throughout America, even in Miami during Super Bowl week in early February 2020. The 49ers had practised at their headquarters in Santa Clara, California, an early virus hotspot, before flying cross-country for the title game. It's possible that someone on the field had already contracted the virus. It's possible that someone I blocked that night was infected. Fans packed into those stands at the Hard Rock Stadium had COVID-19, almost certainly, and they would pass the disease along to others during the game, and afterward.

Numbers don't lie. On March 11, while Flo and I were still hoisting our sails in the southern Caribbean, the World Health Organization declared COVID-19 a global pandemic. A week later, on March 18, the Centers for Disease Control and Prevention reported 3,419 new cases in the US. One week later, there were 13,897. A week after that: 34,864. Up and up the tally went. Alarm kicked in, worldwide. Throughout sports, cancellations or postponements followed like dominoes in lockstep with the rising number of positive cases. On March 12, the NCAA cancelled the March Madness men's basketball tournament. The Tokyo Olympics were postponed on March 24. The Little League World Series was cancelled. The CFL and the National Hockey League cancelled their seasons. Major-league baseball would not hold its Hall of Fame induction ceremony. The NCAA would not stage its baseball, or softball, championships. There was no Wimbledon. No Ivy League football season. And no crowd for the NFL draft, which was held virtually for the first time ever: Commissioner Roger Goodell announced selections from his basement.

That sports leagues, commissioners and health officials were considering the wider world around them was encouraging, and necessary. Everyone, everywhere, was looking at the virus and thinking about how their lives might change, including me. Back from our trip, in quarantine in Montreal, I graduated from reading news accounts to studying the heavier stuff, like the earliest research papers and whatever I could find in medical databases, all of which seemed to point toward the same conclusion: the virus was not only serious, but would get seriously worse.

The question I'd been asked during the Super Bowl week media sessions resurfaced more than once in my mind: *As the NFL's only player who's a doctor-in-training, what do you think of the novel coronavirus?* In hindsight, everything—from the journalists packed around those podiums to the fans sardined into the stands to the one million victory parade attendees—seemed so much more dangerous. Now, my answer to that question was: the novel coronavirus alarmed me, concerned me, kept me up at night.

Everything began shutting down. Borders closed. Schools closed, along with restaurants and other businesses. Countries across the world enacted preventive measures, asking citizens to wear masks, to socially distance and to stay home.

The positive rates took a small dip in April, which only served up false hope that the world might return to normal quickly. Mortality rates for the virus weren't that high; the scary part was how easily COVID-19 spread. From a public health perspective, managing the growing number of hospitalized patients concerned me. If that number, which had gone through the roof, continued up toward the stars, the health care system would become overwhelmed. Then mortality rates would rise due to lack of ventilators and medical personnel. The measures that governments had put in place would hopefully help the system avoid the worst-case scenario, allowing for better care of every patient. But that hope hinged on citizens following those measures, and not in their own self-interest but for the sake of the communities they lived in.

I began to hope no one I knew would be infected. I thought: *At some point in the months ahead, if a vaccine is manufactured and made widely available, the response to the pandemic will slow its spread.* I also thought: *The general public isn't taking the threat seriously enough.*

I kept in close contact with several friends from medical school. Many were physicians; some worked in emergency rooms. One began testing patients for the novel coronavirus; another performed triage on the front lines. They offered a picture of what was really going on, beyond what could be found in the news or in public health reports.

Their view was alarming. They saw hospitals filling up, running out of beds, resources stretched thin, medical professionals suffering a physical and emotional toll, scared they might get sick and concerned they could pass a deadly disease to the people they loved. It seemed clear to them that the pandemic would not be defeated, or contained, in a matter of days, weeks or even, worst case, months. COVID-19 was here—not only to stay, but to wreak havoc.

The turmoil of that first wave of the pandemic led me to reflect. It gave me a different perspective on the events from the previous months, like all the travelling I had done. It made me question my purpose as a football player. Was I playing just for my love of the game, which was, at least in part, egocentric? The idea of putting so much pressure and focus on moving a small leather ball across a field of grass seemed less sensible. Was continuing to play better contributing to the greater good of society in any way? Or was it just for my own benefit? I almost felt bad that I had left the world of medicine at all, even though I knew that leaving was temporary. That world was predicated on a premise that we must help each other, whereas football started to feel more like a quest undertaken to benefit one person: me.

It was impossible for me not to feel the impulse to step in, to do something to help my friends, future colleagues and the system at large to respond to this crisis. Since it was the NFL off-season, the choice was easy. The question was what, exactly, I could offer—where and how I could insert myself in a way that would be useful. Remember, I wasn't yet a full-fledged doctor, rather a student with a medical degree who had yet to complete his residency requirements.

I called my advisers at McGill and asked how I could be of assistance. At first, nobody really knew the answer, because this exact scenario had never happened before. I fell into a sort of grey zone: more trained than most, but not trained enough to be placed in a hospital.

As we hunted for answers, I recognized my privilege, which started with having a choice at all. I didn't lose my job in the pandemic. I didn't have three kids at home learning over Zoom, needing me to fill in the gaps and teach them part-time. In 2018 we had bought a new place and filled it with art, thanks to Flo. I lifted weights at home, and had a football career waiting for me. I had a Super Bowl title to defend. I could choose medicine for now and get back to football later, whenever possible.

It was hard to project myself into the future, as society around me—and everyone else—continued to adapt, shift and adapt again. It was hard to project what would happen in six months or a year. But I'm optimistic by nature, and I knew what we needed to reverse the course of the pandemic: a vaccine. All we had to do until one was created was limit the spread of COVID-19, and the damage.

For my part, to start, public health officials asked me to use my profile and my platform to spread important information to the public. Whenever they enacted a new measure, or urged additional caution, I would do interviews with local and national media outlets, to try to reinforce the proper protocols. I probably answered more questions in those weeks than I did at the Super Bowl.

I filmed a couple of television commercials urging citizens to work together, to do their part. But I wanted to do more. I read about hospitals running out of oxygen and ventilators and basic supplies. I knew front-line workers who hadn't had a day off in weeks, who went to work every day despite the severe risks. Anyone who didn't follow the public health measures didn't truly, or fully, understand the health care workers' sacrifice. They were risking their lives to protect us, or putting their own families at greater risk, at a time when we still knew little about the virus. To return the favour, all we had to do was stay home, minimize our interactions, don masks and wash our hands. Simple, right? Not in reality. Almost two years after COVID-19 began its killing spree, we are still arguing over mask mandates.

Of course, I understand that not every measure put in place was 100 percent effective. Perhaps there were scientific debates about just how protective it really was to wear surgical masks in public. But for me, the possible disadvantages of wearing one were far outweighed by the potential benefits, like reducing the spread and the number of hospitalized patients. We still didn't know all that much about the virus, and even though some of those measures might seem obsolete now, back then we had to err on the side of caution. In medicine, we swear an oath to do good and to do no harm. When we perform tests on patients or provide treatment, we must weigh the potential consequences of our choices. Extend that same logic to the mask debates. Even if wearing one doesn't guarantee safety for every person who complies, there are no major side effects that would justify *not* wearing them even if the exact benefit wasn't known at the time.

Eventually, health officials started to recruit a broader swath of health care professionals to work on the front lines. They desperately needed the extra help, and not-yet-doctors like me were placed in a newly created tier of health care volunteers. I could now wade right into the fray. *Put me in, coach*, as the saying goes.

When the opportunity to work on the front lines became real, reality hit, fast and hard. *How would this all work?* For the Chiefs? For Flo? For me?

From a football standpoint, I knew there was language in my contact preventing me from doing high-risk activities in the off-season, such as alpine skiing, bungee jumping or riding motorcycles. So it was fair to wonder whether the Chiefs would view the pandemic front lines—and my potential exposure to the virus—in the same vein. I needed to know if volunteering to help would place me in violation of my contract. I had so many questions. Would I still be covered if I couldn't play in September because I was sick?

I called the executives in Kansas City. From Mr. Hunt, our owner, to general manager Brett Veach, to Coach Reid, their responses were amazing. They understood what drove me, and they were not only proud I wanted to help but pledged their unconditional support.

I enrolled in a crash course review of medical basics. How to put on a surgical gown the right way. The steps to properly sanitize. Simple elements like those had never been more important.

I soon learned I would be placed in a long-term care facility about 45 minutes from Montreal, in Saint-Jean-sur-Richelieu. I wasn't surprised. The virus had hit the sick and elderly hard, especially in congregrate settings, decimating those populations in Quebec just as it did in many parts of the country and beyond. That was where people like me were most needed. The health care workers who fell ill needed to be replaced, and the demand— for ventilators, for testing, for beds, for shifts—was not letting up.

The gig would be temporary, designed to last until I needed to head back to my football career in the United States.

Or so I thought.

I WASN'T SURE what to expect on my first day at my new volunteer job. I believed that my training in medical school would be helpful, but I also knew that my experience as a medical student on the hospital ward was really different from what I was about to witness in a long-term care facility during a pandemic. My previous experience was in a pre-pandemic world where patients ended up better or cured. In hospitals, we nursed people back to health so they could resume their normal lives. I quickly saw that working in a long-term care facility is not about curing disease. Rather, it's mostly about caring for patients and accepting that they're not, for the most part, going back home. Here, in a place like this, the operative word is not *cure*, but *care*. Add to that: *dignity*. Quality of life. That reality, superimposed with the impact of COVID-19, which profoundly increased our patients' vulnerability and isolation, created a really pessimistic climate and a deep distress that was felt by both patient and health care worker.

My first shift was scheduled for six thirty on a weekday morning. I felt anxious as I drove there, but not in a bad way. These were familiar nerves, born from an elevated sense of anticipation and from my desire to do well. I packed my lunch. I put the address in my GPS and allowed for 30 extra minutes on the

45-minute drive from Montreal. But when I showed up, the doors were locked and the place looked empty. I called my supervisor and learned I'd somehow gone to the wrong facility. By the time I made it to the right one, I was 15 minutes late for my first shift. Not a great start.

In terms of managing football nerves vs. COVID-19 nerves, the situations were totally different, and hard to compare. Back in February, I grasped that 100-million-plus people were going to be watching, and I wanted to win, and I didn't want to be the reason we lost. With the pandemic, my anxiety stemmed from my duty as a doctor and as a citizen. This wasn't the right time to cut corners or act impulsively. I had to do everything the right way, take everything seriously, even when it came to washing my hands and not touching anything without disinfecting first. I know this might sound like a small matter, but the protective measures were—and are—crucial, especially when working with a vulnerable part of the population.

At first, I wasn't working in a COVID-positive facility. And I knew that COVID would not just suddenly appear on our floor out of nowhere. Since the patients were isolated in their rooms and visitors weren't allowed, I knew that *we*, the medical staff, were the most likely to bring the virus inside the building. That idea put a tremendous amount of pressure on us to follow the rules so we did not do more harm then good. I knew that mistakes, if made, could potentially lead to the infection of more patients.

Over the course of the first week, I started to learn the layout of the facility, the patients who lived there and what kind of work I'd be doing. I was assigned to the second floor, which had north and south wings, with 25 patients in one and 35 in the other. The majority of the residents were older, and because they were older, they were living with numerous health conditions or illnesses, some of them brutal. Some had dementia; others, Parkinson's disease; still others, Alzheimer's. Some needed assistance to get around; others required wheelchairs. Some could talk; others communicated without talking. Many were in regular contact with their families; others didn't hear from anyone at all. And because of the very nature of a long-term care facility, we frequently lost residents, who died from a variety of causes.

I'd never worked in long-term care during medical school. But I'd heard stories from colleagues about how these facilities typically provided nice living environments for patients, who enjoyed activities and welcomed visitors while interacting with each other to build relationships. That was not my experience.

When I arrived, the facility was firmly in what officials called the Green Zone, which meant we had very few, if any, COVID-19 cases or close contacts on our floor. "Green" represented the lowest level of threat. But that didn't mean our patients weren't affected by the raging pandemic. On the contrary. Because the patients in those places were older and more vulnerable—or they wouldn't have been living at the facility in the first place—they were also more likely to endure the most severe symptoms if they contracted COVID-19, and to suffer far higher mortality rates than other parts of the population. As such, COVID precautions in long-term care were strict, you might even say severe: patients were confined to their rooms with no visitors allowed. Some were confused by this, unable to fully understand the nature of what was happening. Others were aware of their vulnerability and very anxious, constantly watching pandemic updates on TV and making sure we followed all precautions when entering their rooms. They were quarantined in 10-foot-by-10-foot rooms and saw no one beyond the staff. I would describe how they lived as both difficult and chaotic.

Although we were doing everything we could to protect them and treat them from a physical standpoint, it quickly became clear to me that the psychological trauma of that isolation was almost a bigger issue. Sometimes, driving home, I'd ask myself whether, if it were me, I'd think it was still worth living in those conditions— eating questionable cafeteria food, isolated in my room for three months. But I tried to push those thoughts away. It was not my decision or for me to judge. My job was to try to palliate those terrible circumstances and show as much empathy as I could.

Every time I walked into a patient's room, I reminded myself that I represented one of the few human interactions they'd have that day. We were always running around fulfilling the necessary duties of our jobs, but I tried to take the time to crack a joke or ask a question about their life. I sensed that the little extra time I spent with them could go a long way. I realized that health care is not about treating at all costs, but also about the second half of the term: *care*.

That was, for sure, my biggest lesson from working in that centre, and I learned it by osmosis, from all my dedicated colleagues, who cared without counting.

EACH HEALTH CARE worker on my floor reported for one of three shifts, arriving in the morning, afternoon or evening (for the overnight shift). If any employee contracted COVID-19, or had close contact with someone who did, they were required to isolate. When someone had to go into quarantine, their absence left a gaping hole on the roster. The impact this necessary safety measure had on staffing cannot be overstated. We typically needed anywhere from 12 to 14 people, at a bare minimum, to cover both sides of the second floor on a day shift, and that tally included one nurse for each wing, one nurse's assistant, and orderlies who helped fill in the gaps, along with the doctors who rotated in.

Volunteers like me were deployed on all three shifts as fill-ins for anyone in quarantine. Every week, I met with my supervisor, and we would go over the schedule to identify where we were short-staffed and slot me into the appropriate places. The majority of my day-to-day duties fell under the same broad—and infinitely complex—umbrella called "patient care." I was, at first, an orderly. I replaced bed linens that had been soiled. I changed diapers. I went to staff meetings, either to listen for updates from my colleagues who were finishing a shift or to give out the same information to those arriving for one. I helped stabilize patients who were upset. I called other doctors on behalf of residents, dialing anyone who might be needed to come in, such as a dentist or ophthalmologist. I'd set appointments, or assist when those external professionals came by. I also helped residents reach family members when they needed to. And I spoke to the relatives of those who died, after the doctor on hand had notified them and given a synopsis, leaving the staff to answer any additional questions.

As we lost more nurses to isolation protocols, my role changed. I administered medication and changed the dressings on patients' wounds, put in IVs and drew blood. And, of course, I administered hundreds of COVID-19 tests.

I wasn't there as a doctor, so I couldn't write prescriptions or request tests. Distributing meds might sound like a basic task, but it was not. To start with, the average age of our patients was probably around 75, and their list of medications could be fairly extensive. They'd take certain ones once a day; others, twice; others, once every three days. Some medications were dispensed only when patients asked for them; others we gave out only when they needed that specific type. Some were delivered orally, others under the skin, others crushed. Patients sometimes requested that their medicine be mixed in with chocolate pudding. After seeing the grey powder that resulted from the combination of six different pills, I didn't blame them.

Gradually, I built a relationship with the physicians. I would call them to ask for changes with medications, or report side effects, or suggest changes in dosage. I don't know exactly what you would say my "job title" was, but I did know that we were running around all day, engaged in a real team effort. During lunch, I would help the orderlies feed patients who had difficulty swallowing. At bedtime, I would assist with moving patients from their chairs to their beds. Because of the work demands, combined with being short-staffed, everyone pulled together and helped each other out, which was one positive thing that came out of those otherwise pretty dark first few months of the pandemic.

The strict COVID safety protocols became a routine that I memorized and executed every time I entered, and left, a patient's room: Put on a mask, put on your visor, put on a new gown, put fresh gloves on, enter. Afterward, remove your gloves, wash your hands, remove your gown, wash your hands, remove and clean your visor, wash your hands, change your mask, wash your hands. Move on to the next patient.

That was when everything was going well. If you forgot a medication, a cream or that a patient had asked for a glass of water, you'd have to redo the whole sequence to go back into the room, and then again to leave it.

That was my new reality, a constant reminder that the danger was there.

Due to the number of tasks, the shifting schedule and the preventive mandates, I mostly focused on the negatives at first. Like all the steps required, and how long it took to follow them. Or how burdened the system was overall, which struck me as a level beyond what anyone might glean from a news account. I was seeing the pandemic's impact up close, with my own eyes, and it wasn't good.

Most days early on, I entered that facility with other concerns at the forefront of my mind. I didn't want to get sick. I didn't want to pass the virus on to Flo, or to any of my family members. I didn't want to jeopardize my NFL career. So I believed I should be clinical and efficient, and try to see as many patients as possible in order to have the biggest impact. But that kind of mindset meant I was only seeing the negatives. It was when I started to take more time with my patients and actually *care* more that I began noticing the positives. The global pandemic required a high level of regulation and efficiency in the delivery of health care. That was an obvious, easy thing to say, to believe. But was it exactly what our patients needed? Rushing in and out of the patients' rooms without engaging with them—was that really the best way to care for people?

After my shifts, I would head to an empty apartment that I owned in Montreal, which I used as a sort of transitional zone. I would wash all my equipment, take a shower and change my clothes before heading to the place I shared with Flo.

It took some time for the difficulty of the situation my colleagues and I were dealing with to sink in. At first, I think, I was simply in survival mode, adapting to this new role and its demands, to the rules and protocols. As the weeks wore on, the daily struggle and the distressing effects of the pandemic on the people under our care began to take a psychological toll. I'm usually not a person who shares my feelings all that much during tough times. But one night, returning home after a particularly brutal day when many of my patients had tested positive for COVID-19, I lost it. I cried with Flo for hours.

In medicine, it's one thing to lose a patient. But the heartbreaking decisions we had to make to protect those who were still healthy really got to me. I sometimes asked Flo: *What's the purpose of all this?* I would explain what I was seeing, and how deeply disturbing it really was. I could hardly stomach all the debates on television, with crowds protesting for human rights, participants refusing to wear masks or self-isolate, these small and simple steps that would greatly help everyone while requiring minimal effort beyond minor inconveniences and a little empathy.

The contrast between my days at the care home and other aspects of my life became surreal, the transition between the two uncomfortable, to say the least. Sometimes, the morning after a difficult shift, I'd be jumping on a virtual off-season meeting with the Chiefs to install some plays and watch films with my fellow O-linemen. In the beginning, I thought of my empty apartment as no more than a sanitary station, a way to shift from my days at the facility into my nights at home. But over time, I found I also needed it to decompress.

AS THE WEEKS went by, I began to consider another question. *What makes a hero?*

After all, many in the media were describing me as one, even though I never thought of myself that way. Instead, I considered heroes in general, thinking about when it might be easy to be heroic, like while playing pro football, where the spotlight is immense and unending, and thousands of supporters will stand in line to pat a star athlete on the back. The accolades given to me by various organizations throughout the pandemic were similar, in that they focused on one very public person fighting against COVID-19. But that focus didn't make me a hero; in fact, that very emphasis worked against the idea of what a hero really is. My heroes are willing to sacrifice something—their time, their health—in order to serve the greater good. The front-line workers did not just fit inside that definition, they embodied it, without the glorification of the media. I saw plenty of real ones up close, and while we all wore the same hospital scrubs, their sacrifice seemed even more heroic, because it came with little, if any, attendant fanfare—and no expectations of anything beyond the satisfaction of doing a job well.

Those first few weeks opened my eyes—to how hard my colleagues were working, to the solidarity and chemistry they shared with each other. I once saw a 17-week NFL season as the most difficult challenge, not just for the physical damage it wrought but for its psychological cost. But this was different, greater, more; what these front-line workers were fighting for was bigger than themselves, or even our facility, our city or our country, and they made a fraction of a pro football salary for their efforts. It became obvious: I had to rethink my perspective.

These people, the brave men and women who served as nurses, orderlies or support staff in facilities like ours all over the world, had taken on this virus before we knew how deadly it might be. At some hospitals, the majority of patients would test positive for COVID-19, and many were dying. The staff who cared for them were legitimately scared. Some quit, and that's totally understandable. The ones who stayed worked in hell, basically. They fought both the virus and its spread, while lacking support, in some cases, from their communities and politicians.

They did their jobs with the utmost care, the utmost caution and the utmost diligence.

My sister Delphine was among them. She was going through medical school but her courses had been put on hold when the pandemic hit. She was just at home by herself, so she volunteered to help in long-term care. She was placed on the night shift in a facility that was in outbreak. There wasn't much organization or support, and little in the way of any onboarding process. She was literally sent into chaos. I remember talking about our experiences and it was like two different worlds. My reflex as the big brother was to get her out of there. I said I would talk to my supervisor and get her switched to the same place I was working. "We're going to commute together," I said. "We're going to live this together in an environment that's more structured." She said no. She wanted to do her own thing. "If they put me there it's because that's where they need me."

I was shocked—so impressed by her sense of civic duty but also ashamed of my proposition. Since when did any Duvernay-Tardifs cut corners, take the easy road? I was so proud of her, but her decision was just the same that thousands of others had made. To me, she represented that incredible movement of volunteers with medical backgrounds who had stepped forward to help. Through all that chaos in the early days of the pandemic, that solidarity was beautiful to see.

And so Delphine stayed on, riding her bike to her midnight shifts.

Even though the home where I was assigned to work was better organized, it wasn't immune to the pandemic's devastating effects: everywhere in long-term care, because of the age of our residents, mortality rates skyrocketed. My colleagues confronted death and illness day after day, week after week. Still, they interacted with patients as though they had all the time in the world, in order to understand them as more than numbers on a chart. They smiled through the most mundane tasks (they wore masks, but I could tell). Those smiles were powerful. Even through masks, they radiated hope, kindness, humanity. My colleagues were overworked, exhausted, busy beyond belief, and maybe just a little bit afraid. Yet behind their masks, while interacting with patients and residents, while delivering medication or changing bedding or carrying out any number of crucial but sometimes tedious tasks, they were smiling.

The front-line workers continued to work with great care and professionalism even when the pandemic forced them to cancel vacations or work overtime, sometimes right through their breaks, for weeks on end. I cannot recall a day I worked at the facility where my supervisor Solène was *not* there. I'm not sure if she took a single day off. Once I got to know her, I used to make small jokes.

"Do you ever go home?" I'd ask with a chuckle.

"I can't let people down," she'd say with a sigh, knowing that around 150 people reported to her directly.

The more time I spent at the long-term care home, the more I realized how much, during my years of medical school, I'd drifted away from the main reason I wanted to be a doctor in the first place: to help people. In some ways this change was inevitable, due to the demands of the curriculum and the nature of the work involved. Each rotation at McGill veered us abruptly from one area of medicine to another. Doctors reside at the top of organizational pyramids, putting together treatment plans and making decisions, moving quickly through their days because of the extensive list of patients they need to see. For them to do that, part of the job of everyone who works underneath them is to take direction, doing exactly as they are told so that teams function at optimal speed and efficiency.

I'd come to view the health care world as vertical, hierarchical. There's the head nurse, the nurses and the assistant nurses. Or there's the chief of the department, the doctors, the residents and the medical students. Everyone knows their role, and as a student who wanted to make a good impression, I focused on following protocols, acing my rotations. I saw less of the larger ecosystem and how it fits together—how every person involved in every level of the pyramid plays an important role in optimizing patient care. Now, I see health care as a circle instead of a pyramid, with the patient in the middle. I didn't realize that the most direct impact on patients comes from those who toil in jobs at what I'd thought of as the "bottom" of the pyramid. I had this vision, as a dreamer, of marching into medicine and changing the world by myself. But being a doctor is not that, not in the real world. It takes a team to help people, where everyone values the input and contributions of all the others.

In the care facility where I'd been placed, I came to understand that the nurses, their assistants, orderlies and maintenance staff were the ones who made the ecosystem function. They tended to the mental health of residents, while also doing all the hands-on work: cleaning, stocking, injecting and sanitizing. Ultimately, it's these health care professionals who spend the most time with patients, and their knowledge and communication is crucial for the entire staff. For example, assistant nurses provide critical information to the treatment teams.

To use a football analogy, the doctors in those places are like quarterbacks in the NFL, if QBs rotated teams each week. The front-line workers are more like offensive linemen—more anonymous, sometimes underappreciated, yet essential for the team's success. They reminded me that medicine doesn't have to be hierarchical, not in full; that staff in unglamorous positions can make a huge difference by focusing on smaller details, remaining empathetic. Their level of engagement with patients is heightened by the sheer amount of time they spend with them. They see patients as people, period. My co-workers and I operated in an environment that was, yes, sometimes chaotic. But we also remained diligently focused on the quality of care, navigating the best path forward in unimaginable circumstances. My colleagues carried that spirit into every workday.

One day I noticed how one couple, both nurses, worked opposite shifts. The husband would clock in each morning, and then his wife would meet him at the hospital with their six-month-old daughter strapped into her car seat, and she would head in to work next. He would then head out, to care for their child and sleep. They never saw each other except during those exchanges, or when they happened to be off work at the same time. The virus's personal toll on front-line workers is often overlooked. So many medical workers suffered from, and pushed through, pandemic burnout, the rates of which are higher now than ever before.

I watched an orderly give patients haircuts on his lunch break. I saw nurses take extra time to cut residents' nails, to learn the names of their family members, or to discuss the weather or the game last night. These front-line workers were—*are*—the unsung heroes, the real heroes of the pandemic.

Eventually, I realized that the loved ones who said goodbye to each front-line worker as they headed in for another shift were making their own significant, and nerve-racking, sacrifices. Including mine.

*

BY THIS POINT, Flo and I had been part of each other's lives for a decade. We'd navigated so much together: completing our academic degrees and launching our careers, living a long-distance relationship for half of each year due to my improbable success in making the NFL, starting our own projects together, including our growing art collection—more on that later—and the foundation we were establishing to bring athletic and art resources and opportunities to school kids in Quebec.

The pandemic was a whole other thing. Our lives had gone, in a matter of weeks, from an epic post–Super Bowl celebration and awesome sailing trip to the front lines of COVID-19. Compared with a lot of people, we had it easy. No jobs lost. No one sick. No financial precarity. And yet in some ways it was still difficult. Flo's previous sacrifices in support of my endeavours were one thing. But COVID-19, and me working in a long-term care facility, was something else altogether, and gradually it became something worse. As the weeks passed, the times when I'd confide in Flo after my shifts began to dwindle. I'd steer our conversations closer to superficial topics, changing the subject whenever our talk started to go deeper. I needed an emotional and psychological break from my daily life on the front lines. I'd begun to shut down.

Flo saw the impact without me saying a word. The pain was visible in everything from my slumped shoulders, to my restless nights, to how little time I actually spent at home. Maybe it was subconscious—I certainly never thought about it this way at the time—but when I look back, I realize that I wanted my home to feel safe, and calm, and "normal"—an antidote to a chaotic day, as I shifted my mindset back and forth from football to the facility. There was even more: spring training in Kansas City was constantly being postponed, which only added to the stress. I had to remain in shape, never knowing when I'd be leaving for KC or if I'd be able to fly back before the beginning of the season. Closing off my emotions, though, had unintended consequences and strained our relationship. I erected a wall between us: she could see how much I was struggling, but while she shared her fears, and detailed her pain, she couldn't fully understand mine, because I wasn't helping her to.

Flo remained in contact with our friends from the medical world, and their partners shared some of the daily horrors all front-line workers confronted. With every new local outbreak in or near Montreal, she grew increasingly worried. We knew so little about the virus at that point. But she did know that the facility I reported to every day would create a higher risk for us.

Whenever she could, she broached difficult questions; most centred on our life together, at home. *Would I shower, and change, at the facility? Should we, even temporarily, live apart? What about the car we shared? What if there were five positive cases at work? What if there were 50?*

These conversations opened my eyes to what the workers on the front lines were facing, and the support they needed away from their shifts. I'm sure many partners of front-line workers felt the same way and discussed taking similar precautions. Flo told me she found it difficult to connect with me during those nine weeks. She worried often about my mental health, knowing the transition had been brutal. Three months before, we had celebrated my biggest accomplishment in Miami, and now here I was, trying to help on the front lines in a deeply challenging environment while still having to lift, and stay in shape, for the next season. Flo understood that my default personality is to respond to any crisis as best I can, with solutions. But for COVID-19—and for my job specifically—there were no concrete answers, beyond surviving the next week, enduring the next shift, and trying to help in whatever way possible. In some respects, even though I was living at home, it felt as if we were living on different planets—yet another aspect of the pandemic's collateral damage.

MEANWHILE. especially at the outset, I also worried, a little, about how my colleagues in the facility felt about my being there at all—whether they would see me as some sort of celebrity who only planned to volunteer for a brief time, in search of some positive PR. I didn't want them to look at me as someone who had been drawn in for the wrong reasons, for publicity or an image boost.

I walked the second-floor hallways as a Super Bowl champion who had already forgotten about the Super Bowl, at least temporarily. And yet it was impossible to entirely separate my football endeavours from my COVID-19 ones. I was being publicly recognized for what I had accomplished in football, as well as for my decision to volunteer.

The first few days, I could sense my colleagues looking at me, and the glances I either saw or imagined, however they were intended, led me to put extra pressure on myself. They were respectful and kind, but I didn't feel part of the team. Of course, you almost never do, the first few days working anywhere. But I worried they had doubts about me—and who would blame them, after all they'd been through so far in this pandemic? I wanted to be part of the team, a normal cog; but in some ways, because of the championship and the attendant notoriety that had bubbled over, I ended up feeling part of the team only when I stopped trying to hide the football part of my life.

I tried to remember that I'm naturally paranoid in those types of situations, or at least have been described that way. Perhaps none of my colleagues saw in me what I feared they might see: someone who believed he'd mastered medicine, who would shrink from more menial tasks, who would cut corners, who would want to be treated differently—or all of the above. In reality, I only wanted to be seen as a medical professional with a desire to contribute.

I fought back against any special treatment. When it was offered, it was all well-intentioned, just nice people trying to be kind, and respectful of whatever stature they believed I held. I remember one supervisor telling me they had hoarded food so I could eat, believing I needed the calories to maintain my playing weight. "Don't do that," I gently responded. I wanted to work in the same way as my colleagues. Perform the same tasks. Eat the same food. Sometimes, however, that proved impossible. Like when Solène asked me to exit through a different door from the rest of the staff whenever I headed home. She didn't want me passing the television cameras that were often stationed outside.

As the days grew into weeks, I tried my best to integrate into my new locker room. And I never thought that process would involve football.

At least, that is, until it did.

CHAPTER 10

THE EPIPHANY

One of our patients at the long-term care centre began to deteriorate. It was time for a doctor's involvement. The head nurse handed me the phone and asked me to call Dr. Moser. I didn't know him well. Among the many physicians who rotated in at the facility, he was the one I'd had the least contact with.

I didn't know at the time that this was at least partly by design.

Dr. Moser, it turned out, was a football fan, a very enthusiastic one. When he'd learned that I was coming to work at the facility, he'd told the nurses that meeting me would be like "meeting my idol," and that he might "black out" from speaking with me. Because most of the staff did not follow American football, and because he sounded like a pop music fan who was afraid of attending a Justin Bieber concert, they would just laugh. They told him that I was easygoing, open to questions, that I would understand. But their teasing did nothing to help him relax about my presence. Better, he decided, to steer clear so we could both focus on our jobs.

Five weeks in, the nurses decided enough was enough. That day, they handed me the phone, knowing he was the doctor on call—that he would have no choice but to face talking with me. Having no idea what was going on, I simply introduced myself when Dr. Moser answered.

"You're joking!" he exclaimed.

We quickly managed to steer away from football to the matter at hand. I explained the situation with the patient. He asked what I thought, agreed with my diagnosis and gave some instructions for care. But I learned later that after hanging up, he sat for a good 15 minutes—numb, recuperating—much to the delight of the nurses who'd set him up.

The call served as a catalyst for a friendship with Dr. Moser. But the nurses accomplished more than that. Dr. Moser wasn't the only one who'd been trying to avoid my very public NFL profile on the job. So had I.

I was trying so hard to prove that I wanted to be useful and productive, rather than be seen as a famous athlete, that I did my best to avoid any allusion to that other side of my life—the pro football side. Now that the ice had broken with Dr. Moser, I realized I could bring the workplace a commodity that was in short supply—a bit of playfulness and release—simply by letting people into that strange, rarefied world of professional sports, one they normally wouldn't have such direct access to. Dr. Moser wasn't the only staff member who loved the game, but most, like him, had been too shy to approach me about that part of my life. So I started telling tales from the sidelines, sharing inside jokes, letting them know what it was like to play alongside celebrated teammates like Pat Mahomes. It was a great delight, and a huge relief, to see my colleagues' enjoyment. They ate up my descriptions of the anarchy that takes place in the trenches at the goal line, all the shoves and pushes, the eyes poked, the groins smacked, the faces smashed into dirt.

By opening up, by being vulnerable, I did a better job of

connecting with them, because they could see me, this overly celebrated human, in a different light, more exposed. I called the Chiefs and asked for a box of jerseys and T-shirts, then surprised my team at the facility with some swag (after it was quarantined for 48 hours, for safety purposes). We cheered and smiled as I scribbled my signature straight onto the shirts now worn by my colleagues, essentially autographing their Ts and their backs simultaneously. I had arrived at the facility expecting to help patients, in that mind frame. But I realized that, by sharing my other life, I could bring some relief and joy to health care workers who desperately needed it.

I started to do more of these gestures, whenever time allowed and when I could create the time. After learning that a resident idolized him, I called a professional hockey player I know on FaceTime, and handed the phone over. Dr. Moser would later say I "made a lot of new friends," referring to one patient in particular, who struck him as like a second mom to me.

Sometimes the patients on the second floor would ask me to FaceTime with their families, because no one they knew back home believed them when they said I helped care for them at the facility. We were not supposed to bring our phones onto the unit, but I decided to break that rule—after disinfecting mine twice. After my shifts, I performed a different sort of rounds, making those calls when anybody asked.

I felt the joy in those conversations, and saw how happy the families were to connect, even virtually. But it was also clear those discussions were charged with emotion, which grew as family visits were cancelled for 10 straight weeks. I realized there was yet another layer to the patients' suffering. As I held my cell up for granddaughters to finally see their grandfather, the laughs and smiles often gave way to tears.

Dr. Moser came to call me a "big teddy bear" who doubled as our burly second-floor mascot. He was on to something, I think. Mascot was a start. Add to that cheerleader, confidant, friendly face. My job was never to be a "doctor" in the pandemic. It was, much like my job in football, to fit in, to be part of the team, to make the collective better. I could do that with words, with actions, with something as simple as a smile. I was putting my energy, my enthusiasm, my sports psychology to use in a long-term care facility. My job, at its essence, became about bringing humanity into a place that desperately needed to feel less dire, less isolated, less frantic. Eventually, for patients who were confined to their rooms and mostly cut off from the outside world save for the breathless, and endless, news reports about COVID-19's devastation, nothing mattered as much as that.

IN BETWEEN drawing blood, or dispensing prescriptions, or putting in urinary catheters, I met one resident, I'll call her Janet. She'd lived in the facility for years, after being diagnosed with multiple sclerosis. She used a wheelchair to move around and her own creativity to flout what others might consider her limitations. She could not easily read or write. But she could play Scrabble online by holding a stick between her teeth and tapping it onto a mini-keyboard that rested below her chin. She placed letters on the board by moving her head in front of a special camera.

I used to play Scrabble against my grandmother, a fierce opponent, while I was a student living in her basement apartment. It's my favourite board game. I'd continued to play in Kansas City. It was a comfort, a piece of home.

Janet's process for playing the game impressed me. Whenever I visited her room to give her medication, I would chat with her and ask her yes and no questions, which she would answer by moving her head back and forth, which had been challenging and complicated even before the pandemic. She did not seem diminished by this; rather, she was determined to live in the best way she could.

I began to play with her when I could manage it. She'd ask me to help her brainstorm for bigger words. Sometimes I'd help her set up the stick/keyboard, or assist by typing. One afternoon, we managed to score 90 points in one turn, deploying a seven-letter word, in a game against her ex. I don't think even my teammates at the Super Bowl were as happy as Janet was in that moment. She'd ask for me sometimes when nurses came into the room, saying she needed help with a letter combination. The nurses would let me know, and I would begin the sanitizing process: scrubs, wash, visor, wash, gloves, wash, mask, wash. Head in, play Scrabble, repeat. Whenever I entered the room to play Scrabble, Janet's eyes lit up.

That light in her eyes was no small matter. It had nothing to do with me being a football player, and everything to do with me just taking the time to be there for a few extra minutes—*non-medical* minutes. We tend to analyze this pandemic, like most of life's scariest things, in dry, lifeless, numerical terms. For months, the world focused on the number of new cases, the death rates and the epicentres. But facilities like the one where I volunteered didn't *only* lose patients to COVID-19. Many passed away from loneliness and isolation.

I tried to apply the "Janet principle" to other residents. I found a box in the chapel filled with puzzles and board games. Each day, I'd pick one out, disinfect it and take it with me, searching out people in our care to play against. If I happened to run to the drugstore on an errand, I'd buy more puzzles, more games, and add them to our stash. Even residents who were battling dementia seemed to happily anticipate these visits, regardless of whether they could really do the activities. This was: find a way, or make one, pandemic style. I didn't arrive at that notion alone, but rather by osmosis, by watching my colleagues and following their lead.

Some patients had stored personal home decorations in their closets, only, over time, to forget they even had them. I'd bring everything out, then help them spruce up their room, adding "interior decorator" to my job description. For residents who spent most of their day in a chair, watching whatever happened to be on television—often breathless COVID-19 reports—it was a welcome change. When we would call their families, the patients would show off the room improvements, or talk about a puzzle they had completed or a game they'd won.

One resident with restricted mobility deeply missed her time outdoors, the feeling of a breeze on her face, the plants in the courtyard that she had enjoyed watering. So I asked my supervisor and had her put on a mask and a visor and wheeled her outside, toward the courtyard garden. It was a beautiful day. The sun beamed, birds chirped. Impressively, she was able to identify species by their calls. Sometimes we see older people in hospital gowns with restricted mobility and, without even realizing we're doing it, we underestimate them. It's too easy to forget how much they've seen. How much they know. It was my duty to learn more about them, beyond whether they had low blood sugar, or gastro-intestinal issues, or were more lethargic on a given morning.

As I slowed down, took more time, and invested myself in the residents and their lives, I stopped seeing only the negatives of their situation (and ours). The more I spent time with the people we cared for, the more gratitude and appreciation I developed for our interactions, and the less I dwelt on the horrors of 2020. For so much of my life I had gone non-stop, checking my email, glued to my phone, lifting, studying, working, playing. The residents helped me to disconnect from the outside world, and remember that we're not all that different, if we take the time to understand each other.

Sometimes my touch was the only human interaction a patient would receive in a given day. That made it meaningful, important. So I would shake a hand, or lightly squeeze a shoulder. I took my time when feeding patients or doling out their medications. I was surprised not only at how honest they were but how much they *needed* the interaction, to feel normal in abnormal times.

Even under extreme duress, we made sure our patients ate three meals a day. That they bathed regularly. That we cared as much about them as we did about their blood pressure. Some of my colleagues have been doing this for 25 years in a way that's so tender it's almost impossible to describe. They know which patient needs their medication crushed, who cannot drink liquids, who needs water to swallow pills. They know whose dad is sick and whose grandchild just got into college. I followed their example as much as I could, the same way I emulated veteran linemen when I started in the NFL.

Once, with a great sense of triumph, my colleagues and I fixed an air conditioning unit in a resident's room. That might seem like a minor thing, but when it's summertime and sweltering outside, it's not insignificant. At 320 pounds, I could hardly stand in that space without sweating from every pore underneath my visor, mask and gown. We watched some how-to-repair videos and went to work, until the AC had been fixed and the breeze had been restored. That patient could breathe again, their life a little closer to normal. That's dignity, right?

In theory, we had limited time, and limited energy, to meet our patients' needs. But carving out the time for simple gestures—Scrabble, board games, haircuts, puzzles, warm soup—helped with everything else. That included the overall mood of the second floor. My time with the residents, as well as working with my colleagues, who came to feel more and more like teammates—a different kind of team, facing very different stakes, but a team all the same—proved to me that small things matter *more* in times of great adversity, not less.

Meanwhile, technically, I was still a football player, a member of the Kansas City Chiefs. I partook in virtual meetings with my teammates four times a week. It sometimes felt weird to go from managing a crisis on the second floor to hopping on a call for football.

One time, an older woman was admitted to the floor I worked on, and she was quite irritable and confused. But she also had a urinary tract infection. Together with a nurse, we inserted a urinary catheter. It was hot, and the woman was upset. She just wanted me to leave. I held the catheter in my right hand while trying to keep her still with my left. I told her what I was doing and why, that it would burn a little but she'd be fine. I wore masks, gloves and a visor, and was dripping with sweat. She was growing more distressed by the minute. We finally got the catheter in. It would help the woman, but right now she was miserable. I felt terrible—for her, mostly, but also for my colleagues who did things like this every day.

My shift ended right after that episode. I logged on to a virtual team meeting and tried to concentrate on a tweak we were making to a key play. I would need to utilize my outside leverage on the running back, taking a slightly different angle. This information was important to our season. But it no longer felt as important to me, the doctor-in-training. During meetings like that, I'd hear some of my teammates say things like *COVID-19 is bullshit*, or question the need for masks. I'm sure that happened everywhere, all over the league, all over the world. And, to be clear, it wasn't the majority of the locker room. Even so, it was disappointing to hear men I respected falling for some of the propaganda and outright falsehoods espoused by politicians like the then US president. It became increasingly difficult to reconcile the stark contrast between my worlds.

THE UNTHINKABLE occurred. The thing we feared most, an outbreak, hit the second floor. This represented a real threat to patients and staff. It also threatened my involvement. To some high-up health officials, and surely to many Chiefs fans, my volunteering at a medical facility carried some manageable risk. But volunteering amid a COVID outbreak seemed untenable—the risk elevated, unnecessary and borderline reckless.

My supervisor called. She seemed shaken by the increasing numbers of positive cases, and told me that I probably would not be able to return. No one wanted me to contract the virus and, by the very nature of my public profile, spread fear. They valued my health, and the message that a healthy me sent to my province and my country. The concern was simple: What if the Super Bowl champion tests positive for COVID-19? At this point, in 2022, that wouldn't register as a big deal. But back then, remember, there were no vaccines, and treatments were less advanced. There was more uncertainty around the nature of the virus and the threat it posed. Uncertainty breeds fear.

But they didn't understand what drove me, didn't know that I would never accept a photo op and an easy out. Close friends, even family members, all suggested that I listen to my superiors. But none of their concerns outweighed my desire to not let my team down. I couldn't make sense of the logic, well-intended as it was. Why was I allowed to leave when it got hard while others had to stay? I'm a 30-year-old professional athlete who's in the best shape of his life. But a 50-year-old nurse has to trudge back in for an overtime shift? To me, that was nonsense. *Please, let me help*, I told officials, practically begging to return. I wasn't a coward. I desired to make sacrifices, to live out my oath, and not just at my own convenience.

I asked myself simple yet profound questions regarding my return to the facility after the outbreak: Who am I? What do I stand for? Just because I played a popular game with a leather ball for a team that paid me a lot of money did not shield me from my basic obligations to my fellow citizens. My older sister, Delphine, by then a medical school graduate herself, was also volunteering by then, and nobody in charge had asked her to stay home, to be safe. She made $22 an hour as an orderly, changed the same diapers and worked the same long shifts, sometimes overnight, as I had. I wasn't any better, or more deserving of a break, than she was. What kind of message would leaving send? I knew for certain—it would be the wrong one.

So I stayed, my focus on what seemed most important. I went back in part to show others they should go back too.

During the first 48 hours of the outbreak, the inner workings of our facility changed drastically. We converted the gym and the activity room into makeshift pandemic wards. We put beds in there for patients who had tested positive or who'd been in close contact with someone who had contracted COVID-19. We hung plastic sheets between the beds, for privacy and for social distancing. The conversion meant the staff lost access to the only places that granted them moments of escape or reprieve. We changed before work in a trailer parked nearby. The chapel became our lunchroom. Only authorized personnel could work in areas with outbreaks.

The facility morphed into a maze. The approved workers ascended their own staircase, or rode alone in elevators, preventive measures that would reduce the risk of transmission. Every day, it seemed, the protocols became more deliberate and more intense, and created more separation. I respected, and appreciated, the attention to detail. Workers from each floor left the building via different staircases, each of which was disinfected between shifts.

We continued to seek and find camaraderie, but even with the great care put toward slowing the spread, a lot of my colleagues were sent home to quarantine. An outbreak requires *more* staff, but there were fewer healthy workers available. Some days I was literally running between tasks, and I could feel my weight dwindling as sweat dripped down my back and soaked my scrubs.

Additional measures were enacted. We could no longer interact with workers from other floors, to avoid cross-contamination. We couldn't bring our phones in, or food onto the unit. Sometimes we would power through long shifts and squeeze in a quick lunch on our floor.

I tried to remember what Coach Reid had told me before I went back: *Do what you have to do.* I would. I did. I was satisfied with the decision I'd made. I would make the same choice now, knowing everything that transpired, in particular the number of patients we lost during the outbreak.

Eventually, my supervisor asked me to take a leadership role in COVID-19 testing, another task made infinitely harder by the nature of our facility and who we cared for there. It's hard to imagine that anyone liked having a swab shoved up their nose, especially early on, when we had to insert them 10 centimetres. But some of our patients were in a vegetative state; others refused, or pushed us away, or were not able to give consent; and still others were confused, including some who would push or scream at whoever was administering the test. I worried that all the chemistry we had worked so hard to build with our patients would evaporate. Some of it did. When I showed up with my testing kit, I could see the fear in their eyes, as if I had become the bad guy overnight.

We still needed to be as smooth and efficient as possible. We needed to send the results over to the lab so that anyone who tested positive could be isolated. We'd immediately transfer them to what is known in infection-prevention protocol as the Red Zone. To later hop on a virtual Chiefs meeting in which we were, say, installing inside zone runs for the other "red zone" in my life was surreal, uncanny. Impossible to process.

In the midst of it all, I still had to train, lift and maintain my physical shape for when I returned to the game. All the gyms in Quebec were closed. So I built one on the balcony at my apartment. I could do exercises such as squats, or clean and jerks, finding it harder and harder to motivate myself to lift after those long days spent standing and bending over patients' beds. But I also needed those workouts to channel my frustration and decompress.

Eventually, the outbreak slowed, then stopped. Whew. My assignment at the facility was soon coming to an end as well. I'd worked from the end of April to the end of May, then taken two weeks off to isolate (since I'd been on the front lines, right in the face of COVID, for weeks) before a possible mini training camp in Kansas City later that month. Note the word *possible*.

That kind of uncertainty, which was happening across so many sectors at that time, not just pro sports, took its toll on people. I know it did, because it took its toll on us—on Flo and me. We knew that if I did cross the border, I might not be able to return for some time; two-week quarantines were required for everyone who crossed into Canada except essential workers. I'd be on the opposite side of a closed border from Flo and my entire family, indefinitely. But the pandemic proved a strong deterrent: that June camp was cancelled. So I went back to work in long-term care for another four weeks, into late June. Then it was time to isolate again, and intensify my training, before crossing the border for training in mid-July.

Meanwhile, in whatever minimal time I found to reflect, I started to reconsider medicine and why I loved it. There were a million reasons, but one unintended benefit of the pandemic was the way it narrowed the tally down to the most crucial ones.

Why did I love medicine?

It was partly because my parents taught me to be curious, follow my instincts and help others whenever possible. It was partly the combination of art and science that had drawn me toward medical school in the first place. It was partly because of how my brain works. Thankfully, I had given up on the engineering degree, which would have tied me to a computer far more than I would have liked. I had chosen human interaction, and now I understood the full extent of what that meant, for humanity is what dominated those intense weeks when I volunteered in long-term care.

Over those weeks, amid a fast-spreading pandemic, I'd learned that I had to take time and listen to my patients. That touch matters. And eye contact. And listening, being present, not rushing through a checklist. Yes, you need to be clinical and thorough, you need to check your boxes. But the best approaches are creative and holistic. There's no stronger connection than the one human beings make in a time of crisis.

I decided to host a barbecue on my last day, which happened to be National Orderly Day. I wanted to celebrate my new friends the way they had celebrated my football triumph. A friend who works in the restaurant business catered an outdoor dinner. We grilled. We ate.

As I headed to the barbecue after my last shift, everybody—patients, colleagues, supervisors—stood and applauded. It was embarrassing, and very moving. I should have been the one cheering. My co-workers all signed a poster for me. I placed it in my home office next to another favourite image, of me clad in the Chiefs uniform, celebrating on the field.

WHEN I DO become a doctor, and when I begin to practise whatever specialty I settle on, I vow to respect and prioritize the information I'm given from nurses and orderlies. They are a hospital's eyes and ears. They are its heart. There's more direct care of patients involved in the work of nurses and orderlies, more feelings, more attachments. Basically, everything that happens before and after doctors—with their perpetually busy schedules—swoop in to provide expertise falls within their sphere. They gave me a more complete picture of how medicine works. Working with them, I saw health care at its most basic level, and its most intimate.

I believe, I hope, that my time spent working with them will make me a better doctor, especially if I can remember what they taught me. I will carry the strength and wisdom I drew from our collective efforts in that facility into wherever I end up next. There's more to medicine than drawing blood, putting in urine catheters or crushing pills. I hope to be an empathetic doctor. I will picture myself in my patients' rooms, picture their fear, their hopes and their isolation; their longing for connection, rather than efficiency; their wish to be engaged with, instead of glossed over.

At the end of the day, we're all human. My patients taught me that. They schooled me on my privilege, what I take for granted, what I value, and what I should value more. I remember calling the daughter of one elderly man, and when she noticed his fresh haircut, tears ran down her cheeks. I lived for those small interludes of joy. I wanted to hold on to them, to carry them with me, back to the US.

Would my time at the long-term care facility, and the insights I gleaned from it, also make me a better football player? I hoped so. I began preparing for another season, energized by my long-term care team and all that we had fought through. I was like my teammates—lifting, running, studying the playbook—and yet not at all like them. At that point, in the summer of 2020, I knew that my time in the facility had changed me. But I didn't know that it would inform the decision I would soon be forced to make.

THE DECISION

I shifted gears. Fast. I had three weeks before training camp was set to begin. I resolved to lift, run and diet my way back into top physical condition. I would return to Kansas City, block for the Chiefs, complete another season. I stayed in touch with Dr. Moser, who sent text messages anticipating another fall of NFL football. I would, with a combination of sweat and luck, become the first repeat Super Bowl champion from Quebec.

But this wasn't like the usual ramp-up for training camp. The whole province was locked down, under curfew. Through our apartment window in Montreal, in the park across the street, I would see police officers on horseback moving people along—we weren't supposed to gather or linger, not even outdoors. It's hard to remember now, having weathered the Delta and Omicron variants, on the other side of wave after wave, with vaccines at our disposal, better understanding of and treatment for COVID, and so much widespread immunity in the population, what a big deal the pandemic was in the summer of 2020—how new and terrifying this disease was, how uncertain we all were, how worried about both getting and spreading the illness, and how consumed governments and public health officials were by the very real fear that our health care systems would be overloaded and even out-right collapse.

I'd written a piece for *Sports Illustrated* early on in which I'd predicted that the world would go back to normal relatively quickly. But I was mistaken. That wasn't happening. Positivity rates were increasing everywhere, including in many cities and states where my team was scheduled to play that season.

Friends and family would ask if the virus scared me. No, I told them, not on an individual level. The idea of catching COVID-19 didn't really scare me. What did was becoming a vector of transmission, potentially passing the virus to my parents or my neighbours. I didn't want a person I infected to experience severe symptoms, end up in hospital and require a bed (and the medical and nursing care that went with it) that was needed for someone else's urgent care or elective surgery. We needed to fight COVID together, to save lives and ease the incredible burdens on our health care system. If we failed to do that, the pandemic would drag on and on, its direct and collateral damage beyond measure.

The weeks between the end of my stint in the facility and the date I needed to leave for training camp became increasingly fraught. I wanted to play football. I expected to play football. I *was expected to* play football. The 2020 season would mark my seventh season of pro football, which was about seven more than I'd ever expected to play. I believed in the power of sports, in how spirited competition can pull people together, and saw, in the midst of this crisis, how the game could bring sorely needed entertainment to so many people. Pro sports are a balm to the increasing divisions in our society. No matter who you are or what you believe in, if you are a Chiefs fan, and wearing the red and gold, in that brief moment you are my friend. But my time in the long-term care facility, and my understanding of the medical and societal crisis we were facing, kept muscling in. I watched the rising case numbers, did the math, knew that, for a time at least, the situation would only worsen. If this was happening in Montreal, I had to consider Florida, or Texas, or even Missouri, my home away from home.

It became clear that the NFL was not going to cancel the season. Other industries had paused, including other professional sports. But the NFL said, essentially, "We'll just figure out a way to play." I had the privilege of sitting on the COVID-19 task force for the NFLPA. The Chiefs were one of the first teams to receive the IDER plan, which stood for Infectious Disease Emergency Response. The plan was well thought out and thorough, everything from the ramping-up period before the season started to how teams would handle their stadiums on game day. Protocols included frequent testing, contact tracing, virtual meetings. The league, in conjunction with its Players Association, was taking the right steps. Everything that could reasonably be done to reduce risk was there.

Still, it began to feel more and more strange to even consider hopping on a flight and going back to the business of playing football. As if all I'd just lived through—and all that people in health care were still living through—had never happened. As if the pandemic had vanished, when in fact it had worsened.

I began to wonder, to seriously consider: Did football matter in 2020? And, more pointedly, would I be able to look in the mirror in five to 10 years and tell myself that I had done everything I could to help, to be part of the solution?

I WILL BE the first to admit that I don't like making decisions. I always trust that time will take care of things—that the right path will emerge, become obvious and clear, if I just wait it out. Flo says that I'm not confrontational in my approach to life. I hate tense situations. And I hate having to deal with dilemmas. When I have to make tough decisions, it's not about faith or karma; instead, I trust my subconscious with the choice I have to make. After that, I live with my decision and trust that I made the right call for me in that moment. I feel good about my choices and don't get anxious or stressed after I've made them. My parents always taught me to open all doors, keep all the possibilities in front of me. But you can take that too far: you can cut off options, lose the ability to plan other aspects of your life, even make a choice by attrition, winding up stuck with the only option left. You can also force the people you most care about to languish in your holding pattern.

I remember Flo asking me questions like: *What are you doing? What will it mean for me? Am I not going to see you for six months? Am I not going to be able to come visit you?* And I was just like, *I don't know, honestly, we'll see.*

We'll see.

The way I've been with every big decision in my life: over-casual, trusting time. I have recently begun to see how that's not really all that fair for the people around me.

During those weeks, still lifting and exercising to get myself in shape for camp, I thought about how much I adored the game. How much I had put into it, into getting better, and finding a home, and winning a championship. How I cared for my coaches, my teammates and the defence of our title. I thought back to how unlikely it was that I made the NFL in the first place. The joke is that NFL really means Not For Long. Did I really want to give up one year of playing in my prime, not to mention the money due to me in my contract? There was also the chance that I might not be able to win my job back when I did return. People often take their jobs in the NFL for granted. But I knew how hard it was going to be to stay in shape and win my starting job back in a league where scouts are always looking for someone younger, cheaper and better.

But football wasn't the whole story, not for me. I'm a medical school graduate, a healer, a person who believes in the Hippocratic Oath. Lines like this one began to resonate: *Into whatsoever houses I enter, I will enter to help the sick, and I will abstain from all intentional wrongdoing and harm, especially from abusing the bodies of man or woman, bond or free.* I grew increasingly concerned about journeying to cities, some of them pandemic hotspots, and potentially spreading the disease I had fought so hard against that spring. I asked myself tough questions. Did playing betray my principles? Did I want to remain a part of the revenue machine, seeking additional glory? And at what cost?

Three days before training camp, there was still no opt-out available. I literally had my back against the wall and was still not feeling any better about zipping off to KC, so I contacted the NFL Players Association. Despite the protocols, despite my love for the game, despite my concerns over my career, in my heart I knew there was no way I could play football that year. But serious questions remained around the consequences of stepping back. I was under contract. I'd made legal commitments. I needed to figure out whether I could opt out, and what that would mean. I asked the Players Association, "What is the worst possible scenario?" But, while the NFLPA was keeping players informed, telling us that an opt-out was being negotiated, they confirmed that nothing had been finalized yet.

I watched the way other pro leagues were approaching the situation, and I was confident there was going to be an option for players to break their contracts and not have to report to their teams. Even so, I still had no clue what the contractual implications of opting out might mean for me. I had some specific dates and details in my contract, to ensure my ability to complete medical school and the necessary residencies, so it wasn't simply a matter of pushing my contract back a season. The bottom line was: if I failed to obtain official permission from the league to opt out of the season yet still chose not to play, on top of the salary I was leaving on the table that year, the team could sue me for $4 million. At best, they had no obligation to pay me anything, and there would be no guarantee about what would happen to me in the following season. There was still the possibility of me obtaining an opt-out—that is, official permission not to play, to temporarily break my contract—but there were no guarantees.

I took that in. I discussed it with Flo. I thought, *OK, even with that, I'm going to opt out.* It became clear that I had to tell my coaches. I called Coach Reid and told him I was not going to play. It was possibly the hardest call of my entire life. I was prepared to have to argue my case, defend my decision. But his response was genuinely caring. It was along the lines of: *Are you sure you want to do that?* Logistically, he meant. *I respect your decision, you're set up for doing great things in your life, but I have a lot of doctors in my family. I know how you think and I know you always want to help.*

In some ways, it seemed as if Coach Reid had expected my call. Part of what makes him such an amazing coach has nothing to do with football; it's the fatherly style he uses to reach his players, to get the most out of them. He told me he understood any decision that I made. He would support me, he'd do what he could to help me. "Do what you have to do," he said. "We've got your back."

It was a huge weight off my shoulders. A nice moment. I was so grateful for a coach who, in the face of losing one of his most experienced linemen—he'd have to fill that spot, contend with all the coaching and financial repercussions of my decision—responded with such grace and understanding.

Then I called Coach Heck. He too was calm, sympathetic, compassionate. He wished me luck. I didn't feel judged, or as if I'd let the team down. I told him I would stay in the best possible shape. I insisted that this wasn't goodbye, merely a pause.

When I got off the phone, I was relieved, but not off the hook. Not yet. I booked a flight for Missouri for the following day, the last available flight that would get me there on time. I was still technically, by contract, due to report at training camp, and unless some legal framework was found that I could fit into, I'd be liable for something like $30,000 for every day of camp I missed. So even though I'd made my decision, and the league had not announced any opt-out options for the players, I was still packing clothes and gear, preparing to have to quarantine—all the while planning not to play football.

We got on the phone to the Chiefs' administration to try to find a solution that would allow me to stay home while waiting on the ruling about my opt-out request. After many frantic calls and conversations, the Chiefs allowed me to delay my arrival at camp for 48 hours. The team knew that the NFLPA was going to confirm an opt-out plan shortly, and given the quarantine rules in Canada, they knew it was counterproductive to make me travel to the US.

Finally, I had some room to breathe. I put my suitcase away.

A little while later, Flo and I stood together on our balcony. I had decided. And yet, I remained torn. "Am I crazy not to play?" I asked.

She shook her head.

"Don't just say that because you want me to stay," I said, and we laughed.

The following day, just as training camp was about to get under way, the opt-out became available. That evening, Flo and I took a stroll through our neighbourhood, a bustling part of Montreal known as the Plateau. She understood the stress I felt in making the choice I'd made.

But Flo also understood me, and she knew that I cared about how this decision could be viewed, interpreted or mischaracterized. It wasn't just that strangers on social media might react negatively. I cared how everyone in Kansas City would feel, especially if no other player took the option to opt out. I didn't want to stand on that island alone, when other players with COVID-19 concerns had decided the risks were worth it, at least for them.

We stopped to order takeout from a place a few blocks from home. While Flo waited for the food, I made some calls to my football friends.

I wanted them to know: I was stepping away from football. It was temporary. I hoped they would understand.

NOW THAT MY opt-out was official, it was time to go public.

I sat on the balcony, working up a tweet. Sasha reviewed it, and so did the Chiefs' communications department. We needed the organization to sign off on it so we'd know they would back me up in the face of any backlash. How I communicated my decision mattered on their end too. The pandemic, unfortunately, had already become politicized and divisive. My wording had to reflect my opinion while not hurting or criticizing other players, the team or the league, which wasn't my intention anyway. And though I'm now fully bilingual, I can't always distinguish the connotation of this English word versus that—the difference, for example, between being "a vector" and being "responsible for the transmission of the virus."

It was a gruelling two-hour process, working and reworking that tweet. Finally, after all those weeks of indecision, after all the buildup and legal logistics, I looked it over one last time, read it aloud and hit Post.

This is one of the most difficult decisions I have had to make in my life but I must follow my convictions and do what I believe is right for me personally. That is why I have decided to take the Opt Out Option negotiated by the League and the NFLPA and officially opt out of the 2020 NFL season.

Being at the frontline during this offseason has given me a different perspective on this pandemic and the stress it puts on individuals and our healthcare system. I cannot allow myself to potentially transmit the virus in our communities simply to play the sport that I love. If I am to take risks, I will do it caring for patients.

You hit Send, and you feel like the world explodes. Reaction was swift and intense. I was the first player to opt out. In both Canada and the US, the media took it up. It was trending on Twitter. I googled my name, and 20 new articles popped up. Boom. You try to get a feel for whether people are respecting your decision. Are they criticizing it? I knew it was not going to be an issue in Canada. But how were they reacting in Kansas City?

It was a Friday night, around 8 p.m. A friend came by. We drank beers, as my phone pinged like a slot machine.

*

I DECIDED I wouldn't comment in the media about my decision. I didn't want to get pushed into a corner and asked questions about whether football should be happening at all in 2020. That wasn't for me to judge. I wanted to stay out of that conversation. I could only govern myself.

But my teammates *were* put on the spot. At the virtual team press conference held to mark the start of training camp, reporters asked how they felt about my choice to opt out of the season. I watched, both curious and nervous. I didn't want them to feel as if I'd let them down. Earlier in my career, another Chief had decided to retire a few days before practices started. I remembered how that felt. A sense of betrayal creeps in. That's human nature. This pandemic was a completely different situation, yet it wasn't hard to believe that some of my teammates might consider my decision a little extreme, and even unfair to the team. Several of them had reached out to me already to offer their support. Even Clark Hunt, our team's owner, had sent me a text offering the unconditional support of the "Chiefs family." But it's one thing to support me in private, another thing altogether to do so in public.

Coach Reid told reporters he was "happy and proud" of me. It meant a great deal to me that he'd met with the media at all to address the question; his positive statements were beyond what I could have hoped for. As other teammates echoed his sentiments, my tension eased. "I respect his decision," Chiefs quarterback Pat Mahomes said. "He's a guy that's been on the front lines working with the people that are suffering from COVID day-to-day, and putting in all that time, and all that work. He understands it, and his decision was he wanted to stay there."

There was negative stuff online, for sure. There were reactions that completely misrepresented my motives, which was hurtful. But having the team back me up was huge. In some ways it felt like 2018, when I flew back to Missouri after that big medical exam and everyone in one part of my life, the football part, embraced the other part of it. That's the beauty of the football locker room: everyone is different, in their cultures, their hobbies, their religions, and in so many other ways. Throughout a season, I would learn what motivated my teammates, what they cared about off the field, what their callings were. I respected what mattered to them, cheered them on. And they did the same right back for me.

In this case, it was in the most powerful way.

However, it was over. The back and forth, the hand wringing, the duelling duties—to my team, to my conscience—the tough phone calls, the negotiating, the frantic tweet editing—all of it. There was just me at home facing a pandemic, a locked-down city, a year without football, and the crushing awareness that the game would go on without me.

Not even my team's amazing support could shield me from the void I'd just walked into.

And it has to be said: I don't do well with voids.

Chapter 12

THE NEW REALITY

The nurse was heading straight for me. I could tell by the look on her face it was urgent. I knew her, we'd worked together in the spring. She told me in a rush that a patient was doing poorly. There was a doctor on the way, but this woman needed help now.

Then my supervisor approached. "We need your help, come with us."

This was my first day back at the long-term care centre after opting out of the NFL season. I had literally just arrived for my shift. Same facility, same floor, same people. It felt surreal. On the one hand, my internal clock was telling me I was supposed to be in Missouri, on a football field with my teammates, diving into workup training for the season. On the other, it was as if my few weeks away from here, working out and mentally preparing for a football season I'd ultimately decided, after much soul-searching, to forgo, existed on another plane, in a separate reality.

I hustled down the hallway toward the patient's room. The nurses wheeled an oxygen tank and a crash cart—a trolley stocked with medication and equipment that might be needed in an emergency. I knew the head nurse would have way more experience than I did with whatever situation awaited us. But I was it; I was the person available.

I leaned on the best approach to any medical crisis: follow systematic steps. The woman, when we arrived, was super lethargic. Elderly people are often vulnerable and fragile, so doctors must be careful and deliberate. A-B-C first: airway, breathing, circulation. All good. Then we checked her vitals. They were decent. Her oxygen levels were low, but I had no baseline. She had hypoxemia, or low blood oxygen. That raised further questions. Did she have something infectious? Was it a cardiac or a pulmonary issue? What was her normal oxygen level? Was something blocking her airway? The nurse and I ran through the possible scenarios as swiftly as we could. Was it COVID-19? What was her normal level of consciousness? Was she diabetic? Had she taken her medication?

We decided to put her on oxygen, and gently asked her some questions. After a few minutes, the doctor showed up. I went back to my other responsibilities—or, rather, to my newly reclaimed responsibilities. There was no ambiguity about the choice I'd made, no more putting off its implications. I had not gone to the Chiefs' training camp in Kansas City, had not spent August practising, sweating, icing sore muscles and complaining about the heat. I was, for the foreseeable future, a health care professional working in long-term care in the midst of a pandemic in my home province of Quebec. Unlike my stint in the spring, my situation this time was less temporary, more open-ended, and so it had been decided that things should be formalized. I was no longer simply a volunteer. I was officially on staff.

Technically, I was an orderly, but really I was there to help wherever I was needed with whatever skills I had. Sometimes that meant helping patients with meals and their hygiene routines.

Other times it would mean helping the nurses, who were short-staffed, with doing a blood test or inserting a catheter or an IV; distributing medication; or, as with the elderly patient I'd been rushed to upon my arrival, holding the fort in a crisis till a full-fledged doctor could get there; and, of course, running the testing crew for COVID-19. This—this struggling care centre with its dozens of dedicated health care workers, these tense, high-stakes shifts, this global health crisis—made up my new reality.

SOME WEEKS had passed since I'd posted my painstakingly worded opt-out tweet. Much had changed.

For the previous six years, I'd been used to going non-stop, moving back and forth between my medical studies and the NFL; between training to be a doctor and training for the football field. Every year, during football's off-season, I'd work in the hospital until the last day before showing up to training camp. And, after the last game of the season, I'd fly back to Montreal—after losing in the playoffs (because obviously you don't make the Super Bowl every year)—and jump right back into hospital work as a medical student. The schedule would be tough, but the toughest thing was changing my approach and my perspective. I'd have just spent five months playing in huge stadiums in front of tens of thousands of people, under media scrutiny and constant pressure from my coaches (and myself) but with a whole team there to support me—trainers, physios, a mental coach, even nutritionists—as I tried to optimize my performance, pushed the limit, flirted with that line. Then, within a week, while still processing the fact that we'd failed in our quest for the Super Bowl, I'd be back in medicine, at the bottom of the medical hierarchy, where it was my job to listen; to learn; to sit on the sidelines and pay attention to my superiors and mentors when appropriate; to show empathy and aim to optimize, not my personal performance on the gridiron, but the care and health of a patient.

Flipping between these worlds every year was hard. But each time I settled into the flight from one world to the other, I embraced the challenge of hitting reset. The back and forth grounded me; it gave me a different perspective on the game, and vice versa.

Now, though, for the first time in a decade, I was letting go of one-half of my life in order to focus on the other. The last time I'd done that, when I'd quit football to focus on medical school, it had not gone well. I'd lasted two months. This time, it was going to be for at least a year, and maybe forever, because I knew how hard it was going to be to find a way back onto an NFL roster. I was anxious about that commitment and the impact it would have on my mental health.

As I looked into returning to serve in the overtaxed health care system, I felt weird. Unsettled. Anxious. It was the time of year when I would normally be going away from home, stepping outside ordinary daily life into what felt like the hardest mental and physical challenge I could possibly undertake. Training camp is intense and all-consuming. It grinds you and pushes you to your limits. Without it, an emptiness loomed, one that I could tell threatened to upset my equilibrium.

I was still in touch with some of my colleagues from long-term care. We did group texts. We talked on the phone. The front lines remained harrowing. The virus was formidable; staff burnout and shortages were a problem. But before I could head back into the fray, there were arrangements to sort out. There was paperwork. That took a few weeks. During that time, I'd be sitting in my office, looking out the window at the park we can see from our apartment. Usually a busy urban park, cheerful and bustling, it was mostly empty. I thought about, on the one hand, the people across the country who'd lost their jobs because of the pandemic and, on the other, those who were now overworked or on the front lines. I knew I was privileged to have any options at all. I didn't want to take that privilege for granted. I tried to think clearly about the upcoming year and how it might play into the future. What might I do in the off-hours that would give me focus and motivation? I knew I'd always done well with dual challenging pursuits, and I wanted to put my time away from the Chiefs to the best use I could.

My thoughts turned to public health.

Part of the beauty of football is that it's not just a sport; its widespread popularity makes it a megaphone for players to promote what they most believe in. It's still weird to me, going on these national talk shows, speaking to writers from top magazines and newspapers. But all that airtime and attention is also an opportunity. Someone like me can reach an audience I never would have spoken to otherwise. It would feel stupid to me if I used that public face only for talking about football. Before, I'd always seen working in medicine as a series of individual interactions with patients: you see 40 or so people a day and you have a pretty good chance of helping each one improve their life. But now, with the platform I'd built through my years in the NFL, and with the experience I already had in long-term care, I began to think, *What if I could reach a hundred thousand people, or a few hundred thousand, and improve the lives of even 1 percent of those people?* That's public health: promoting health at a population level.

My interest in the field wasn't solely about my (hoped-for) potential to reach a wider audience with important health information. Each time I returned to Montreal after the football season to practise as part of my medical training, I found it more and more difficult to remain anonymous—to be seen as just any other doctor-in-training by patients. So I'd begun to wonder how, when I became a practising physician, I would be able to balance even my relatively small level of fame with my patients' privacy. Doctors must ask the people they care for difficult questions. They must probe. They must counsel. And the better-known I became, not just in Montreal or Quebec but beyond, the more delicate, and in some cases awkward, those exchanges had become. It was as if, in comparison with others, it was sometimes harder for me to gain trust and confidence from those I was trying to treat. It began to make sense, at least for the early part of my career—and for however long the lingering notoriety of being an NFL player might last—to use my platform to promote something I believed in. Some of my teammates used their voices to speak up about the importance of voting, or against racial inequalities. I wanted to use mine to advocate for primary prevention and health.

So now, during those weeks when I would have been in training camp, when a full year without football was opening up before me, I began to think, well, if public health is going to be part of my career, why not study it? Right now. Immediately.

And here's where I might have taken a step back. Maybe I could have asked myself, *Do I really need to do this? Why do I think I need this?* It's where Flo, who knows me and my pitfalls—my competitive nature, my need to always be jumping to the next thing, to be pushing the limits—challenged me. *You don't need to optimize everything,* she said. *You don't need to keep proving to yourself that you can climb higher, go farther, do more. Is it necessary? Is it the right thing? Is it really the message you want to send, especially in the context of a pandemic?*

We had some good, tough, serious conversations that COVID summer, Flo and I. I considered what she said. But I also couldn't help wanting to strive, to study, to have something that felt productive and meaningful in the works. I wanted to do my part during the pandemic, during that year I'd stepped away from football—to do something for my community. But I also wanted to do something for myself. This was my way of coping. *I'm going to do a little bit for others and a little bit for me. I'm going to do a little bit for my intellectual advancement, so I come out of this pandemic with something more in my back pocket.* Was it good or bad? I still don't know, but that's what was going through my mind. I began looking into graduate programs at different schools, and decided to go all in: I applied to the T.H. Chan School of Public Health at Harvard University.

I put a lot of effort into my résumé and the essay I wrote on my motivation for studying public health. I pulled together letters of recommendation. I was proud of my application. Still, when I was accepted, I almost couldn't believe it. Harvard. A master's degree. Even though my coursework would take place purely online, it was still amazing to contemplate. Football, I knew, would be over someday. When that happened, I would need to shift toward a different life, a different way to be and to contribute. I hoped the degree would boost my credibility and lend more weight to the messages I wanted to help spread in the future, about health and prevention.

IN LATE AUGUST, not long after my return to long-term care, I logged on for my first biostatistics class, clutching a pen in my right hand. After a quick introduction, we dove into the first chapter, which focused on case-control studies versus cohort studies. I strove to grasp the concepts. I hadn't been in a classroom, actual or virtual, for years—not since before I'd started my clinical rotations in 2012. All the work toward my degree from that point on had taken place out in the field. I remembered the grind of studying internal medicine: the cardiovascular system, the nervous system, the immune system, and theories related to all three. The hardest block of classes I'd taken in med school had lasted for eight weeks, with work starting at 6:30 a.m. I sometimes wouldn't finish studying until after 11 p.m. Now, years later, wrapping my head around this new material, I immediately liked that familiar feeling, of being challenged intellectually, pushing beyond my field of knowledge.

I dug into the curriculum, sitting through virtual classes in health and social behaviour, nutrition and epidemiology with students from all over the world. It was a rich experience. Much of the material focused on people—groups of people—and it made me realize how fragile the societal ecosystems we live in really are, and how seemingly minor changes in a society can have profound effects on individuals, especially the most vulnerable. In statistics and epidemiology we took deep dives into the numbers: how to distinguish which are important, how they're skewed, what they reveal.

In a normal time, I might have found such classes long—even, sometimes, boring. But we were barely six months into a historic, raging pandemic. We used the numbers related to COVID as examples for group discussions. We investigated positivity rates and selection bias, and how such information was being disseminated, and whether the choices made by public health officials were helpful, misleading or somewhere in between. We looked at newspaper accounts of statistics, and where reporting and analysis might mislead, or be misconstrued by, the public.

We checked for biases. The data was profoundly relevant, and teasing it apart was fascinating. My teacher kept saying, "Anyone can make the numbers say whatever they want. It's your job to find the data that is unbiased, and interpret the result." I began to see COVID-19 in a more complete and analytical way, one that provided context during my shifts in the facility and, later, when considering COVID outbreaks in the NFL.

I didn't love the homework, which we submitted on Wednesday nights. But that became my new game day. I started to lean into the familiar learning vibe again.

Meanwhile, I'd returned to the intensity and emotional grind of working on the front lines. There is no easing back into that kind of environment, you only jump in and immerse. After my stint in the facility in the spring, I'd invited my co-workers to our place for an outdoor barbecue. In my mind, there was a good chance I wouldn't see them again—I would soon be leaving for Kansas City. But a month later, here I was, back where it had all started. Just seeing everyone again was uplifting. It was a good team, I'd been happy to be part of it.

But things had changed. We were no longer at the height of the first COVID wave, and some of the health care workers who'd been pulled into long-term by the provincial authorities to help with the crisis—retired nurses, physiotherapists and others—were no longer there. Now we had a roster of new order-lies, who'd been quickly recruited and trained by the province to help ease the widespread staff shortages. This cohort of train-ees were excited to be there. They were energetic, positive, opti-mistic. And their optimism was infectious—even, to an extent, shared by the core staff at the centre, those who'd been there for years and had been through the worst. The pandemic was still going on, but case numbers had fallen, we weren't in active outbreak, restrictions and protocols had eased somewhat. There was a sense of relief, of reprieve.

It wasn't going to last, though, and we knew it. Solène, my supervisor, had frequent meetings with her superiors, who in turn reported to the health minister. She knew that the lull in the pandemic was only temporary. One day, as I sat in her office, she said, "Right now, it's OK. But everybody's telling us to brace ourselves for impact." I could feel her worry, her fear. It was going to be bad, potentially worse than what we'd experienced the first time around. The difference was, this time we knew what to expect, and we could prepare. We could make sure we had supplies on hand. We could put plans in place for setting up isolation units in the building.

And we did.

As we got ready for what felt like a looming Armageddon, my course load was challenging my busy mind during the days and hours I was away from the facility. It provided a substitution for football, for the physical intensity of training camp. It was crucial that I have *something* to step in for football, especially as the season approached and the reality of the choice I'd made, in pressing pause on my NFL career, sank in.

Every day, it sank in a little more.

My team, the Chiefs, would soon be gearing up for their home opener against the Houston Texans. And they'd be doing it without me.

MOST YEARS, I knew exactly what I'd be doing in September, every day, down to the hour. A weekly schedule packed full of tasks was part of my DNA. I knew that Wednesdays were important, because we would install and tweak the offence based on our next opponent. I knew that practices would get easier as the week went by, that I would sit in a hotel at home or on the road and make my final preparations on Saturdays, maybe take a bath if time permitted. I knew what I would eat the night before a game, the music I was going to listen to driving to the stadium, that we'd warm up at 10 a.m. local time before every noon game. I knew that I would find my rhythm—and so would my team—in the second half of the season. I knew that I would fight through injuries, add rehabilitation to my schedule, lift weights, kick ass. This was football. In the midst of that rigorous schedule, the stress is intense. But when I looked back, it hit home that it was actually reassuring to exist within that clear framework.

Earlier in the spring, before I'd opted out, the Chiefs had signed tackle Mike Remmers along with three young O-line prospects. But the position group in general, though anchored by mainstays Eric Fisher and Mitchell Schwartz, remained a question mark. Then, the day after my decision not to play became public, KC had made its biggest, splashiest O-line signing yet. They inked Kelechi Osemele to play my old position, right guard, while adding guard Jovahn Fair. Both would compete alongside Andrew Wylie, my close friend, another skilled guard who could play on either side. Osemele was an interesting choice, and a good one.

NFL rosters are fluid ecosystems that change dramatically each year. In Kansas City, there were always new players for the coaches to develop, and always evaluations of individual players and how they fit into larger position groups. These latest changes were at least in part prompted by my opt-out, and they proved, at least in the early going, highly promising. The Chiefs kicked off the 2020 season with four victories, toppling the Houston Texans, the Los Angeles Chargers, the Baltimore Ravens and the

New England Patriots. The team looked awesome, formidable, as though they were ready to march right back to the Super Bowl and win again.

I had, if not conflicting emotions, then at least a broad range of them. First and foremost, I wanted my teammates to do well. But I also didn't want my old spot to be taken permanently. I wanted the team to succeed; but I also wanted the team to need me. I was only human, how could I not want that? It was a slight relief that the Chiefs signed Osemele to a one-year deal—but a marginal one. I didn't need to remind myself that in the NFL, no job is guaranteed.

I followed my teammates on Instagram. I missed them. I missed playing. I longed to be studying pass protections in my position room, rather than studying biostatistics. Strange as it might sound, I missed hitting people. I missed the drudgery of camp, the all-in nature of preparing for another season. I even, to my surprise, missed doing interviews. The news cycle had moved on, and my decision to opt out faded from public view.

I had made a choice. With football season now under way, and me far away, living a completely different life, it hit home that now I had to stand in that decision. I had to work through any uncomfortable emotions related to it, and accept the radically altered routine that came with it.

I learned an important lesson during that time. It was one thing to stand before the media and say that the choice I had made felt like the right one, the only one. It was another thing entirely to make that choice worthwhile, and to live with it on a daily basis. Don't get me wrong: I remained grateful to even have a choice. But I also want to admit to the doubts that followed me around that early fall, especially as the rate of positive cases declined and the NFL season began without much in the way of pandemic catastrophe. I sometimes wondered: Had I *really* made the right call? Had it been necessary, or right, or wise, for me to give up football this year? All NFL careers are limited, finite, painfully so. They're also fragile: the slightest shift—a poorly timed injury, a rising star out-competing you—could knock even one of the strongest players off the field for good. And I had just willingly thrown myself onto the sidelines.

Would I ever make it back?

Sometimes I worked on Sundays, during Chiefs games. I would be dispensing medications to a patient, or putting in an IV, or changing bedsheets, and in that room, my team would be playing on TV. Those moments were surreal. There was my old life. And here was my new one.

I WAS part-time at the long-term care facility, trying to fit three shifts a week into my schedule, and doing coursework and training on my off-days. The lectures were virtual, and often recorded, so I could be flexible, fitting them, as well as study and assignments, in around my shifts. After some shifts I would visit with Solène, my supervisor, so we could schedule my next one. Sometimes she'd be missing two nurses, and I would slide in to take one of those slots. Other times she didn't have enough bodies for the night shift, and I would assist with staffing, combining shifts, working through lunch and sometimes through dinner.

Solène was amazing, having served in a dual role as nurse and night doctor for years. She had taken on more of a managerial position as the pandemic continued to spread. She was a critical mentor to me, helping me get up to speed. She was also worn down by the pandemic, and I saw the toll it took on her. Sometimes during our meetings she would tell me about problems and setbacks, and her own grief around the effects of the pandemic—on her staff, and on those in our care. Sometimes she'd become emotional talking about the situation, but she couldn't present that face to the hundred people in her care. She let me see that vulnerability, though, maybe because I was something of an outsider. Maybe she just needed an ear.

After my shifts I'd go home to the apartment I shared with Flo. As a curator and writer in the art world, she was dealing with her own stuff. She was stuck at home, her workload dwindling. And I know, looking back, I wasn't truly there for her—not as much as I should have been.

When I'd first decided to take the year off football, Flo had expressed some concern, having heard from other partners of pro football players about how difficult it could be when they retired, everyone adjusting to the new dynamic when someone who'd seldom been home suddenly always was. At the same time, we'd both been looking forward to spending more time together, having a more "normal" schedule than we'd had in years. But our new reality was completely the opposite. Between the care centre and my Harvard courses, I was working nonstop. Plus, I had to train. I was determined to stay in shape, to maintain my strength, my ability to be explosive on the field. It was one thing to imagine going back to the NFL to play. That was the easy part of dreaming. The hard part was actually doing what I needed to in order to make sure I could. I'd put together a plan with my trainer and set it in motion in September, at the same time the season kicked off. The plan was to lift weights after work or after dinner. But it took some time to get into a routine. Gyms were closed, and finding the weights and equipment to train at home was a challenge; this stuff had become a rare commodity.

Between the workouts, the shifts at the facility and my studies, I was, if possible, more absent from my life with Flo than ever
before. And as the weeks passed, my mood grew darker. I found
it difficult to watch my team win football games. I often found
myself wondering whether I could still play, whether the Chiefs
missed me, whether it even mattered. I tried to remember, even
as I went through the most difficult or mundane tasks at work,
that this new life was temporary. Even if I could not make it back
to the NFL, I would not be on the front lines forever.

Sometimes I would go straight from a shift at the facility to
the grocery store, and I'd hear strangers spout nonsense about
vaccines or even about washing their hands. Those snippets of
overhead conversation triggered me. I had left the NFL for a
year to assist as many people as possible—to help the very people
who sometimes didn't seem to grasp the bigger picture.

It was hard to keep upbeat. And hard to talk, even with Flo,
about my mood or my frustrations. I wondered whether the shell
I'd put around myself was, at least in part, tied to the lack of
normalcy in our lives—brought on not just by the pandemic but
by the fact that I was home, rather than where I would usually
be at that time of year: with the Chiefs, caught up in the fever
of athletic competition. I also wondered if, as an offensive lineman who spent my football life protecting others, I was shutting
down, however subconsciously, to protect myself. Many doctors
I know are like that. They spend their days telling patients how
to live a healthy life, while not necessarily taking such great care
of themselves.

When I feel out of balance, exercise usually helps. But that
fall, the colder it got, the harder it was to train. My shifts were
long, I got home late. I sometimes wondered why I cared. *Why
am I lifting 400 pounds? Why am I running these stairs?* But I tried to

remember how these sweat sessions both calmed and motivated me. And how crucial they were. But there were times I would go to squat a typical amount of weight and would simply not be able to. Was it the fact that I'd been running around at work all day? Was I too tired? Too stressed out? I didn't know. But the idea of losing strength was freaking me out.

SOMETHING had to give. And something did, in part through the flexibility and creativity of my supervisor. Due to staff shortages and absences, Solène was struggling to adequately cover meal-times. The morning shift was 7 a.m. till 3 p.m., and the evening shift was 3 p.m. till midnight. But we decided it would make sense for me to work 11:30 a.m. to 7:30 p.m. That way, I would be able to train in the morning and then drive to the facility for my shift.

It was a small but significant change that lifted my spirits. It helped me a ton with my workouts—with feeling that I could keep up my strength and fitness level. It was also good for the centre, as I was now on hand to help during lunch and supper. And because I overlapped two shifts, I saw more of my colleagues. I was sometimes able to bridge the gap, passing along informa-tion that might have been missed during the handover at shift change. And—this was key—I was able to work out before com-ing to work. It was so much easier for me to lift in the morning.

I began to see my workout sessions through a different lens, less *why am I doing this* and more *I'm doing this for me*. The pan-demic had unfortunately robbed so many people of their typical levels of activity, keeping them at home, locked onto screens, logging on to Facebook. I still fear that down the road we'll see the harmful results of that period of reduced physical activity. And I know it increased the general level of anxiety. I felt it myself. I turned to training to combat it. I needed the endorphin rush of competition, the goal of getting better, not to mention the muscle fibre and the peace of mind that come from cleaning 315 pounds of weights. I decompressed a little more with each lift.

In much the same way as a football team takes shape over the course of a season, I found my rhythm at the facility over time too. In football, there's a choreographed dance that evolves which can only be reached through repetition, which requires the full effort of dozens of players, and the coaches willing them to reach their full potential. Usually after the first five or six games of a season, we started to feel in sync, a full—and highly functioning—team.

At the care centre, I started to open up, to share more and to look for ways to support the rest of the team. I don't have kids, but many of my colleagues did. I tried to be flexible with my schedule to allow them time with their families, especially when someone needed to stay home with a sick child. Watching how *they* balanced their work and home lives inspired me. I wondered about them the same way people often wonder about me: How were they able do all these things at once?

Sometimes I put a lot of pressure on myself. I would think: How can I complain when I have everything I could ask for? But asking for help actually lets others know they can ask for it too. So I let myself lean on my co-workers a little. I stopped hiding from my family and from Flo. I found my public health coursework increasingly motivating—and amazingly relevant. I'd remained on the NFL COVID-19 task force, which included doctors, scientists, researchers and interested players like me. Sometimes I'd log on to a meeting right after taking a class online. World-renowned specialists like James Andrews would be discussing protocols or statistics, how best to protect the players and their families from infection. Sometimes they would cite the very material I'd just studied in class, my new life intertwining with my old one.

The pandemic during that time was hard for me, but for reasons that I can't entirely convince myself are really justifiable, especially when compared with the challenges that many others faced—the loss of jobs, the deaths of loved ones. Maybe I should have just accepted a period in which I accomplished nothing meaningful, in which I didn't move forward in some way. It seemed at times as though I wasn't able to do that, and sometimes that scared me.

I remember talking to my sports psychologist around then. We were discussing high achievers, how they must get better at *something*, whether they're growing a business, building a career or helping their community. The pandemic froze so many of those plans. I realized as we talked that that was what I'd been struggling with. But I also knew something else: I simply needed to find *other things*. Changing how I looked at that situation changed how I felt about it.

Each time I logged on for a course, each time I came back from a shift or finished another workout, I felt better. As October turned to November, my new life began to crystallize. I would sit at my computer, sometimes after midnight, and I would think about my shift the next morning and the people who needed our support. And I started to feel more of a sense of reward, of pleasure. I had found a way to help while continuing to advance my personal development. That's one of my favourite feelings—one born from the best kind of work, the hardest kind, the roll-up-your-sleeves-and-get-at-it kind.

*

THE CHIEFS, meanwhile, were rolling. As well, that is, as any team could in that pandemic-shadowed season.

In the early fall of 2020, to mitigate risk and avoid cancelling the season, the league implemented a raft of strict protocols. Players and coaches met virtually when possible. Teams shipped workout equipment to their players so they could train at home. Daily testing was mandatory, and, as with health protocols in so many other contexts, anyone who tested positive or who'd had close contact with a positive case was required to isolate. The testing alone cost around $100 million, split evenly amongst the 32 franchises.

The measures were effective. COVID rates across the NFL were strikingly low throughout the early season, especially compared with the rest of the United States or many other parts of the world. But there were outbreaks, and they were expected.

In Week 4, Tennessee experienced a rash of positives. A full 23 people—players, coaches, staff—were reported to have contracted the virus. The rest of the sports world watched to see how the NFL would adjust both its protocols and its playing schedule. The outbreak was also proof of what league doctors had been saying all along: it wouldn't take much for any one position group, or any one team, to find themselves in a huge mess, due to the virus and how quickly it could spread.

This was life in a pandemic, and it required flexibility, adjustments. There would be new cases the very next week. For teams like the Titans, their schedule was adjusted by moving their off-week to later in the season. And the NFL deployed other, more creative solutions on a case-by-case basis. When quarterback Cam Newton was infected, just as the Patriots were scheduled to play the Chiefs in Week 4, the league moved the contest from Sunday to Monday, and New England even took the rare step of flying to Missouri on the day of a game.

League officials continued to sketch out hypothetical scenarios to address potential outbreaks. They also made some important changes to protocols on the fly. A month into the season, the league mandated that players and coaches be tested on game day, the only day they had previously been permitted to skip. They stiffened other protocols, further limiting in-person meetings and granting less access to the locker rooms and weight rooms. Games scheduled in facilities where it was determined that ongoing outbreaks existed were moved. Commissioner Roger Goodell told the owners that games would be postponed only for medical reasons, not for competitive ones. If any one franchise was missing an entire position group but there was no "ongoing transmission," that contest would move forward. The same would happen if, say, Tom Brady contracted the virus, putting his new team, the Bucs, at an obvious competitive disadvantage.

Amid all this, I began reaching out to my teammates. I wanted to check in. I texted with Fisher, the O-line veteran, and Wylie, a guard I had grown close to. I wanted to know about their seasons, the team dynamic and how it might have shifted. I wanted to hear the war stories, glean pivotal moments, live vicariously. At the same time, I understood that I shouldn't ask too much. Most years, early in the season, I would sometimes stop by the coffee shop after practice and work on some of my outside projects. I would visit, hang out. But as the weeks and months passed, I would chiefly be concerned with conserving energy. Every finger hurt, along with my elbows and my shoulders. Finding the energy to face down the stakes of a Sunday game, and the expectations of fans, was still easy; after all, that was my job. But the grind of practice and creating the energy and focus day in and day out to prepare yourself for the game—that was the challenge. I knew that grind, and how annoying well-intentioned people can sometimes be when they reach out for the insider scoop, for the juicy anecdotes and tales of glory. I didn't want to be that annoying person.

In Week 5, the Chiefs suffered their first defeat of the season, against the Raiders, and the O-line began a downward spiral. Osemele went down with a serious injury. I felt awful for him. But it's the NFL, which operates on a "next-man-up" mentality. The team had to adjust. Yet again.

Which it did. Remmers would spend some time at the guard spots, as would Nick Allegretti and Wylie, who was manning my old position—and playing like a beast. On October 19, the Chiefs beat the Bills. They trounced the Broncos, then the Jets. On November 8, they toppled the Panthers. Nine games into the season, the Chiefs walked confidently into their bye week. They were 8–1.

Now, all they had to do was get back to the Super Bowl—and win it without me.

CHAPTER 13

RED ZONE

One day in October, the first snow of the year fell on Montreal. I watched as flakes descended in white sheets outside the windows of the long-term care facility. The first snowfall is always a surprise and a wonder. It transforms the grey atmosphere of bare trees and dead grass into a world that's both hushed and glittering. I saw by their faces that the residents were delighted. One woman was so happy to see the snow that I opened a window in her room. Then I went out on her balcony and scooped up handfuls of wet snow and shaped a small snowman on the little table near her bed.

Obviously, the fellow couldn't stay there long. But we indulged in a few moments of make-believe. We turned her empty hot chocolate cup into a hat. I found some aluminum foil and fashioned our dude a shiny nose. We both grinned, admiring our work.

By this point, a couple of months into my second tour of duty in long-term care, I'd settled into an approach to the work that felt both useful and positive. On paper, I was an orderly, whose job is chiefly to assist with basic patient care: hygiene care, feeding, changing bedpans, replacing bedding. Orderlies also restock medical supplies, sterilize and set up equipment, help to relocate patients, and essentially lend a hand wherever a hand is needed. Because I had completed medical school and was very nearly a full-fledged doctor, I was able to help with some medical needs as well, from administering medication to inserting catheters. Some of this work, such as the time-consuming and delicate task of changing a dressing on an ulcerated sore, was extremely helpful to my overworked colleagues. But I also remembered from my first nine weeks in the facility back in the spring that there was something else I could offer, which was as important as anything practical: care, comfort, company.

Whenever possible I'd go beyond my checklist to do something friendly, silly, fun—like building a miniature snowman. Or helping a patient with a puzzle. Or, while delivering medication, stopping to watch a bit of whatever newscast, show or sporting event a resident had on their TV. "What's the score?" I'd ask. I'd catch parts of Chiefs games, or highlights from them. One woman was an avid sports fan with indiscriminate tastes; she loved hockey, tennis, football, everything. A T-shirt featuring her favourite hockey players hung on the wall of her room. At some point while I watched part of a game with her, it sank in for me what it actually means when they say that "millions of people tuned in." It means they're watching from all kinds of environments, including the small, tidy, sparsely furnished room in the long-term care facility in which this woman lived.

For all that such interludes were uplifting, providing some warmth and humanity in an institutional environment, we, the facility's staff, moved through the early weeks of that first COVID fall in a kind of holding pattern. We tried to be optimistic, and sometimes we truly felt that way. But we were also tense and watchful. Though months past the outbreak we'd struggled through in the spring, we were enjoying a reprieve that, deep down, we knew couldn't last.

IT STARTED like most outbreaks: small. Potentially manageable. First, two cases were confirmed. Then three. Every day after that, there were more, which themselves only led to more, and to the extreme measures required to combat them. We had to establish a red zone, and fast.

In football, "red zone" means an offence is close to scoring a touchdown, when a team is within the 20-yard line. If you're on the right team, this is good news, even great. In our facility, though, "red zone" was a phrase you didn't want to hear. Ever. It meant the risk for transmission was as high as it could possibly be. It meant transforming gyms and cafeterias into makeshift virus wards. It meant severe restrictions for medical personnel: no lunch boxes allowed, no cellphones. The floors were kept completely separate. The nurses, orderlies and doctors who treated the patients who tested positive did not interact with the workers on other floors. Our whole facility became a maze of red, yellow and green duct tape, everything laid out on the floor to direct us this way or that, to ensure we didn't contaminate one another.

Meanwhile, our lives once again became ruled by personal protective equipment (PPE). Before the outbreak, we were, of course, careful to use and wear PPE on shift. But once the outbreak hit, that protective gear—using and wearing it properly, without even the most minor exception—became one of our most crucial tools for containing the virus's spread, to protect the people in our care, as well as ourselves. Becoming infected would mean having to take time off, leaving the facility even more short-staffed than it already was. And the last thing any of us wanted was to become infected and thus a vector, passing the virus on to a vulnerable resident or to one of our own family members back home.

During the years I studied medicine, PPE wasn't something I really gave much thought to, apart from in the operating room or when it was needed for a sterile procedure. We wrote exams on anatomy, diseases, treatment protocols—not on gloves, masks and face shields. Now, because of, on the one hand, my years as a professional football player and, on the other, my time in long-term care during the pandemic, I can see that my life has been punctuated by two very different, but equally intense, "suiting up" routines. These routines involve lists of gear so different from each other it's almost funny—shoulder pads, say, versus lab coats. And moving through those lists to put everything on, item by item, prepares you for two entirely unrelated forms of battle.

Dressing up to play ball on game day is an important routine, part of getting both physically and mentally ready. I show up to the field three hours before kickoff not just to exercise and stretch; I need to prepare. First of all, I go to the locker room to put the right under-layer on—leggings, topped by a pair of shorts. I'll jog out onto the field and move around some. Then I come back, remove the shorts, put my pads inside my pants and put my pants on. Stretch a bit. Throw on my jersey with the shoulder pads still loose. I'll pull out the bullet-point notes I've prepared the night before, sit and review the first 15 plays to be called in the game plan.

Then, 45 minutes before the game, we show up on the field as a team. That's the moment it becomes real. We run through a couple of plays. We exercise. The equipment guys come out and help us strap our shoulder pads tight. You build a relationship with these guys; they know how loose or how tight you like your pads, what kind of cleats you like wearing when the field is wet or frozen, what you like to put on when it's minus-10 or plus-30 degrees. Then you tape your wrists and fingers. Like a boxer getting ready for a match, you do this yourself. That's part of the process. Nobody else is going to tape my wrists and my fingers. Finally, I pull on elbow pads, I pull on gloves. I know for certain that when I remove those gloves and unwind the tape around my fingers and wrists, the game will be over. There's going to be a winner and a loser. As I look down at my taped and gloved hands, I think to myself, *You'd better come out on top.*

The very last thing you do, just as the game's about to begin, is put your helmet on. You run out onto the field with your teammates. You're not just dressed, you're ready. You know what to do in order to win. You can dominate, you can be in control, you have the weapons you need in order to fight. And what you're fighting is tangible: it's right in front of you.

Let's shift gears now, back to my other life. When it comes to the virus, as compared with football, you can't see the danger. But you know it's there. You're keenly aware of the threat it poses. At any point, if you let your guard down, you could expose yourself. One unmasked interaction with a colleague during your lunch break, one conversation without enough social distancing while you are walking to your car at the end of your shift—just one incident of not respecting the safety measures and you might become infected. Then you could be the one seeing a patient and giving them the virus.

You never know how the virus is going to get into the facility. All you know is that it's going to get in there at some point. And it's not going to appear by magic: it will be you or one of your co-workers who brings it into the building. You're there trying

229

to do good, but your first priority is actually to *do no harm*. That put a stress on me.

When facing a wave of infections, the only way we could judge whether we were doing well was not whether we kept the virus out of the facility entirely; from a statistical standpoint, that was unlikely. We had to gauge our success by how strict we were with the measures that would ensure any infected staff member or patient was diagnosed quickly, and that each of those infections was immediately contained, was not passed on. You find the virus, isolate it, stop it in its tracks. The best way to do this, in fact the only way, is to strictly follow prevention and containment protocols. These begin the moment you show up for your shift.

You arrive for work dressed in your regular civilian clothing, the same way you walk into the stadium on game day. The similarities between the two routines stop there. You enter the trailer set up outside the facility and put your scrubs on. Upon entering the building, dressed in your clean scrubs, you put on a mask and a visor. And a clean white lab coat. This is a critical step, one you might not expect. Partly because of how medical workers are portrayed on TV, people think the lab coat is cool, maybe even that it differentiates the doctor from the nurse. I used to wonder, what's the point of it? Well, during the pandemic, I learned the true purpose of a lab coat. You wear it from the moment you walk into the building until you arrive at your unit, which might be several floors away. Then you take the coat off. Attached to it are any germs you may have picked up as you travelled through the facility. Your scrubs, which were safely hidden underneath, remain clean, uncontaminated. Now you're ready for your shift.

But you're not done with suiting up. Or rather, un-suiting and re-suiting. Before entering a patient's room, you do the following:

wash your hands, remove your visor, clean your visor, wash your hands, switch masks, put your visor back on, then put on clean gloves. Upon leaving, you do the same, beginning with removing the gloves. Then you get dressed all over again for the next patient.

The outlook my colleagues presented day after brutal day blew me away. They showed up for every shift not quite knowing what they were walking into, and they climbed the special staircase into the infected area with smiles spread across their faces. They made jokes with visors, masks, gloves and gowns on. They embraced the trailer, and changing out in the cold, sometimes after waiting in line outside. Even with only a few shifts a week, I felt as if I was part of a team again, and this team was even more important than our squad that won the Super Bowl. Our patients' lives were at stake, every day, and it was our job to protect them as best we could. We couldn't let them see how we felt, how terrifying it really was.

ONE DAY, a bathtub on the COVID floor broke. There was water everywhere, seeping through the linoleum and pooling on the floor below. Of course, we called the maintenance team right away. The problem was, due to the pandemic—every problem you could find, really, was due to the pandemic—the maintenance crew was already stretched thin. With more pressing issues eating into what time they did have, nobody could fix the tub. Already, due to our staffing shortages, even with a working tub, some residents and patients were only bathing once a week. It wasn't the facility officials' fault; it was simply the reality of what we were dealing with. But to lack access to such a basic necessity as personal hygiene struck me as inhumane.

I asked my supervisor if I could take a crack at it. She said OK, so I went to the basement and grabbed some tools—screws, wrenches and whatnot—and I went to the bathroom to take a look. After an hour, somehow, I'd fixed the tub. A small win. It felt good. We wheeled a patient to the bathroom and helped them in. It's crazy how, during my time in the facility, the tasks that I was proudest of and the things that removed the biggest burdens on my team were often not medical (remember the installation of the air conditioner?). When I got home that night, I felt good. When I told Flo how my day went, I had a big smile on my face.

Working in long-term care during a pandemic, you cling to small triumphs like that. Because most of the time, that isn't the way things work. More often, it's like what happened on Day 2 of the outbreak, when an elderly woman I'd grown to respect and care for tested positive for the virus. She needed to be isolated immediately. Worse, because we were still setting up our red zone and our ward for infected patients wasn't secure, we were going to have to move her to another facility.

This woman didn't want to leave. She'd been living under safety protocols that meant she hadn't left her room for six months. Now she was being told it was necessary, and she couldn't understand why. As we tried to move her into the hallway, she screamed and tried to hold on to the door. She was terrified.

Those types of situations were traumatizing for all of us, and I sometimes struggled to cope with them. I kept reviewing the facts: In order to protect the rest of our residents and patients who had yet to contract the virus, we were sending this frail older woman to a hot zone. We had little choice. But we knew, the minute we took her from that room, that her chances of coming back weren't great; they were certainly lower than if she'd stayed put. She wasn't even exhibiting symptoms yet, which made forcing her out that door even harder to do. And with the potential for a false positive test, who were we to force somebody out of their room against their will in the name of public safety? I knew the action made sense statistically, from a population-based health perspective, but it was still hard to execute, especially knowing the patient and understanding the risk the move would pose to her.

I believe I will hear her cries for the rest of my life.

Over the next two days, as we continued to set up our red zone, we had to send four more patients to other facilities. The first woman eventually came back. She'd survived. But another woman didn't. She had lived on her floor for 15 years, keeping her small refrigerator stocked with various beverages that she would offer to volunteers, using her own money to buy the drinks. I spoke to the orderly who had to transfer her body, someone who had known her for years. I felt terrible for them both.

An older gentleman I liked very much—a talker, and a joker—contracted COVID and had to be moved to the red zone. He survived and eventually came back to his own room. But he wasn't the same. He was weak. He could barely talk. He had hyperglycemia, meaning his glucose readings were too high, and his electrolyte levels were all over the place, which caused his brain to swell. Not long after his return, he died. He no longer had COVID and didn't directly succumb to the disease, so his death wasn't counted in official pandemic statistics. But the pandemic had taken him from us, nonetheless.

THE SAFETY ZONE that I'd used in my spare apartment, where I would return after shifts to shower and decompress, had been rented, so I no longer had a place to take additional precautions before going home to Flo. I didn't want her to feel unsafe, and so I hesitated to give her the full picture of the devastation at the facility. But it was also her right to know, in case she wanted to take additional precautions, or have us figure out other arrangements, like one of us temporarily moving out.

In my mind, Flo represents the thousands of significant others who've supported the workers on the front lines throughout the pandemic—people who, like me, have put themselves, and sometimes those closest to them, at risk. She saw the toll the job was taking on me. Witnessing that, while also navigating our new reality and the anxieties that came with it, took a toll on her too. I know it did.

The stress the pandemic was putting on people's personal relationships and home lives was a common subject on our floor. I knew workers who refused to see their kids, and who slept in their garages so they wouldn't infect anyone in their families. Some relationships between staff members and their significant others actually ended. I was so grateful for Flo's support during that time. Being in her position could not have been easy, in so many ways.

Working in the contemporary art world during the pandemic was tough. Flo had lost big contracts and work opportunities. I was trying to be supportive, but I also kept reminding her how privileged we were, and that it wasn't the end of the world. Looking back on those conversations, I see I was not the best boyfriend. It's as though I'd used up all my empathy during the day and struggled to show her some.

I knew from experience that the best strategy for clearing my mind and feeling in balance was to keep myself active and busy. And so I turned to woodworking, a pastime I'd picked up as a kid while working on school projects in the basement, often with my dad's help. It had begun with a model of the city of Troy, complete with the Trojan Horse, for a school presentation, and escalated into me making wooden toys and selling them to my classmates—swords and castles, stuff like that. One year I made a bunch of reindeer out of big raw pieces of wood and sold them in a little Christmas boutique. They went quickly, all 10 reindeer selling in a single weekend. The owner called the house and left a message. My mom picked it up. "You have to listen to this," she told us. The woman from the store wanted 36 more reindeer. I saw dollar signs—I was more than ready to fill that order. But there was no convincing my parents that it would be OK to skip school to carve reindeer. I had to let the Christmas shop woman—and my bank account—down.

Way back at the outset of the pandemic, when Flo and I, on the boat in St. Lucia, realized we might have to quarantine when we got back to Canada, I fretted about how I would manage staying home with nothing to do. I knew that I needed a plan. Then I remembered woodworking. Possibly more quickly decisive than at any other time in my life, I went online and found all the things I'd need: wood, a drill, a table saw, a router. I placed my orders and sat back relieved, knowing that, when we got home, I'd be fully equipped. I'd have something to do. Something that, if I felt restless or out of sorts, would help.

It proved to be a wise move. I like finding my way to the centre of a piece of wood. In part, it's planning, and in that respect it resembles sailing. You can't simply go at the wood with a saw or drill, or the piece might crack, and then you will just have to start over. You need to go back to the basic stuff we all learned in geometry. Maybe you need to sand the piece first, before putting a hole through the wood. You put yourself in a bubble where you have to give your full attention to what you're doing, otherwise you make a mistake.

Disappearing into that effort was my escape during the toughest weeks that fall. Many, many evenings, I would descend to our garage, grab a block of wood, and begin to carve, sculpt and shape. I built an outdoor garden, then a table for our patio. I made a stand for my iPhone, a holder for a toilet paper roll and a wooden extension for my desk. At one point Flo told me that the next piece of furniture I built needed to be approved by her first. Perhaps she was not a fan of my pieces, especially the ones that weren't square enough, or were too wobbly. But she knew I needed that time.

I needed it because out in the rest of the world, starting with our facility in mid-outbreak, so many things seemed broken, from the number of available beds to the number of people available for any one shift. Everyone was trying their best. But our resources were stretched thin, and some decisions made at a macro level negatively impacted our ability to work and to comfort our patients, including the prohibition on all visitors, a pandemic restriction that included family members and friends. On the one hand, it made sense to restrict visitors, to help keep the virus out of facilities and away from vulnerable seniors. On the other hand, in normal times, these "visitors" actually served as caregivers, and their presence played a significant role in ensuring patient needs could be met. They also knew those patients better than anybody else did, so they could sometimes identify and understand their needs more naturally. They were familiar, they were close, and their presence provided great comfort, especially to the most vulnerable.

It was widespread knowledge by this point that nursing homes and seniors' residences had been the hardest hit during the first wave of the pandemic in Canada; they were where more than 80 percent of COVID deaths occurred. The numbers were especially grim in Quebec, where, of the 5,718 deaths reported from February to July 2020, 4,836 were in long-term care. Management issues, staffing shortages and working conditions in long-term care that saw staff forced to cobble together a living by working part time at several facilities—often taking the virus with them as they moved around—were now being widely scrutinized by policy-makers, the media and the public. Some progress had been made, including a push in Quebec to quickly train and hire 10,000 personal support workers. Prospective workers were paid during their training and promised $26-per-hour positions in publicly funded nursing homes upon completing the program. (Some of those new hires were now my colleagues.) Later, in January 2022, a report by the province's health and welfare commissioner, Joanne Castonguay, would be released, recommending a wholesale transformation of the health care system. Castonguay makes a case for prioritizing patients' needs rather than medical services, and describes a current system that has three crucial blind spots: prevention, public health and senior care.

Back then, though, in fall 2020, it felt some days as though the system was crumbling around us. It didn't help that, outside facilities like ours, news crews would set up and report breathlessly under headlines such as ARE WE LEAVING OUR ELDERLY TO DIE? Some of our patients watched those very segments on the TVs in their rooms. It's one thing to do good journalism and give people access to important information, but in those critical times you have to think about the impact of your tone and approach—to remember that patients also watch TV, that you have an obligation to report the facts and not use sensationalist titles to attract viewers. I remember eating my spaghetti and my pudding at lunch the day I saw that report and being so frustrated

I composed an impulsive tweet. Before hitting Send, though, I decided to wait until the end of my shift.

By then I'd calmed down a little and decided to hold off. It was probably a good call. What good would it do anyone, especially the patients on whose behalf I'd felt so angry, for me to add my own frustration to the rancour and division already rife on social media?

WHEN I'D OPTED out of the NFL season, I thought that people might judge me for the choice I'd made, especially in Kansas City, where pro football fandom runs deep. I figured that many football fans would struggle to understand why I had committed to medicine at what they saw as their team's expense. I even wondered if they'd see my decision not to play as an affront to the opportunities I enjoyed.

So I was a little shocked that fall of 2020 when recognition began pouring in. I shared the Lou Marsh Award, given annually to the top athlete in Canada, with soccer star Alphonso Davies. I won the Muhammad Ali Sports Humanitarian Award from ESPN. Astonishingly, my medical scrubs and lab coat were sent to the Pro Football Hall of Fame.

I really appreciated what these honours seemed to suggest: maybe, after all, my choice *wasn't* widely seen as crazy, or entitled, or reckless; maybe it was actually regarded as a reasonable, and maybe even a good, thing to have done. But the accolades also made me uncomfortable, especially when I considered my co-workers. The day a *Sports Illustrated* cover dropped, naming me one of its five sportspersons of the year, I walked in for a long shift with my head down, almost sheepish. Hadn't my colleagues given up more? Received less for their sacrifices? I knew I couldn't control what people thought, or how they looked at me, but I worried they might think I was taking advantage of a global pandemic, millions of deaths, to bolster my own celebrity, for my own gain. Then, one day, after winning another award, I again walked in for my shift with eyes cast down. One by one, as the day went by, people congratulated me: doctors, nurses, supervisors, patients. That meant a whole lot more to me than making the cover of *Sports Illustrated*.

The notice I was periodically receiving from the sporting world served as a potent reminder of that other world carrying on alongside the one I was now immersed in. In that world too, in ways that were very different from what we were experiencing but every bit as real, the pandemic was in the driver's seat.

It now seemed clear that the NFL would play its pandemic season without pushing the schedule out an extra week, but not without glitches, challenges, setbacks. Just before the slate of games scheduled over American Thanksgiving, there were 65 positive cases league-wide, a significant figure that sparked concern among NFL higher-ups.

The cases had risen even though, in late October, the league had tightened and expanded its protocols. Five days in quarantine were now mandatory for anyone—players, coaches, executives—who'd been identified as a "high-risk close contact." To determine who fit that description, officials—much like public health officials everywhere—used contact tracing, while factoring in more nuanced data, such as length of time in company with a positive case and whether masks were worn or distancing maintained. League officials were dealing with a moving target, adapting and tweaking their response as they went. The goal—exactly like ours, in long-term care—was to break the chain of infection when positive cases or outbreaks occurred. But protocols are only effective when people follow them strictly and consistently. And people aren't perfect. There are always gaps through which a virus will make its way. And in some ways it was easier to err on the side of caution in the real world, away from the NFL, where every extra day in quarantine can have enormous repercussions on your team if the player in question is your starting quarterback. It's a fine line between being safe and optimizing team performance by making sure you're doing everything in your power to have your 53 players healthy on game day.

The Baltimore Ravens seemed to take the worst of it. Their strength-and-conditioning coach came down with the virus, leading to 25 additional positive results. Among them: the reigning league MVP, star quarterback Lamar Jackson. According to multiple reports, that strength coach had not been wearing a mask, did not immediately report his symptoms and had not worn the tracing device that had been mandated for all team employees. That was unfortunate. The league would later discover that much of the spread of COVID-19 during the season originated with strength coaches, massage therapists or chiropractors, many of whom worked with players outside team facilities.

The Ravens isolated everyone quickly. The NFL postponed their Thanksgiving game. That game would eventually move three times, which meant the franchise's Week 13 matchup versus Dallas was shifted twice too. Adapt, right? The Ravens played the Cowboys on a Tuesday, a modern-NFL first, to make sure the NFL schedule could be completed.

So it went, on and on, each team doing its best to play in the midst of frequent schedule changes, infections that sometimes sidelined top players, and ever-changing protocols and risk levels. Eventually, masks were even mandated on the sidelines. Even with the more stringent protocols, however, there wasn't much for players to complain about. They still had their jobs. They had resources, such as daily testing, nurses and masks, that enabled them to keep working. I knew full well that some of those resources would have been very welcome and useful in other contexts where they were often in short supply. Some observers, watching the NFL push through its season, found this a frustrating example of inequity.

It does raise the question of how far we should go, or should have gone, in order to keep the football season on track. Of course, pro sports weren't essential at the height of the COVID crisis. But I must admit that I also feel pro sports were the last live events that brought people together and provided a connective tissue that helped people, for a little while, take their minds off the pandemic. Because a game like football unites people around a common goal—rooting for their team—it can, at least in a small way, counter the divisiveness that has come to infect so many other aspects of our lives. I felt that pro sports were a bit of a silver lining.

Against this fluctuating backdrop, the Chiefs returned from their bye week and kept right on winning, toppling the Las Vegas Raiders, the Tampa Bay Buccaneers, the Denver Broncos, the Miami Dolphins, the New Orleans Saints and the Atlanta Falcons. Many of these games were close, but my teammates prevailed. It was heartening, and occasionally gut-wrenching. Even though I no longer really doubted my choice, I sometimes let myself wonder whether playing the season—as pretty much everyone else had done—would've been simpler. At one point I even asked Sasha if we could work out a way for me to return to the Chiefs later in the season, for a fraction of my salary. But what about the protocols? I couldn't exactly jump straight from working in long-term care in a pandemic—one of the riskiest places on the planet at that time—into a football locker room. And what about my physical readiness, or lack thereof?

As it turned out, none of those questions mattered. Stepping on the gridiron this season was contractually impossible. My decision was irrevocable.

I let that fantasy go.

By early January 2021, only one regular-season game remained. Having already secured the top seed in the American Football Conference, Kansas City didn't need to play all its starters. So Pat Mahomes rested, and Chad Henne played well in a loss to the Los Angeles Chargers. (The afternoon Henne filled in, shaking off any lingering rust, would soon prove more important than anyone realized.)

That same week, Cleveland experienced a mini-outbreak. The Browns took on the New York Jets without any of their main receivers available, on the same Sunday that the Detroit Lions played the Tampa Bay Buccaneers while missing several coaches who were in isolation. The New Orleans Saints played without an active running back against the Carolina Panthers.

It sounds like a lot of upheaval, but in fact, as the regular season wrapped up, a grand total of only 22 games had been moved, and none had been cancelled. Because of the measures the NFL enacted and enforced over the duration of the season, only 37 people who'd gone into isolation due to their status as high-risk contacts had wound up testing positive themselves. In a scenario where a deadly virus cannot be eliminated, where risks can only be mitigated, this was a very good outcome.

Earlier in the year, I'd been on a call with the NFL Players Association during which one of the reps had pegged the chances of the league having to abandon the season partway through at about 50 percent. I'd flinched. I wanted my teammates, and players across the league, to be safe. I wanted the right protocols enacted. I also wanted the season to run its course. But I knew the risks—everybody knew the risks. Players would leave their facilities and head home into the real world, where they would interact with people who weren't subject to the same stringent rules as they were while "on the job." With no one, at that point, vaccinated, with roughly 1,300 players based in communities across the country, and with half the teams travelling each week, some level of COVID-19 chaos seemed all but certain. I didn't want to be pessimistic, but it was sometimes hard not to be.

Now, at the end of the year, as the Chiefs geared up for the playoffs, I was relieved. And a little defiant. Here was one aspect of life, at least—an aspect I cared about deeply—that had squared off against the pandemic and not been beaten.

Back in Montreal, I'd been squaring off against it as well, and—along with Flo, family, friends and my tired, overworked colleagues—just managing to hold my ground. I went in for shifts, studied on off-days, kept up with my workouts. Like the woodworking, the physical exertion helped—at least for the time I was focused on it. After a snowfall, I would brush off the balcony and lay down some padding. I'd dress as if I were going out for a ski: goggles, hat, gloves. Then I'd warm the bar with a propane heater before lifting so that my damp gloves wouldn't freeze when I grabbed hold.

We spent roughly four weeks in the red zone. An eternity.

One day our threat level decreased to orange.

Then yellow.

Finally, it dropped back down to green.

CHAPTER 14

THE PLAYOFFS

By the time the Chiefs bounded into the NFL post-season, they'd gained a six-foot-five, 300-plus-pound superfan. Perhaps you've heard of him. Medical professional. Super Bowl champion. Speaks French. Big, bushy beard. Likes to carve wood in his spare time.

I did not create or follow any superstitions. I wasn't that kind of diehard supporter. No designated T-shirt, no forever jersey, no usual spot on the same couch watching the same flatscreen. I just wanted the Chiefs to excel, to defend our championship. I *needed* to follow and support my team, especially after the big COVID outbreak. I needed the distraction, the connection and the energy I got from, of all things, sitting on a couch. I'd only ever tuned into football on TV during the few times I'd been injured during a season in KC and wasn't travelling with the team. Now I was glued to the screen.

The camera angles and slow motion gave me a new perspective on how physical, how painful the game was. In some critical situations, when everyone in the stadium knows we're about to run the ball, there is no more room for strategy and finesse. It's just brute strength and will: who has the most desire to win.

Sometimes, watching, I caught myself saying out loud: *À quel point tu veux gagner?!* (How much do you really want it?!)

How much did I? Did I still have it, the willingness to hit—and *get* hit—that hard?

Earlier in the season, I'd mostly avoided watching the Chiefs play. For a while, Flo didn't really notice. I wasn't the type, after all, who lounged around on Sundays watching whatever NFL game happened to be on TV. When she finally *did* see what was going on—more like what wasn't going on—she understood. For years, she'd trained to become a professional dancer. When an injury abruptly, devastatingly, ended that pursuit, she stopped teaching younger students and couldn't bring herself to attend shows. It was hard for her not to be involved in the same way anymore. She also understood me and how I operate, so she didn't pry too deeply. But when I started to actively, avidly watch the games, she definitely noticed. Because *that* was unusual. And she knew then that I hoped, eventually, to return.

As my fandom increased, I began to think more about the hardships faced by the team I'd left. From afar, I came to see my teammates through an empathetic lens, in the same way I'd come to see my patients during that super-difficult year. Though I'd played alongside many current Chiefs for years, and some of them were really close friends, they suddenly struck me as more human than they'd ever seemed before. I felt grateful that these were the people I'd marched onto a field with every Sunday. I wanted to know more about the weeks and months they'd lived through since I'd opted out.

I was well aware of some of the tough decisions people had made in order to keep the game alive. Take our beloved offensive coordinator, Eric Bieniemy, who'd been a coach with the Chiefs for my entire career. The summer after the pandemic hit, Coach

EB moved into a hotel, where he stayed from July through to January, and not because he liked fresh linens on his bed every day. His oldest son, Eric III, has cerebral palsy and respiratory issues, which put him at particularly high risk for contracting COVID-19. If he did catch the virus, it would be potentially life-threatening. In order to protect his wife, Mia, and both his sons, Coach EB mostly stayed away from them.

I loved Coach EB. I admired his energy, how he never seemed down, how he'd show up every day like a can of Red Bull, ready to attack even the most mundane of tasks. He'd supported me, as he did so many others, through my steepest learning curves, my injury, our championship run. Through every high and every low, Coach EB was a constant, the kind of person who receives little credit for contending but who's a crucial block in the team's championship DNA. He's the kind of person around whom a franchise is built.

I thought of the other coaches, in particular Coach Reid, who I knew habitually spent way more time working than we players do. We players sometimes forget the amount of time our coaches put in to get us ready for games: watching film, preparing game plans, sometimes showing up at the facility at four in the morning and not leaving till 10 at night. I never arrived in the morning without seeing Coach EB's car already in the parking lot. Sometimes, when we'd get back to the facility at 5 a.m. after a Sunday night away game, the coaches would head straight into the building in order to start breaking down film on the next opponent. Every December, when we'd be dead tired and about to go practise on a frozen field, I would think about their sacrifices—the fact that they'd already been in the building for maybe 12 hours, and still found the energy to teach us and make us better.

That's in normal times. Add in COVID protocols, players in isolation, trainers in isolation, postponed games, etc. Plus the usual injuries and ordinary challenges and setbacks. Everyone, on some level, had dealt with a season more trying than any they'd taken part in before.

That was true outside the NFL as well, where these days, it seemed, division now ruled and we considered only what separated us, instead of what could unite us—such as the fact that we all hated COVID and the havoc it had wrought, the lives it had taken, and the sacrifices, discomforts and inconveniences it had forced upon us. What if we all just gave it a shot and tried to consider other people, regardless of colour, religion, occupation or political bent, and how they were surviving during, or had been affected by, this really trying time? Weren't we all suffering? All making do? All isolated? All missing human contact?

Unfortunately, because it reduced our social interactions, the pandemic, in a sense, made us all focus more on ourselves. It was easy to ignore what our friends, colleagues, neighbours and community members were going through, what they had to do to adapt during those two years. This was especially true as so many of us replaced in-person contact with the kind you get on social media. We're so lucky to have digital communication; in so many ways, it has helped. It allowed isolated people to "gather" with family and friends. It permitted people to continue pursuits that were important to them, such as, in my case, studying for a master's degree in public health—*at* Harvard, but *from* home, while fitting in shifts at a nursing home. But when it comes to places like the Twittersphere, we tend, helped along by insidious algorithms, to follow our "likes," which means we constantly, almost exclusively, see content that confirms our world view. In that world, we engage mostly with those who share our opinions, either ignoring other voices or simply never coming across them. Without even realizing it's happening, we gradually lose our ability to listen when we disagree, to consider opposing ideas, to have debates and grow as individuals.

To some extent, pro sports crosses those barriers and brings people together based on a principle that has no correlation to any other aspect of a person's life or any belief they may hold dear: that is, supporting the team you love. I see sports as a connective tissue in society. It's a space where liberals can cheer alongside—and as loudly as—conservatives; where millionaires can hang out with the middle class, the young with the old, people from this background with others from that background—all of them rooting for the same players on the same team.

Perhaps the world could learn from an American football locker room, the way people from different places and walks of life come together to hold that Lombardi Trophy above their heads. Like people everywhere, the members of our football team disagreed over politics, over lifestyle, over religion. But we didn't let those differences define us. We respected each other's opinions. Even when we disagreed about a hot-button issue, we still listened to each other's arguments. We tried to understand rather than judge, because we still needed to work together, block for each other, trust each other. It may be that having a shared goal in mind, which was to win on Sundays, helped us do that. But shared goals aren't hard to come by, even in the wider society. Take "collectively protecting the most vulnerable among us during a pandemic" for a start.

The year 2020 was marked by a public health crisis, but it was also, in my opinion, a year of social cleavage, and it's going to require a collective effort for us to reconnect and rebuild our solidarity. We have to get better at reaching out and listening to other people's stories in order to find empathy and broaden our perspectives. For me, in early winter 2021, that began with paying attention: with watching my team in the playoffs.

KANSAS CITY had opened the season as Super Bowl favourites, the odds in some books at +600. By the time the calendar turned to December, after a victory over Tom Brady and the Bucs that improved KC's record to 10–1, the payout had dwindled to +275. The Chiefs had improved their standing in the eyes of oddsmakers despite a series of injuries to offensive linemen, as well as some positive tests that included two members of my old position group.

Heading into the post-season as the overall number-one seed in the American Football Conference, the Chiefs didn't have to play a game in the wild card round. Instead, they could sit back that first week of playoff football—always a glorious weekend on the pro sports calendar—and study the team they would play. It turned out to be the Cleveland Browns, who topped the Pittsburgh Steelers in a shootout, setting up a trip to Kansas City in the divisional round. The Browns had been without their head coach that afternoon; Kevin Stefanski had watched their win from home after contracting COVID-19.

I wanted so badly—so very, very badly—for the Chiefs to win that first playoff matchup. I wanted to be there, at Arrowhead Stadium, where a limited number of cars would gather to tailgate in the January cold, and where the smell of smoked meat would waft half a mile away.

The Chiefs proved their mettle that Sunday. Even without Patrick Mahomes, who was injured, they dominated with Chad Henne at quarterback. Though the severity of Pat's injury concerned everyone—including me, way up north in Quebec—the Chiefs had proven they could seize an important, make-it-or-break-it game without the most valuable player in the league on the field. The victory over Cleveland reminded the pro football world that there were upstart teams and there were established ones. And it was obvious which label applied to the Chiefs.

That didn't mean they preferred to play Henne the following week, against Buffalo, in the third consecutive conference championship game they'd host. But that's what's beautiful about football: it's never about one person, or one player, or even one position. Close, high-stakes games are won by teams with depth, with qualities like will and guts. It's not the team with the most talent that wins; it's the team with the fewest weak spots.

WHEN I SAT down to watch the conference championship, I was thinking about the final two years earlier, when we'd dropped a heartbreaker to Tom Brady and the Patriots. I remembered how crushing that defeat felt, because of how close, and how far, we had come.

This time, the Bills caused trouble for the Chiefs from the get-go. With an emerging MVP candidate of their own in Josh Allen, and several hundred members of their rabid fan base, known as Bills Mafia, in town, they jumped out to a 9–0 lead. Then the O-line got in the game, despite a couple of injuries. Coach Reid always said that the teams with the healthier bigs (O-line, D-line) had an advantage in the playoffs. We lost Fisher in the last quarter with a torn Achilles. That was a blow. I knew that was going to affect us in the big game, and I knew how much it would affect my friend. He was so close to the end of his contract and free agency. That injury would be a career-defining one for him, which proves that timing is everything and how much of a role luck can play.

In this game, though, even with Fisher out, the Chiefs kept gaining ground. As I watched yet another comeback take shape from afar, my thoughts went straight back to our run of post-season thrillers the year before. Perhaps that stretch had built the Chiefs into what they were now—a burgeoning NFL dynasty. Kansas City won, 38–24. After a 50-season absence, the Lamar Hunt Trophy, named after our founder and given to the AFC champion, would remain in Kansas City for another year. Confetti fluttered in the sky as the limited number of fans present roared, and hugged, and celebrated.

Man, did I wish I was there.

But the main thing was this: the Chiefs were headed back to the Super Bowl. Though Fisher's and Mitch's injuries hadn't made things easier, my season away hadn't cost them that chance. Now all they had to do was win.

SUPER BOWL LV was to be held in Tampa, the Bucs' home stadium, marking an NFL first. The new COVID protocols meant Chiefs players would stay two full weeks prior to the game in Kansas City, flying to Tampa Bay only the night before. Meanwhile, players were subjected to *two* tests every day. As a result, the NFL hadn't seen a single positive case in over a week.

That was good news. But I also knew that even the best protocols and highest degree of caution did not mean the virus would back off. It was always there, in the background of every situation, in every kind of business, even professional sports, waiting for a gap to slip through. Despite the constant adaptations—the virtual meetings, the testing, the half-empty stadiums—the NFL would not be immune.

One week before kickoff, a barber who'd tested negative but then tested positive came into contact with some of my team-mates. Wideout Demarcus Robinson and centre Daniel Kilgore were both placed on the reserve/COVID-19 list just six days before the coin toss for the game that would determine the NFL's pandemic-season champion.

This virus scare would be the last of the 2020 season. Months later, the Centers for Disease Control and Prevention would publish a scientific research paper about the league, its doctors and scientists, analyzing how it moved forward during a global pandemic. The paper concluded that the investments made in such measures as frequent testing had been effective, and that all the protocols—including mask requirements, social distancing, limited in-person meetings, and closed dining rooms across the league—had been beneficial. The time that players and coaches spent away from their families, the time they took to get tested, the decision not to carpool to team headquarters—every adjustment added a layer of protection. Those measures might seem insignificant compared with the potential virus incubator an NFL game represented, but collectively they helped reduce global exposure and the risk that any one player brought to the field on Sundays.

The paper also declared that the outbreaks that did happen were preventable. They were due, more than anything, to people not following the rules.

At the Super Bowl, masks were required. A limited number of fans were in attendance—22,000, all socially distanced—with roughly one-third of them being vaccinated health care workers. A normal Super Bowl could play out before an audience of

60,000 to 100,000 or more spectators, depending on the stadium where it's held. I was actually invited to join them, but the border was still closed. And it was more in line with my approach to the pandemic thus far—to avoid possibly becoming a vector for the virus—to stay home rather than travel to Florida for a football game, regardless of how important that game was to me.

After five days of isolation and negative test results, both Robinson and Kilgore were cleared to play, and placed on the active roster before kickoff. The Chiefs flew in on Saturday, having kept their bubble as tight as possible since the conference championship. Given that the Super Bowl was in Tampa, the Bucs didn't have to travel at all.

The Chiefs entered Super Bowl LV without their mainstays. They were even missing some backups. They didn't have Osemele, the player they'd signed in the aftermath of my departure.

The Chiefs had taken a patchwork approach to the O-line all year, out of necessity, and now more recent losses meant that Coach EB had to be creative. Schwartz, one of our most consistent linemen, was out. Fisher was out with his torn Achilles. Coach EB shifted Wylie to right tackle and Remmers to left tackle, while Nick Allegretti and Stefen Wisniewksi (an experienced player who'd been part of our 2020 campaign and had been signed midway through the season) manned the guard positions. Austin Reiter started at centre.

I watched the game from home, logging on to a Zoom call with Sasha and a handful of mutual friends. It all felt very 2020/2021. I worried for my reconfigured linemates, many of whom weren't in the positions they normally played, which is much harder than it sounds. Every position on the offensive line is different. Some skills and techniques translate, but not as many as might commonly be assumed.

It didn't take long for the game on my screen to turn into a nightmare. The Bucs went up 7–3, then 14–3, then 21–6, as I considered throwing things at the screen.

The O-line didn't play well. All the injuries and substitutions really made it hard for them. It's *so* much harder for an O-line to block when you're trailing in a game, because everybody in the stadium knows you're going to pass, and the defence brings on the pressure full-force, with no respect for their rush lanes. On top of that, Tampa Bay's defence was one of the best in the league.

One image that sticks with me from that game is Pat's body nearly parallel to the ground as he attempts a throw after getting tripped in the backfield. If most pictures are worth a thousand words, this one served as a game summary. Because our offensive line was beset by injuries, Tampa Bay recorded three sacks *and* two interceptions.

This time, there was no comeback. The Chiefs fell, by the lopsided score of 31–9. It was, after the best three-year start to a career for any quarterback in NFL history (he'd never lost a pro game by more than one score), the worst game of Pat's career.

It was impossible not to wonder whether I could have made a difference. Several people told me in the aftermath that I could have at least given the Chiefs a better chance, through depth alone. The truth is, no one will ever know. I feel I *could* have contributed. Perhaps I *want* to believe that. In reality, I have no idea. Considering the number of players it takes to win any one game, in any one season, let alone the championship year, I'd be foolish if I claimed otherwise.

I felt for my teammates that day, and in the weeks and months after: for their struggles, for how much that loss must have stung. I felt for Coach EB, who, after the loss, would yet again, incredibly, be passed over for NFL head coach openings. I sympathized with him, a legend who had won, and lost, Super Bowls, who I knew wanted that win badly. The fact is, the Chiefs were one of the two teams out of 32 that made it to the big game; but I knew that rationale wasn't going to help. As a competitor, you want to win, and every time you come up short, even if it's close—maybe even more when it's close—it feels like an all-out defeat.

But I wasn't only thinking about my team. I was thinking about me. I now knew one thing for certain: I wanted to play again. I wanted to return for 2021.

Speaking to the *Ringer* before the 2021 season, Brett Veach, our general manager, admitted what seemed obvious to the analysts: what cost Kansas City another title was apparent and needed fixing. He said that had someone told him back in August that amid all the uncertainty in the world—with the opt-out and the pandemic—KC would go 14–2, register the best regular-season mark in franchise history, win the conference title game and keep the Lamar Hunt Trophy in Kansas City, he would have been thrilled. And yet, because the Chiefs had Pat Mahomes on their roster, because they were so good, so primed, *how* the Chiefs lost—and how badly—also made him feel as if they were "the worst team in the league." Both things can be true, I guess.

I knew I could bring something back to the table. At the same time, Veach had cut Fisher and Mitch in a clear attempt to show he was determined to rebuild the unit. The old guard that I'd played the last six seasons with was being replaced, and maybe, in the eyes of the organization, I wasn't part of the solution. Dedicated as I was to returning, I sensed, for the first time, that I might not be welcomed back with open arms.

But I knew I at least had a chance. And that I would, in all likelihood, go to training camp. The next question was: *How?*

CHAPTER 15

THE COMEBACK

So. Remember that chat I had with Mitch way back in the winter of 2020, pre–Super Bowl championship, pre-pandemic? When he said to me something like, *Wouldn't that be a great way to go out? On a Super Bowl win? And get on with becoming a doctor?*

He was right. I'd played with the same team for seven years. I'd helped that team, after a 50-year dry spell, take the Super Bowl. Given all those years of hitting and taking hits on the line, my body felt OK. I could end the story there, on pure triumph. What better time to walk away? If, instead, I played on, the ending—short of another NFL championship—wouldn't be as satisfying, as perfect. I might go out on an injury instead, or a devastating loss. Or I'd be outshone by a new recruit. My importance to the team could fizzle, peter out.

I made my pros and cons lists. On one side I had things like: risk of injury, the longer gap before starting my medical residencies, the need to catch up. On the other was the familiar structure and routine; the excitement of playing at such a high level, of pushing myself to my absolute physical limits; the security of being part of a team, of something that felt important, bigger than myself. And finally, even if I promised myself not to consider it too much, there was the money.

These things are all objective. A person's love of the game, though, is subjective. And how much you love the game can trump any rational argument.

I'm not a gambler, but when talking it over with my sports psychologist, I used the analogy of the guy at the casino at five in the morning. He's had a good night, he's got a lot of chips in front of him. Does he cash in his winnings and walk home? Or does he keep playing instead?

What he decides to do, it's not really about the money.

After the Super Bowl, while I was weighing my options, I was pretty sure about one thing: I really didn't have the stomach for going back to Kansas City to train and fight for my spot on the team only to lose it and have to leave. That scenario did not appeal to me, and I knew it was a possibility. Meanwhile, the team management got in touch. They offered me a 100 percent guarantee—a promise that I'd remain on the team for next season—if I took a 50 percent pay cut. Sasha looked at the market, and that new contract was actually significantly under my real value. But I felt that we were building something special in Kansas City and I wanted to play another year there. It was a huge cut to accept. But in reality, by any normal measure, my paycheque would still be enormous. Refusing such a deal would be more about pride than practicality—or about what I really wanted. I thought about that, and about the situation we were in: the rising concern of the pandemic, and the uncertainty that was upon us all. I thought about how great it had felt to win that Super Bowl. About how it felt to be part of a winning team. My team. The Chiefs.

I said yes.

I signed the deal in April 2020, just before I decided to go volunteer in long-term care. Once I'd made the choice, there was no going back. I would play as a Chief again for one more year before turning back to medicine. The only obstacle now was the pandemic. But it wasn't necessarily insurmountable. Later on, when I took the opt-out, my agreement with the team wasn't nullified; it was simply postponed a year.

All this meant that, when the Chiefs lost to Tampa in the 2021 Super Bowl, though I was still working shifts in long-term care, I was already preparing, in my mind, to head back to KC.

It was time to lift.

During a football season, you don't get stronger. On the contrary. You're constantly running, getting banged about on the field. You're sore. The game-day bouts of adrenalin that make you feel indestructible, ferocious, eventually leave you depleted. You're worn out from travelling. You're growing weaker, or at least fighting to keep the same amount of strength you started out with.

When you're at your peak is actually when you show up to training camp in July. It's all downhill from there.

That season I was away from the game I did everything I could to maintain that peak pre-season strength. It wasn't easy, with mainly my balcony to work out on—in the dead of winter— and I knew I'd lost some ground. But now we were off-season, which is actually when you need to get right into conditioning mode. If you don't, you can lose sight of your objective and show up for training camp in the worst possible shape. I've seen plenty of guys do that, and it costs them their careers.

I started lifting four to five times per week. I'd hired my old strength coach, Olivier, who'd got me ready for the NFL draft back in 2014. His workouts were the worst—but the results were impossible to argue with. He came to my place in a mask and snowsuit and coached me out on the balcony in the snow. Shades of *Rocky*, for sure. He gave me that extra bit of discipline I needed. And the more I trained, the more I realized I needed to, the harder it became to fit in those shifts in long-term care. I dwindled down to one shift a week, and finally went to my supervisor and told her it was time for me to move on and get ready for the next season.

My public service, for now, was over.

I know some people, aware that my future would not ultimately lie in football but in medicine, saw my decision to step away and work in health care during the pandemic as a kind of soft exit strategy. You "opt out" this year with a really good excuse, and then you just never come back.

But that was not my plan. If it had been, the notion of sacrificing a year of football to serve my community during the pandemic would have lost a whole lot of meaning. No way was that the idea. I'm a really stubborn, competitive person. I was coming back. For sure.

I was going to prove to everyone that I could still play ball. I'd train, and I'd show them. And not only that—I was going there to try to win the Super Bowl again. I meant business.

I did have at least one hurdle to overcome. During those eight months I'd been away, the combination of closed facilities and winter had prevented me from working on my runs, sprints, jumping, cuts. It's hard to do a plyometric workout, where you're using speed and force to build power, on a balcony. I had to find a way to gain my explosiveness back.

One day in March, my trainer and I went out to the nearest city turf we could find. There was still snow on the ground. We hopped the fence and ran our sprints.

The clock was ticking.

*

MY PLANE touched down in Missouri. It was June 2021. For the first time in nearly two years, I'd flown south from Montreal for the Chiefs' mini training camp that took place every spring.

It felt weird. I was going home—to my home away from home. I'd been to mini-camp every year since being drafted by the Chiefs in 2014, except the year before, 2020, when I'd opted out. But the team had changed so much in that year, I might have been reappearing from an alternate timeline. The O-line, beset by injuries during the 2020 campaign, had been completely rebuilt. I now knew only two of the 12 guys on the line, and I'd be the second-oldest O-line player among them.

I didn't know how they'd react to me. Would I have to prove myself all over again? If so, I was willing and ready. I wanted back on that starting unit. I was braced to fight for my spot.

But first I had to head to the locker room and face my team—the old players I knew so well, and the new.

As soon as I arrived, the months I'd been gone just fell away. I walked to my old locker. Everything was still in place. It's a friendly environment. It was great to see everyone and say hi. And my reception by the newcomers was better than I could have expected or hoped. Joe Thuney, who'd gone to three Super Bowls with the Patriots, was one of our new offensive linemen. He came right up, shook my hand and said, "I'm proud of what you did, man. It's a pleasure to meet you." Ditto Orlando Brown, coming from the Ravens. Some new O-line members asked me questions about the Chiefs playbook and so on. There was an immediate sense of mutual respect.

The June mini-camp is really just a chance to shake off the off-season. Limber up. Get to know each other. The real thing starts later in July, when we head to a college campus out of town, move into the dorms, eat cafeteria food and go all out for three weeks. Before we all took off for a short summer break, I had new guys looking for advice, asking me what they should bring for food and that. My old O-line didn't really have a pillar—we'd all kind of grown together into a unit—but things were different now. There was a chance for me, I could see, to serve as a leader of the unit.

WHEN I'D LEFT for Kansas City in June, I wasn't sure whether I'd be able to come back to Montreal during the summer break. There was a two-week quarantine in place for travellers returning to Canada, and with just a four-week break, I wasn't sure it was reasonable to come back home. Luckily, the restrictions were lifted for vaccinated travellers by early July. So I flew north and spent some good-quality time with Flo.

Then it was August: time to get serious. No more mini-camp. The pre-season was upon us.

On the drive to Missouri Western State University, which we call St. Joe's, where the team holds camp each summer, I strangely looked forward to the challenge before me. The cramped dorm room. The packed schedule. The full contact. Focusing on only one thing in order to push your physical and mental limits: breathing and dreaming football. Even in the time away since June, I'd missed the team atmosphere, the focus, the camaraderie—including the ball busting from my fellow linemen, who'd tease me about the fact that I was only speaking one and a half languages. I basked in it. Bring it on.

I wasn't the only one who felt, on some level, that I was coming back to something temporarily lost. The pandemic hadn't disappeared, but things were less dire than they'd been in 2020, in large part because of the availability of vaccines. Every Chief, save two, had rolled up his sleeves to be vaccinated—twice. It was summer, and the most recent wave had waned. Omicron had yet to strike. All that to say, protocols were far less stringent than the year before. We were tested once a week and wore tracers at the facility that would record how close and for how long we were in proximity to others, data that would reveal, in the event of any positive cases, who'd been a close contact and would need to isolate. Coaches and trainers wore masks; players didn't, except when we were in transit. For my teammates, compared with the virtual meetings, training at home gyms and daily testing of the previous year, this was way less intense. For me, after months working in long-term care donning full PPE, it was a haven of relaxation.

That said, those first few practices leading up to the first full-pad day of camp, I was a little anxious. Fortunately, the pads are a great equalizer. Doesn't matter where a player comes from or how much money he makes, once he dons that protective gear, he's like every other guy out there, fighting for his spot on the roster. In our practices, which lasted three hours, we learned each other's strengths and weaknesses, how to pick each other up and how best to complement each other.

During those practices, I looked left, I looked right, and I saw 16 offensive-line hopefuls, including many accomplished, high-priced veterans. In my seven years, I had never seen a group with that much depth or that much skill, which, of course, was precisely the point of the off-season overhaul.

Every day—every practice, every drill—I tried to run through all of it as if I'd never have the chance to do so again. It was a really hot camp, unbearably humid. I tried to love that too. I had long ago fixed my technical issues, become a starter, then a pillar, then a champion—all while strengthening my mental fortitude. But now I had to knock the rust off and compete as if I had nothing to lose. I lasered in on what I did best. I wanted my final days of football to be positive, memorable.

If I was honest with myself, I had no idea whether the Chiefs really wanted me there. It wasn't that I doubted their support, or thought they were upset that I hadn't played the previous season. What I wondered, in moments of self-doubt, was whether the Chiefs, having dramatically reconfigured their O-line, felt they were stuck with me.

Still, I loved the pressure of those practices. I'd spent an entire career—a life, really—proving that I could compete, that I was being underestimated in one way or another. Why not now? *Especially* now. I honestly had no idea what would happen. A rule tweak in the collective bargaining agreement meant that teams could dress more players, meaning most would dress more linemen, meaning any one team might keep 11 O-linemen, as opposed to, say, eight. I saw three more spots—and the guaranteed money in my deal—as factors improving my odds of remaining on the roster.

But as Sasha always said, don't count the spots. Just focus on your game and on improving every day. Training camp is not a sprint, it's a marathon. Some days you perform poorly, but you have to find the mental stamina to get back the next day. And you can never be comfortable when you have a good day, because there's always something you can work on. You can't project yourself into the season ahead, or dwell on the previous day. You have to be in the present, bringing all your energy and competitive drive every time you step on the field. When you're tired, and you've just lost nine pounds of water during practice, you can't start thinking about the practice tomorrow—you have to focus on the hours in front of you, on recovering and getting back into shape for the next day. Training camp is one day at a time. One play at a time.

I knew I had to keep my "starter" mindset. I was determined not to have anything break my concentration. I ate right, focused on recovery and sleep, and drank my fluids to get ready for the next gruelling practice. I roomed with Joe Thuney, a cerebral guy who, like me, loved the thinking side of football—analyzing the strategies and plays. We became great friends. Every night, back in the dorm, we played a game of chess, a ritual that, for me, balanced everything out.

Out on the field, the more we blocked and shuttled, the more our chemistry developed; way more than I'd hoped, given all the change. When I saw that talent and those bonds, I started thinking we'd amassed the best collection of offensive linemen in the entire league.

THE GENERAL MANAGER came to me and said he hadn't been expecting me to perform as well as I was. I was doing all right. Nonetheless, I started out as a second-team guy.

A rookie, Trey Smith, had my spot on the starting O-line. I knew he was going to be really, really good. He had all the athletic ability. He was extremely explosive and strong. But like any rookie, like me in my first years with the Chiefs, he lacked consistency. He would sometimes make mental mistakes. I was working with him, trying to help him the way more veteran players had once helped me. To me, that is the greatest thing about the NFL: even though everybody has his own career to worry about, you always see the older guys—who technically are competing with the younger crowd that threatens to push them out—giving advice and teaching tools. That's the beauty of team sport, and that's when you know you have a good team, when the older players are willing to pass on their knowledge and potentially sacrifice their own prospects to help the rookies, and ultimately the team.

Sometimes, when Trey made too many mistakes, the coaches would send me onto the field in his place—to send a message: Laurent's there to push. That was extremely motivating, to know that, OK, I have to be ready to jump in at any time.

Then the unthinkable happened. On August 10, during a practice, I tried to block somebody, and I punched him in the face mask. Boom. I broke my hand. They call it a boxer's fracture: I'd snapped the fifth metacarpal. At first I thought—or, let's face it, I hoped—that it was all right, maybe just squished. But we did an X-ray that showed, no, it was definitely broken. I wasn't overly concerned about the injury itself; I knew it was the kind that would heal well. I didn't even call Flo, which I would have done if it were truly serious. (But I have to admit that I was never great at communicating with her during training camp—it is so immersive, you kind of disappear into it.)

Even so, the bone did have to heal—it had to be permitted to heal. It was in the joint, and too small to do surgery and pin it. The doctor recommended a cast for four weeks.

Insert your favourite curse word here.

Exactly.

Now, you can play with a cast if you want to. Plenty of players have done it, but those are mostly defensive guys. When you're on the line of scrimmage, playing with a cast is challenging. Plus, it was training camp. Even so, I was ready to play. But the general manager and head trainer came to me and said, Laurent, you showed us great things, you showed us you can play. Sit this one out, take care of yourself, work on your footwork and all that stuff. We're going to need you at some point this season. Rick, the head trainer, also pointed out that I had a second career waiting for me, where I would for sure need my hand and full dexterity. It wasn't worth risking. I thought that was really nice.

At that point, I knew they were going to go with the younger guy. There's always a gap between college and the NFL. If it's not year one, it's going to be year two. They might as well give him as many opportunities as possible to play and learn. When I'd started playing, I wasn't the best guy for that position, but they saw my potential and knew that with time I would get better. And I did. It would be the same for him.

WHEN THE TEAM left for a pre-season game in Arizona on August 19, I stayed behind. One night, I went to dinner with a friend, an oncology nurse I'd met in Kansas City—a brilliant thinker and a go-getter. Our friendship was one of the few I'd found in Kansas City outside football, a precious thing. It was really good to spend time with someone who didn't live within the pro sports bubble, especially when I couldn't be fully inside it myself.

We caught up. We—of course—told each other our pandemic stories. She'd worked at two medical centres during the past several months. Like me, she'd been placed on a COVID-19-specific floor. She focused on oncology there, mostly meeting with patients, just like I had.

We had a lot to talk about, the overwhelmed health care system for a start. And the misguided politics that had helped, and continued to help, the virus hold sway. I was curious to compare her experience in the US health care system during the pandemic with what mine had been in Canada. By then we both understood that the perfect situation—the ideal pandemic response—just didn't exist; everyone simply did the best they could with the situation they were handed. My friend, who's from Lebanon and had been overseas when the port explosion devastated Beirut, was especially sensitive to this reality. Unlike me, she was still working on the front lines. She had so much on her mind, and no time to process anything. She only had time to react, to keep showing up, day after day. To do what she could.

Our conversation made me both angry and sad. Not enough doctors. Not enough beds. Not enough time off for front-line workers to attend to their own mental health.

I thought about other medical colleagues I knew who were fatigued, overworked, heartsick, frightened—and those desperately trying to pick up the slack for others who'd had to take time off due to sickness or stress. Everything related to the pandemic snowballed in that way; as resources shifted in one direction, hospitals or facilities were left short somewhere else. Short on people, short on time, short on resources—everything. It was fucked up. It only *seemed* normal because we'd lived the pandemic existence for so long, and with such intensity. I thought about the patients I'd had to force from their rooms to the COVID-19 floor. I will never hear the phrase "red zone" again and think only of a moment in a football game. I'll remember the eyes of my patients, how distressed they looked, how disoriented, how confused. I saw fear. I felt fear.

I suddenly realized that during the 18 months between the Chiefs' Super Bowl win and my return to Kansas City, I'd been in survival mode: working and studying and training, aware of how messed up the world had become, but too busy to really try to dive into how I was feeling. Or notice how I might have changed. It was strange, because every year for the previous seven years, training camp had been a time when I would try to reflect and think. Training camp is so demanding that I don't do email or anything related to my side projects (like my foundation). I just embrace that one thing—football—and it grounds me.

I came away from that dinner with my friend knowing that, from now on, I needed to give myself room to breathe, pause, reflect. I hoped all my colleagues on the front lines—including her—would do the same.

Here's one reflection worth sharing: Football wouldn't rattle my nerves in 2021 the way it used to. My injury was a terrible blow, for sure. But my year away had put things into perspective. On the one hand, it reminded me, viscerally and sometimes painfully, how much I loved the game. On the other hand, it confirmed something I already knew: football isn't life and death, it just seems that way when you're in the middle of it.

The thing I did in that long-term care facility that I'm proudest of had nothing to do with medicine. It was fixing that bathtub so all the residents could use it. And that had less to do with cleanliness than with dignity. The more I thought about it, the more I knew it was the small things that mattered. The small things always matter.

And that's what I'd take with me, back onto the field.

MY FIRST PRACTICE after the hand injury was a reminder of just how physical and intense football can be. The practice was jarring, but in the best way, and I could see right away the results of my work on agility and balance.

In some ways, my situation with the injury reminded me of the Olympics, a competition where not all medals are created equal, where context matters. Where mindset matters—a notion I learned long ago from my sports psychologist. There are swimmers who win a bronze medal and feel disappointed. And there are swimmers who finish sixth and celebrate the greatest accomplishment of their life. They're happy simply to be at the Olympics, to qualify and compete.

I was determined to play one last season with the Chiefs, even if in a backup role, and then retire. To finish my medical training, I had to complete a residency, to find my specialty as a doctor, and I needed to begin that process in 2022. So this was my last chance to play in the NFL. I needed to leave everything on the field, as they say. Most football players don't get to choose when they retire, or how they step away. I was lucky to have that choice.

I was also lucky to have the chance to bask once more in the world of pro ball. Football is both a physical game and a communal one: 53 players rely on each other to become greater as a whole than they would be apart. The bonds that effort creates come in part from how hard it is, how violent it is—and also how strategic it is. We're immersed in the project, mind, body and soul. That might sound like a speech from a sports movie, but it's the truth.

During the off-hours at training camp, I hung out with my teammates. I relaxed a bit more than in past years. Over our chess matches, Joe Thuney and I walked each other through tips on technique and told war stories. I found a connection with Remmers, a lineman I hadn't known before but had definitely watched on TV in 2020.

As the start of the 2021 season approached, I didn't know what my role was going to be. I believed that, at some point, I would play and contribute. I had to believe that. But I also needed to be realistic. I'd spent a year away. I needed to remember that just getting back onto a pro football field would be one hell of an accomplishment.

And so, I looked forward, uncertain of my footing but (mostly) OK with that.

I was ready for whatever was going to happen next.

CHAPTER 16

THE SIDELINES

For more than a year, the thing I'd desired more than anything, besides actually playing, was to stand on the sidelines once more at Arrowhead Stadium. And that's exactly where I was.

The Chiefs' home opener against the Cleveland Browns took place on Sunday, September 12. It was hot—30 degrees Celsius—and sunny. Flo had flown in from Montreal for the game. She'd stay in town for a little while. We'd scout out an apartment for the year (I'd obviously let the old, pre-pandemic place go) and lease a car. It was time to get settled. Resettled. Though my hand was still healing, and I wouldn't run out onto the field that day to help anchor that O-line, it felt good. Really good.

After all, I didn't want to return too soon and be forced to play cautiously, or worse, refracture the bone. That's what happens when you jump back in, in pain, your future weighing heavily on your mind. It's when even worse injuries are more likely to occur. I needed to be patient. I needed to be able to trust my hands. Especially my right one, which I use to rock defenders in most of my blocks.

So I was philosophical as the announcer ran through the starting offence, and when it came time to name the right guard, he called out Smith instead of Duvernay-Tardif. It wasn't ideal, but at least I wasn't back in Montreal, watching on a screen. I was here, with my team. That was step one. I soaked up the energy as fireworks exploded, as cheers rose from the thousands in the stands wearing our colours, as adrenalin whirled through the stadium. The last time a capacity crowd had packed into those stands, the Chiefs had won the AFC Championship and gone on to take the Super Bowl.

I was so happy to be back. The hype was infectious—the kind of "infectious" you welcome.

But it wasn't so long ago that I'd been working day in, day out amid the ravages of the pandemic. Now I stood on the field in a packed stadium while the virus continued its deadly rampage. Looking around, I had to wonder: How many unvaccinated fans had come to Arrowhead that day?

Despite the very real risks at play in that jam-packed stadium, I knew where I stood. There was no pretending COVID away. Protocols and safe practices were crucial. But we as a society also needed, especially now, the benefits that came—for fans and players of all kinds, from the neighbourhood lot to Arrowhead Stadium—from sports.

THE ANTHEM rang out. By kickoff, I was fully immersed, my mind in football mode. NFL players don't watch games the way fans do. We're looking for assignments, technique, adjustments. We're less focused on the art—dazzling throws or acrobatics—and more on the math and physics.

I studied the Browns, looking for where we'd need to make adjustments, which is tougher to gauge early into a season.

Cleveland jumped to a 22–10 advantage. That didn't bode well. But we came back and took the game, 33–29.

It was a great start to the season: we'd beaten a very good team. But we'd also made mistakes, too many of them. If we saw Cleveland in the playoffs, we'd need to play better than we had that Sunday to beat them again. What stood out most was our lack of swagger, the kind the Chiefs had been known for in recent seasons, with all the talent on our sideline. To regain that cockiness, or confidence, we needed to be arrogant, to know how good we were. I wanted us to be like we were in '19, when we scared opponents into mistakes before we even snapped the ball, simply because we wore the red-and-gold jersey.

We dropped the next two games, then won against the Philadelphia Eagles in early October, then lost again to the Buffalo Bills on the 10th. The Chiefs didn't look like a team loaded, as we were, with All-Pro talent.

I knew we had to get better. If our O-line improved, our team would improve, and that might be the difference between 2019 (Super Bowl championship) and 2020 (Super Bowl defeat).

I could contribute to that improvement, even from the sidelines. During practice I played on the second team offence against the first team defence; it was our job to play out what the opposing team's offence would do in our next game. It was also our job to go hard, but not too hard—you don't want to injure a fellow Chief in practice. It's a fine line to tread: you want to show the coaches what you're up for, but at the same time you have to protect your teammate. The time to really show your skill and go all out is in training camp. By the time the season starts, the lines are in place; it's what happens on the field on Sunday that will dictate the following week's lineup. I had to find a way to make the team better while still staying ready myself.

As a veteran right guard, it was also my job to counsel Smith. I remembered what it was like my first year on the team, absorbing new strategy and technique, learning not to just rely on explosiveness and strength alone—figuring out how to approach a given block in different types of situations. I shared my way of approaching certain plays and told him to always remember what the defensive lineman in front of you is seeing, and use that to your advantage. It's like the judo principle of using your opponent's own force against him. I spent time with him watching film in the mornings and studied the playbook with him before games.

Relatively safe as we were inside our NFL bubbles, it was almost possible to push COVID to the back of our minds. But we all knew it wasn't over. Far from it. We still had protocols in place, including testing and masking rules. As in 2020, reporters were barred from locker rooms; interviews were conducted via video conference. (For me, that rule was one of the only positive side effects of the protocols. Imagine having a reporter in front of your office—which in our case was our locker room—three times a week during your lunch break.) And even from the get-go, positive cases wreaked havoc with teams' game plans. The Dallas Cowboys, for example, had lost their season opener to the Tampa Bay Buccaneers without six-time Pro-Bowl guard Zack Martin, who'd tested positive that week.

The league considered mandating vaccinations for all players, coaches and staff. In the end, it limited the mandate to personnel who worked with players. Players themselves, though encouraged to get the jab, were left to make up their own mind. Some stars, like Indianapolis Colts quarterback Carson Wentz, chose not to get vaccinated, despite criticism from owners, general managers, teammates and fans. I believe in personal freedom. And I understood that players like Wentz often had a variety of reasons for their choices. But I didn't understand how anyone could arrive at that choice logically, through a knowledge grounded in science.

The rancorous conversation around vaccines, and even masks, troubled and amazed me. How political it could be. How often basic science could be ignored. I could be flying to Kansas City through New York, taking off in a city with safety mandates and landing in one with far more lax restrictions. Some places carried on as though COVID-19 didn't exist. In many ways, it felt like the recent presidential elections in the United States: everything tinged by division, with reason taking a back seat to standing firm, being "right." I read an article in the *Washington Post* about the lives of health care workers on the front lines, their struggles with the deadly Delta variant, and the toll the pandemic had taken on their mental health. They were "baffled" by the vaccine debate. Many were quitting, considering another line of work.

I am still triggered when people—including fellow NFLers—insist there's a conspiracy or nefarious purpose behind asking citizens to mask up, self-isolate when exposed to the virus, or get a vaccine. There are those who see an uncle who came down with COVID-19 after being vaccinated as evidence that we're being lied to, or that the authorities are overstepping; and there are those who take a mild COVID case experienced by a family member as proof that the whole pandemic is overblown, or even a hoax. I get it. Maybe that relative's bout with COVID seemed like a common cold, but a COVID infection is not like that for everyone, especially the most vulnerable. When it comes to public health policies, we have to consider data at a population level.

When these subjects arose during the 2021 season, or my teammates sought my opinion, I tried to point out the facts in the least political ways I could. I told them about my colleagues in 2020, my patients, the outbreak. I tried to humanize my experience but not dramatize it in a way that would polarize the debate the other way. I tried to just be clear about what we were up against, and how important it was to join forces, to be in this together. We couldn't beat the pandemic if we were divided. We needed everyone to pull in the same direction.

I liked what Cowboys owner Jerry Jones said in mid-August 2021, when he emphasized that "we" needs to take precedence over "I." Perfectly stated. Focus on public safety, rather than politics. That's what we mean by the "greater good," and that's what's often lost in arguments over so-called "freedom."

I was glad to have pandemic-related conversations with my teammates, even when they were difficult or had the potential to turn political. Most readily bought into the notion of saving lives. Some wanted to keep their families safe, especially children too young to be vaccinated. Others were simply practical: they didn't want positive tests to cancel games. I respected all viewpoints. I believed they respected mine too. If that leads to more vaccinated players, that's great; that's part of what makes an NFL locker room such a unique place.

In some ways, that's what I love most about football, how so many people from disparate worlds can come together. It's the adrenalin, the camaraderie, the deepening bonds that dissolve whatever differences you might have, as you push together toward a common goal.

MY HAND healed. It was in great shape—pain-free. *I* was in great shape.

And I was still on the sidelines.

As the season progressed, it became clear that no matter how well I practised, I wasn't going to take anyone's spot. The five guys on the O-line were locked in. My only chance now of moving to the starting lineup was necessity—a gap in the line caused by an injury. It's an awful position to be in, knowing your fortune depends entirely on someone else's misfortune. I hated the way that felt.

But what could I do? The team had moved on. I focused on being a good teammate, a good practice guy. I wasn't angry. I knew so many guys this had happened to. It had happened, in fact, to my mentor Jeff Allen, who'd helped me learn the ropes—and who got benched because, back then, *I* was the rookie with potential whom the coaches had wanted to give the best chance to. I'd always known it would happen to me at some point. I just wished it wasn't this season, right after my year away—the one year I'd planned to come back to football, give it my all, leave everything on the field, and then walk away toward a medical career. It was frustrating to have broken my hand. It was equally frustrating that there were people who thought I'd only returned to KC to collect a paycheque. My contract was guaranteed that year, after all. I didn't have to play to get the money the team owed me.

But I wasn't there for the money. I was there to play. I kept up my hard work in practice. I volunteered to take practice reps on the defensive line, which was depleted, beset by injuries. That was where I'd started out so many years before at McGill. In theory, it was an injury risk, playing on the opposing line in a less familiar role, but I wanted to stay active, I wanted to sweat. I just wanted to have some fun. The coaches often thanked me for the guidance I provided younger players. Their praise was well-meant and appreciated, but I also saw in it the reality that my role wasn't likely to change.

I also looked to the future—my future beyond football. It was natural, given my situation. It was also important. I'd taken a one-year leave of absence from the master's in public health at Harvard in order to return to pro football this season. So that was hanging, unfinished, awaiting my return. And I'd graduated from medical school in 2018, after which I had four years to apply for residencies. The deadline for me to start specialty training was July 2022, and that was fast approaching, less than a year away. I reached out to medical school friends for advice. They warned me that applying for residencies was complex and convoluted, with lengthy lists of requirements for documents, paperwork and letters of reference that would take time to gather. I reached out to Dr. Primavesi, the associate dean at McGill who'd helped me all those years ago to figure out a way to juggle medical school with football, to talk through my options—and to ask for a reference letter. I also contacted Solène, my long-term care supervisor, and a physician I'd worked with, and asked them for letters too.

I was debating between emergency and family medicine. I was drawn to the ER's high-stakes environment. I was used to working under pressure; I liked it. But as I asked more questions and spoke to friends who'd already done their residencies, I learned that if you specialize in emergency, emergency is really all you'll be able to do. Whereas if you specialize in family medicine, you can add to it over time. You can do a "plus one" with public health, with emergency, with sports medicine. I knew I had many different medical interests that I might gravitate toward at different periods in my life, and family medicine would give me more flexibility to get back into the rhythm of that world. I would have the freedom to figure out what I wanted my practice to look like while still keeping up with other activities—such as working with my foundation and maintaining a media presence with a message centred on public health and primary prevention—and exploring new knowledge and expertise.

Dr. Primavesi told me he believed that my year away from the NFL had helped me see these possibilities and figure out the best path forward. The break from football gave me perspective, broadening what I thought possible but also revealing connections between my pursuits that I might not have seen.

He was right. For one thing, I find myself increasingly interested in helping make the game as safe as possible, and hope to draw on my experience on the NFL's Healthy and Safety Committee. I was fortunate through that work to have met with numerous scientists, and companies like VICIS that are on the cutting edge of available technology. I've also delved into research on traumatic brain injuries, and looked into helmet technology and mouthguard sensors with Athlete Intelligence, a company that specializes in sports data and analytics.

My combination of experiences on the field and in health care could help these companies understand their products from the medical perspective of someone who's played the game and understands the science. Researchers also need to better understand how the NFL works at the players' level, and that's another place where I could come in. I could point them toward strength coaches, performance coaches, physical therapists and team doctors, break down who's responsible for what, and when. Sometimes it's game officials they need to speak with. Or representatives from the players union. I could assist in discerning whether to market products based on performance optimization, or reducing injury risk, or returning to the field more quickly. Ultimately, we want the same thing—for teams to buy in, to build out the right kinds of resources, to better protect their players.

I knew that completing a residency in family medicine would offer me the most flexibility, leaving the door open to further pursue this kind of work, and other initiatives or projects, down the road.

I submitted my applications and prepared for the long wait to hear the results.

IN A DISAPPOINTING loss to the Tennessee Titans in late October, the Chiefs' O-line suffered some injuries. None were too serious, but they were enough to leave holes that needed filling. For our next bout we'd square off against the Giants for *Monday Night Football* on November 1. That day, the coach came to me and said, "Laurent, you're putting your pads on tonight." I'd be dressing for backup, which is normally not my favourite job. I've only done it a handful of times, and it's incredibly stressful. You never know when somebody's going to break a shoelace or something—and you'll have to run on the field in top readiness, able to explode into action. So you need to be "on" for the entire game, and chances are, you'll never be called on. Never get in. Not play at all.

That day, though, I was pumped. I was excited. It was the first time I'd be running out through the tunnel, onto the field, at the start of the game, since the Super Bowl of 2020. It wasn't the way I wanted it to be, but it was real enough that I felt emotional. I felt happy.

I also felt that, with luck, it might mean I wouldn't have to make a decision I was both dreading and uncertain of. Rumours had been swirling that the Chiefs wanted to trade me. They couldn't without my buy-in—my contract included a no-trade clause that only I could waive. A trade wouldn't happen *to* me; if I *were* traded, I would be an active agent in the decision. That made things complex. I had a choice, which meant I'd also have to bear some responsibility for the consequences if I switched teams. But no player wants to feel like dead weight, like their team is stuck with them. I wanted to know the Chiefs' wishes. The Saturday before the Giants game, I'd met with some of my coaches and our general manager and asked for transparency. The reality was this: the franchise had too many injuries, and could really use my roster spot to fill the gaps. I held no ill will toward the executives. I understood the NFL was a business, and that's how business operates. And I appreciated hearing the truth.

The other truth was this: I did have options. Teams were coming calling. But for a trade to happen under the conditions of my contract, three parties needed to agree on the terms: the Chiefs, the other team and me. In the case of some of those teams, the Chiefs would soon be meeting them on the field in the regular season. They'd never trade me to a team they were due to play, because I could share the whole playbook with them.

Still, possibilities were swirling. Change was, potentially, afoot. If I were willing to embrace it. That weekend, back in Montreal, Flo was working furiously, wrapping up some deadlines. She was flying down on the Sunday with her sister to spend 10 days in Kansas City. We hadn't seen each other in a month and a half, and I was excited that she was coming. I also warned her that offers were coming in.

I told her I wouldn't accept a trade. I said I wanted to finish the season in Kansas City, even as backup. Even not playing. I meant what I said. The thing was, an injury might occur at any time, including, if I did leave the team, after I was gone. I was picturing myself on some other team, watching the Chiefs, with their right guard injured, head to the Super Bowl. Without me. I wasn't sure that was something I could ever get over or forgive myself for. It wasn't beyond the realm of possibility. During the

2020 campaign, everything had started well injury-wise for the Chiefs' O-line. Then, boom, they lost a ton of key players. That was a significant part of why they lost the big game. Being backup means being available for those moments, and part of me was telling myself just to be patient. What if the time came when my team needed me—I mean *really* needed me—and I'd already left?

Flo was meant to arrive the night before the game, but a combination of bad weather and pandemic-induced staff shortages meant hundreds of flights were delayed or cancelled that weekend. She missed her connecting flight in New Jersey and had to spend the night there. The following day, she flew to St. Louis, rented a car and booted it to Kansas City. She was still on the road when, with a sense of anticipation, I pulled on my familiar red-and-gold uniform with number 76 on the jersey. She got to the stadium on time, but barely—she arrived just before kickoff, which was particularly memorable that evening.

My friend Alex Smith, the quarterback who'd helped me settle in and learn the ropes when I'd first arrived to play for the Chiefs, was back at Arrowhead in a completely new capacity: as a *Monday Night Football* analyst. As part of a franchise ritual, he banged a huge drum before kickoff. The sold-out crowd was on its feet, keen to honour him, as was I. We all stood, clapping and cheering. *What a cool dude*, I thought. *He's awesome.*

After that uplifting moment, after her frenzied journey to arrive on time, Flo watched as, for the entire game, I sat on the sideline, all dressed up with nowhere to go. I didn't play a single snap.

Being dressed for that game reminded me how awesome it felt to be on the field, ready to play. Now it sank in, full force, that if I didn't entertain the possibility of playing elsewhere, I might not play again at all. I was so close, yet at the same time so far, because that last step was out of my control. And I knew without a doubt that, to exit the game without regret, I needed to get back out onto the field. I started to seriously consider whether I wanted to pick up and move in the middle of the season. I remember telling Flo around 1 a.m. that I didn't know what I was going to do. It was weird. It was emotional. Even thinking back on it, months later, I'm emotional.

The next day we went to grab breakfast. Sasha called with an update. One of the offers on the table—an offer that would expire that afternoon—was from the New York Jets. Sasha said, "This is what we've got: the Jets have a right guard we think you can beat." He meant, if I accepted the trade, I actually had a fighting chance of making the starting lineup. That was significant, since I was on the offensive line, a tough role to jump into partway through a season. It's not like a wide receiver, who can just plug in as he is learning the playbook. On the O-line, you're in or you're out. You can't just sub in and take cues on the fly: you need to know the whole damn playbook.

Ever since offers had begun to surface, almost everyone I was close to had told me they would lean toward staying put. Only nine weeks remained in the 2021 NFL season—hardly enough to learn a new offence and fit into a new team. If I went for this deal with the Jets, I'd be moving from a powerhouse to a franchise that had been struggling for the better part of a decade. And there was always this: if I stayed where I was, I'd end my career with my original team, the Chiefs, which had always been my preference. Helping out during practice, acting as a mentor from the sidelines, I'd be less at risk of injury. I had a whole other career waiting for me, after all.

I knew the logic. I knew the challenge that was ahead of me. But it came down to four words: I wanted to play.

Flo and I talked.

When a player changes teams, it's not only his own career that's at stake. Changing teams means changing cities. And there are other lives involved, lives that must be hastily reconfigured. In my case, that life was Flo's. During all the years I'd played in Kansas City, the tenuous nature of my roster spot, combined with my medical school obligations, meant she and I could never plan further than six months ahead. We lived more than half of each year in two different countries, separated by thousands of miles, a border and our own busy lives. Being a freelancer in the contemporary art world meant Flo also had a great deal of uncertainty with regard to her schedule and commitments. She would be travelling to art fairs to scout artists, sitting on acquisition committees for museums, working with private companies to advise them on building their collections. Fitting our complicated lives together was an ongoing project, a complex puzzle. And her willingness to allow my football career to encroach so significantly on our mutual agenda was built on the understanding that I wouldn't play forever, that I would take my best shot in a limited time frame. I'd already told her that, at the end of the 2021–22 season, I would retire. She had made peace with that.

But if I switched to the Jets, what would that mean? Switching mid-season just to finish the year and play was a weird move for somebody with a fully guaranteed contract. It would mean uprooting from Kansas City and integrating all over again, into a new place, with new people and a new team culture. What player with a no-trade clause would go to all that trouble for just eight games and then call it a day? By even considering the possibility, I was sending a clear message that I wanted to get back on the field—to build my résumé and perhaps sign a new contract. I knew it was kind of nonsense, but it wouldn't be the first time love for the game had led me to make what might seem like a weird decision. I really wanted to play.

To do something this drastic, I needed Flo onside. I also knew that even putting the possibility before her was unfair.

We talked it through. We looked at the angles. The pros and cons. We looked at the sacrifices it would entail. At the possible upsides. At what was at stake.

And finally, we made a call: I should go for it.

IN PRO SPORTS, the trading of players is carried out with brutal efficiency. It's a business arrangement, after all. After Flo and I finished our meal, I called Sasha and said, "It's a go, man. Let's do it."

I'd barely decided in time. It was around 1:50 p.m. The trade deadline was 2:00. Both franchises were made aware. And that was that. On November 2, 2021, seven years and six months after the Chiefs had picked me in the sixth round of the 2014 NFL draft—profoundly changing my life—I was traded to the Jets for tight end Dan Brown.

While the teams finalized the trade, I was sending texts. The first batch to my family: my sister Delphine, my sister Marilou and my parents. There have been times when my closest relatives have learned about a major development in my life through the media, because I hadn't called them quickly enough. The news sometimes gets out fast. I didn't want that to happen this time.

Their responses were just what I expected: a big wave of love and support. They wouldn't be shocked. They wouldn't be blown away. They wouldn't be over the moon with excitement—or dismay. They'd just want to know that I was happy with my decision. And if I was, then so were they. I'm not a special case in my family, the one person pushing their limits. I'm just the one the rest of the world happens to know a little something about.

Before embarking on medical school herself, Delphine was a member of the national cross-country ski team. Though she's no longer competing officially, she hasn't let go of her love for the sport, or her need to break through boundaries. She recently planned a three-week wilderness trip skiing more than 400 kilometres on the ice roads in northern Quebec, towing her tent, cooking fuel, gear and provisions on a sled. Me, I come home after a two-hour ski and I'm cold. I'm ready to warm up, not set up camp in the middle of nowhere in harsh winter conditions.

Then there's Marilou, who's on the national rowing team, does 20 to 30 hours of workouts a week, and has her sights set on the 2024 Summer Olympics in Paris. She'll row 30 kilometres then weight-lift and train. Unlike me, waltzing into pro football locker rooms with all the equipment and trainers I could ask for, she does this with far less support. She has a coach, of course, but the team only trains together at certain times of the year. She has no trainer who's there day in and day out to motivate her in the moment if she's down, to help her assess a minor injury on the spot, to teach her a better way to do this or that exercise. She tracks her heart rate on an Excel document. This is in the midst of finishing her studies. She spends a few nights a week at our place in Montreal so she can easily get to her classes at the Université de Montréal, and arrives with her rowing machine in the back of her old car. She sets it up in the garage with a space heater going, to keep warm but not too warm. The amount of work she's putting in is incredible, and she does it with almost no support, monetary or otherwise—and certainly no cheering section of thousands.

This is our family. Our parents, not so young anymore, still go on serious kayaking trips. Our mom comes home smiling after 40-kilometre cross-country ski outings. We all share athletic genes. We've all got our own dose of the drive or competitive nature to go with those genes. And everyone's car is jammed with skis, bikes, tents—ready to go, pretty much any time, on some outrageous adventure. The reality is, I'm probably the member of my family who takes the fewest risks—or the risks that have the lesser stakes. My sisters do all this amazing stuff, and nobody's really talking about it. That's partly the difference between amateur sports and pro sports: not just the money, but who pays attention. They don't need the attention. They do it for themselves. So when I send them a text that says I've just agreed to be traded from the Kansas City Chiefs to the New York Jets, it's a big deal, sure, but it's a lot less daring than 160 kilometres of skiing in full autonomy that my sisters are planning for the upcoming weekend. It's way less of a leap than training for a single competition several years away with no guarantee of reward or success. I love football, the game, but I also love its trappings: the atmosphere, the pressure, the crowds. I don't think I would enjoy it as much, or be as committed to it, if it had the same media reach and attendance as the national rowing championship. Is it bad to be like that? I don't know. But it makes me respect my sisters' endeavours a whole lot more.

AN HOUR AFTER I made that call to Sasha, we'd already packed up my apartment. Flo and her sister had planned to spend the week in Kansas City, working remotely, hanging out with each other, and with me in our off-time. Now we had to hightail it to the airport to head straight back to New York, which they'd only left the day before, after being stranded Sunday night.

But first I drove to the Chiefs' facility. I hugged Coach Reid and Coach Heck, high-fived my teammates, emptied out my locker. I've seen guys get traded or cut and they're frustrated, which is totally natural, what you'd expect. I felt good, I felt light, I felt hopeful. It signalled to me that I'd made the right choice.

At the airport, we ran into Alex Smith and his wife, Liz. They were booked on the same flight. I told him how great it was to see him showered with love the night before. Then something clicked, and he gave me a sharp look.

"What are you doing here?"

I told him. His eyebrows shot up. I laughed. "This is crazy," I said. "Everything started with you in Kansas City. And now, as I'm leaving, it's finishing with you too."

Flo had gotten to know Liz during my first three years in KC, and loved her for her warmth and the way she brought people together. Now, she knew exactly what Flo was processing—she'd been there before—and offered what the moment required: comfort.

We talked and reminisced till boarding was called. I'd protected Alex on the field for three years before he left Kansas City. When I started, he was already a big deal. But he was a calm presence. And when he was talking with you, he showed interest. He looked you in the eye. He listened. We had a great chat in the airport that day. It was a really nice way to wrap up my time in Kansas City.

The next morning, I was on the field in New Jersey, practising with the Jets.

CHAPTER 17

THE FIELD

I threw my helmet. Hard. It smashed against a locker.

It was January 2, 2022. The game was over. We'd lost, 28–24, to the Tampa Bay Buccaneers. I had never in my life thrown my helmet after a game. I was so frustrated. We'd been leading for the whole freaking game. We were so close to winning. We *should* have won. I knew some people thought, all things considered, it was a pretty good performance. We'd held our own against Tom Brady, the ultimate opponent, for most of the game. And the game was close.

But 80 percent of NFL games are lost by less than one touchdown. It didn't really matter if we lost by four or 14 points. We lost.

"We" were the New York Jets. I'd just played my third game with my new team, as a starter on the offensive line. A week before, over Christmas, I'd been on the COVID list. Omicron. I was in bed for three days. I missed one game. I'd come back feeling fully recovered, but it turned out I wasn't—not quite. During the game I got so out of breath I had to take oxygen on the sideline between plays, through some bronchodilators. (I wasn't the only player that had happened to during the pandemic.)

Even so, I'd played well. I knew I had. And I'd played, period. And as I calmed down, and picked my helmet up off the floor, I knew that was the point. That was what mattered.

I'd played.

Well, it wasn't *all* that mattered. When I'd accepted the trade to New York, all I'd wanted was to play. But I wasn't sure how much I was going to enjoy the idea of losing most of our games with a new team in a rebuilding phase. As part of a less successful team, would I remain a true competitor and fighter? After losing three in a row with the Jets, I got my answer.

God, I hate losing.

But it was so good to be back.

Those close games—whether you lose them or win them—give you that rush of adrenalin and the mental challenge I find so addictive. It's hard to lose. Especially again and again. But it's the reality of team sports. No matter who you are or at what level you play, 50 percent of the guys on the field each and every week are going to lose. And there is, for sure, a lot to learn from that. In this league, you have to lose with professionalism but also with emotion. You have to take every defeat personally and get back to practising with a little bit of that bad taste in your mouth. That's how you get better: when you let your emotions from the game fuel your desire to improve.

The best-case scenario is when you feel everyone on the team is doing that. No matter the results. For me, win or lose, as long as everyone sticks together and nobody is pointing fingers at each other, every game is an opportunity to turn the tide and start a winning streak. In New York, that was exactly how it was.

Plus, so many of our games were so close in the fourth quarter. I really pushed myself, and relished the experience. That was what I'd been missing—not just playing, but going hard, to the absolute limit of my ability.

Every game, I left it all on the field.

IT HAD BEEN two months since the trade—since my risky, whirlwind move from Missouri to New York, from the Chiefs to the Jets. Two intense months: on the football front and on the pandemic front.

Let's start with football.

After the trade, I'd released a statement on my social media accounts. It read, in part:

> *Words cannot express how grateful I am to the Kansas City Chiefs organization. They made my dream come true by drafting me in 2014. Thanks to Coach Reid who believed in me and supported me throughout my whole career to pursue both medical school and pro football, my two passions. Winning the Super Bowl in 2020 with this team will forever be one of my proudest moments. To the Chiefs fans, thank you for the support throughout all these years. You embraced me with open arms and made a French-Canadian feel right at home in the middle of the Midwest ... Saying goodbye to KC is not an easy decision. When I opted out last year, I promised myself to do everything in my power to come back to the field. Joining the Jets gives me the best opportunity to play.*

When reporters in Missouri asked Coach Reid for his thoughts on my departure, he answered with typical grace. "It's great that he has an opportunity to play right now," he was quoted as saying. "Whether he does it for a year, or 10 more years, he has an opportunity to play. That couldn't be promised right here at this time. So, if he decides to go be a doctor after this year, he's going to have an opportunity to play, and he can take that with him." From the very first time I met Coach Reid, before the NFL draft in 2014, he'd understood my motivations—what drove me, at my core. Leaving him and the others I knew so well on the Chiefs' coaching staff, to put myself under the guidance of coaches I didn't yet know, was going to be no small thing. It was seismic.

I paid close attention to the Jets' media responses to the trade. I was curious, of course, to see how they would frame it. Joe Douglas, the general manager, told reporters the team had sought the trade because of my "championship pedigree" and my veteran experience. My new coach, Robert Saleh, said he hoped I could help push a young locker room in the right direction.

I liked the sound of that.

STROLLING INTO the Jets' locker room the first time was surreal. The equipment guys were just finishing up putting my name on my locker and filling it with my new uniform: helmet, shoulder pads and new jersey, all of them green and white instead of red and gold. My new office. Soon, my new teammates would enter it to dress for practice, filling the silence with the sounds of football. It's like the first day of a new school year. I didn't know anybody in New York, but I walked through the locker room and introduced myself to the guys. (To facilitate the learning curve, I'd googled the roster the night before to get a head start on learning everyone's names. First impressions matter, right?) After months of feeling as if I was no longer a part of something, it took only a few minutes to feel I belonged somewhere again.

But my immersion wouldn't be as quick as all that. I moved into the hotel near the Jets' palatial headquarters in suburban Florham Park and started cramming—on field and off. I had a lot to learn. I studied the new offence and watched film of our upcoming opponents on my iPad. I started out practising as a backup, which meant I was likely to at least make the active roster for upcoming games. But it was no walk in the park. I was learning a whole new playbook, a new team culture, on speeddial. I had to show the coaches as quickly as possible that they could trust me on the field, that I wasn't going to make a mistake that would get our young quarterback Zach Wilson killed. There were only nine games left in the season; the clock was ticking.

The plays themselves weren't new to me. Every team in the NFL has the same run concepts in their playbook. They might use more of one type of scheme than another, but the actual plays are essentially similar. The difference is in the way a team approaches them—the technique. In KC, let's say we're running a run play. You block your guy, get leverage, and the running back's going to read what's going on and put the defender on you. With the Jets, that same play was way more aggressive. It was all about hitting full-speed vertical, and it's you, the offensive lineman, who defines the way for the running back. That might sound like a minor adjustment, but in reality it was huge. For me to run the play in New York the way we did in KC—the way I had for seven years—was almost silly. I'd think I was making a good block, but the four other guys on the line would be working in a completely different way. I'd be left looking sloppy and weak.

So it took time for me to get on the same page with everyone. Time and focus. It also took learning the Jets' terminology and signals, which, to be honest, is like learning a new language. On the field, communication is every bit as crucial as technique. Football teams use a shorthand or code that can be shouted amid the mayhem on the field, on the fly. It's got numbers, it's got colours, and it's got its own slang. There's a structure to it. What we called a "36-smack" in KC, in New York we called an "18-Wanda." Seriously. There's no way to remember that except to, well, remember it. Repeat, repeat, repeat. Drive it into your head. With the Chiefs, a four-angle run had a range of suffixes that could be attached, such as "smack," "weak" or "zombie," which all meant different things in New York and were associated with different numbers and signals. They're instructions, and they matter. You respond to them on the field without hesitation. With the Jets, there were a whole series of cues that used "Wanda" with various numbers—it was all based on the number, and I had to get them down, pronto.

In KC, the colour grey meant "on one," while in New York grey meant "on two." In KC, Patrick Mahomes would come to the centre and switch whole plays from pass to run with one word that meant both a new play and a new cadence at the same time. With Zach in New York, it was all different. I had to learn to know when the ball would snap as instinctively as I did with the Chiefs. In the middle of a game, everything moves so fast, you can't stop and think, *OK, in KC, this play means this, so I'm going to block like I did in KC, but with the approach of New York.* No. There's no time to move step by step in your mind. A football play in a huddle is between eight and 15 words that all mean something, from personnel formation to cadence to angle to routes, and so on. You need to know exactly what to do—right away. You need to act. I had to retrain my natural reflexes and gain the ability to communicate with my team in a loud stadium environment.

On top of learning the basic playbook, I also had to know all the once-in-a-game—or even sometimes once-in-a-season—plays pertinent to special situations. For example, in a football game, if one of your players catches the ball and it's not clear whether it's a catch or an incomplete pass, you can decide to quickly run a play to prevent the other team from challenging the catch. (An opponent can't challenge something two plays back.) In KC, that play was a quick pass with a simple pass protection to allow us to snap the ball as quickly as possible. The signal was "attack attack attack." With the Jets, it was a totally different play called a "Nascar," which was a run to the right. There were so many different elements involved with that specific situation, and it's the sort of thing that would happen maybe twice a year. It hadn't come up in practice since my arrival. No one had told me about it. You can see what's coming. In one of my first appearances with the Jets in an actual game, the quarterback was suddenly yelling, "Trigger, Nascar," and I was like, *What the fuck? Nascar?* I had no clue what to do. Instead of running the run, I did a pass protect on that play. And trust me, it looked bad. In that situation, it doesn't matter that it's not your fault, that you couldn't have known. As an offensive lineman, you're being graded on how consistent you are. One bad play out of 10 is average. So if I don't know what to do on one play, to make up for that, I've got to do nine plays really well. It was intense, and it was sometimes frustrating.

The adjustments I had to make, after seven years with the same team, were numerous, and they weren't just on the field. Meetings were structured differently, as were our strategy sessions. In KC we watched a ton of film; in New York it was way more about stats and diagrams, *X*s and *O*s on a sheet. The weekly practice routine, which I'd grown so accustomed to, wasn't the same. Of course it wasn't. In Kansas City, I knew exactly what we'd be doing every day of the week. I knew that a Wednesday practice would involve this type of play and this sequence of practices. Same thing, every week. In New York, the drills were different, as was the approach, all the way down to whether we did a full-speed or walk-through warm-up. And I had to calibrate my practice play extremely carefully. You can't go too hard in practice—you don't hit people in a practice the way you would in a game. At the same time, though, as the new guy, I had to go harder than I normally might, to prove myself. So, go hard, show what you're made of, but not so hard that you're a total jerk-head, your new teammates are pissed, your coaches unimpressed. I'm not saying I expected things to be the same, of course not. But the uncertainty in that new environment was a monumental challenge; every practice for me was an exercise in constant adaptation. My nerves were taut, my adrenalin high. When you're in a familiar routine, you can save that coursing adrenalin for the Sunday game, when you need it most.

And it was there, at the game itself, that I found the biggest difference of all.

When your team record is 2 and 10 versus being 10 and 2, your approach to the game is different. Your entire team mentality. In KC it was like, *You can bring whatever you've got. We're never gonna lose.* With the Jets it was like, *We're able to win if we work together.* That's a really big nuance. There's no doubt in my mind that the whole coaching staff wanted to win. Coach Saleh was young and charismatic. He created a really different vibe than I was used to in KC, but he was the type of coach you want to play for. Being able to rally the team and get the best out of every guy is a monumental effort when you have a losing record, and he was able to do it with brio. But as a coach you have your team's record to contend with as well: you have to find a speech that's positive while also being realistic.

There are 32 teams in the NFL. I'm sure there are 32 different coaching styles and philosophies, 32 ways of prepping your team for a game, a season, a run for the top. You don't build a winning culture overnight. In KC it took us six years: the first year we didn't make the playoffs; the next three we made it and got knocked out early; the fifth year we got to the conference championship but lost; then, finally, we took the Super Bowl. New York wasn't there yet. So instead of what I'd come to expect in KC, which was along the lines of *They're coming to our house, there's no fucking way they're going to win*, there was always that qualifier: *if. If we work together, there is no chance they can beat us*.

I saw the contrast between those mindsets again and again after I was traded. In New York, sometimes we were up by three points, and our opponents would score a touchdown and you could feel the momentum shift. In contrast, in the divisional playoff game that put Kansas City on the road to the Super Bowl, we were down 24–0, and we came back and won it. Because we were confident. We trusted each other. To be a winning team in football, you need that confidence and that trust. And you can't ever waver. The thing is, football is not like hockey. Say you're a hockey team in the playoffs. It's best of seven games. If you slip up in one game, you have six more chances to make up for it. In football, it's go big or go home—every single game. You cannot wait for the debrief in the locker room to change stuff. Every game, you have to feel like you're still in it, even if you're trailing.

Even the pandemic was playing out differently with the Jets, and not just because Omicron, a more contagious variant, emerged soon after I was traded. In Kansas City, well over 90 percent of the players were fully vaccinated. In New York, that figure was way lower. At least a dozen guys on the team were not vaccinated. I found that pretty interesting, and as a medical professional, it made me wonder if there's a better way of educating people about the benefits of vaccination. Advocating for the safety and importance of vaccinations is a huge challenge, especially in the face of all the medical misinformation circulating in the world, particularly online. And when I got to New York, I experienced first-hand what happens when the people around you choose not to get vaccinated.

A football locker room is 53 guys from all over the country, from all different communities and backgrounds. And in every NFL locker room across the country, players and staff were facing the same NFL-imposed pandemic restrictions and protocols. I am sure an epidemiologist would love to work in that type of setting to study the impact of proper counselling on vaccination rates, because the variables between two locker rooms would be pretty much the same. If you didn't get vaccinated in Kansas City, you had to be tested daily and wear a mask to meetings. Ditto in New York. So what was the difference? The head trainer and the doctors: what they were communicating to the players and how. The messaging from health care professionals.

That fall, though vaccines still provided excellent protection from serious illness or death, Omicron proved better than earlier incarnations of the virus at evading them. Meanwhile, cooler weather set in and people were spending more time together indoors. These factors combined meant COVID cases surged all over North America, including in the NFL. In the two-week period between Halloween and November 13, 81 players and staff members tested positive, marking the season's highest caseload. During the two months prior, there had been just 97 positives cases in the league.

In mid-November, the league re-strengthened its COVID protocols, and also found strategies for minimizing spread over the Thanksgiving holiday, such as encouraging teams to create drive-through testing sites for visiting family members and friends. As cases continued to tick upward, everything except practices and games went back online. Then, one week, there were so many positive cases around the league that a decision had to be made about what to do to ensure that teams were able to keep playing games. The answer the league and the Players Association agreed to was to do away with mandatory weekly testing across the board, and restrict testing going forward to those who were symptomatic. When you looked at it rationally, you could defend such a move. It's what we do in normal life, after all: get a test if we have symptoms of an illness. And we weren't in the same place we'd been in at the start of the pandemic: we had vaccines and many other protocols in place. So you could justify it. Except that you needed to make clear what the consequences of that new testing protocol would be. I called the president of the players union and said, "Hey, if we want to do that, I'm comfortable with that, but you have to release a statement to all the players saying that, if we stop testing, 99.9 percent of us are going to get COVID in the next three weeks."

Really quickly, things went haywire. Within a few days, players who said they had symptoms were being asked, "Are you sure? Do you really need a test?" And that's messed up. You give just a little bit of room and suddenly it's all the player's responsibility. That's when I got COVID myself. I was far from alone. By December 24, 20 members of the Jets franchise, including Coach Saleh and quarterback Joe Flacco, were sidelined by the virus. I took my highly contagious Omicron virus back to my hotel room, away from anyone who might catch it, and went to bed. And that was where I spent Christmas Day.

*

EARLIER that fall, amid my frenzied efforts to fit, mid-season, into a new organization, reminders of the Chiefs were all around me. For one thing, they were on fire, bagging game after game, likely to make another Super Bowl run. It seemed as though every time I spied a television in the Jets' cafeteria, the segment centred on the Chiefs. Analysts on the NFL Network were debating, analyzing and scrutinizing their chances at a championship.

But I was immersed in a new team and a challenge, intently focused on learning the Jets' style of play and adapting to the new terminology on the field and in meetings. I went from my hotel room to practise and back. The days flew by. Ten days after the trade to New York, I was suiting up for a home game against Buffalo. I donned my new uniform and ran out of the tunnel with the team at the start of the game. However, like the game earlier in the fall when I was called to dress for the Chiefs, I was backup and didn't get a chance to play. It was probably better that way because I was still a bit fuzzy on a few of the finer points of the Jets' game plan.

The Tuesday after the game, I got a call from my new position coach, John Benton. There was no preamble. "We're going to go ahead and make you the starter, at the right guard position, this week. Are you up for the challenge?"

"Yes, sir," I responded. "That why I'm here."

He urged me to keep asking the right questions, to keep leading, keep learning the playbook as quickly as I could. We both knew the difficulty inherent in an offensive lineman becoming a starter on a new team that quickly. All I needed now was to ace every day in practice, in meetings and, eventually, on the field the coming week, against the Miami Dolphins.

No pressure, really.

The current right guard, an awesome dude, was a veteran with 10 years under his belt. In order to get on the field on Sunday, he was the guy I had to beat. We shared a similar approach to the game. He was a really cerebral guy. He was also a key leader of our room—the O-line room.

That week, he helped me get up to speed on a ton of key things related to Jets-style play. It was a weird scenario—those situations always are. The level of professionalism you need to teach the guy who's about to take your place is unbelievable. We're talking the fate of careers worth millions of dollars here. But it's as though you forget about that when you are in the moment and you just want to be a good teammate. You can't help but put your team first. It's ingrained in you to do so.

Day after day in practice, he gave me guidance, offered tips. I for sure played better because of his advice. Sunday approached.

I called my friends and family, to let them know.

ON NOVEMBER 21, I woke up early. I wanted to maintain the same pre-game routines I'd established in Kansas City, so the previous night I'd scarfed down my usual meal of spaghetti with a mountain of Parmesan cheese on top, followed by asparagus and carrots. I'd gone to bed early and slept for almost nine hours. I made a coffee in my hotel room and climbed back into bed with my playbook in hand. I went over the game plan, all the various situations I might encounter. Then I spent 20 minutes in the shower, where I closed my eyes and visualized the first 10 plays of the game. By the time I grabbed my towel to dry off, I had the material down cold.

I made my way down to the team breakfast buffet and ate some eggs with oatmeal before driving to the stadium early enough to arrive three and a half hours before the game, just as I'd done 70 times over the past eight years. I dressed, jogged onto the field and commenced stretching. I stole glances at the stands, where I spied my mother, who'd driven all the way to New Jersey to surprise me, sitting next to Flo and Sasha. I fought back tears. It hit me how much I missed them all—just spending time together. The previous months had been so intense. Heart full, I retreated to the locker room and climbed into the hot tub to warm up my muscles.

Before long I was sprinting out through the tunnel with my new teammates. I listened as the announcer went through the introductions. My name boomed from the loudspeakers. The standings, the circumstances, the stands—less full than those at Arrowhead—none of that mattered as the national anthem started. I didn't yet know that in a few weeks I'd be out for five days with COVID. That my first time playing after being infected, I'd need oxygen to help my lungs keep up with the rest of my body. I didn't know I'd be so invested in this team, so furious over losing a game we could have won, that I'd whip my helmet across the locker room; or that I would have managed to build such great camaraderie with my fellow O-linemen.

All I knew was this: for the first time since lifting the Lombardi Trophy in Miami in February 2020, I was back on the field.

It's an extraordinary feeling to put your shoulder pads on and run out onto the field on game day. Globally, each year, only 1,500 guys get the chance to play professional football. Literally. And only some of them will step onto the field as starters and look out across that expanse of green turf, the familiar markings, the distant goalposts. Against the odds, and with a few curveballs thrown at me, I'd proven that I deserved to be one of those guys. It's such a privilege. A pro football field is bigger than some

Olympic stadiums. It's three times the size of the Maple Leafs' rink in Toronto. It's huge—and it's buzzing with the players' adrenalin, the energy of the fans. There's a show, it's about to start, and you're the main event. It's an indescribable high, that first play of the game. The first time you hit someone and make a block, you're going to look them in the eye and know this is it: *OK, for the next four hours, it's going to be on.*

And I'm gonna bring it for every play.

It's about to get real.

"Let's go!" I yelled.

Into the game. Into the most thrilling competition life has to offer. Into this new version of my old reality. Into clarity. If I'd known, before I took a sabbatical from football to wade into the front lines of the pandemic, what the consequences would be, I'd still have chosen to opt out. Standing on that field, I knew, right down to my bones, that was true. I carried everyone—my colleagues from the pandemic, my patients, my friends, my parents, my sisters and, of course, Sasha and Flo—with me onto that turf. It hadn't been easy to get back there. It had been one of the toughest challenges of my life. It would have been easier for me to exit football after the Super Bowl. Expected. The sensible path. But I wasn't ready to take it.

Every decision, every step on the journey, had led to this: to the play we were about to execute, to all the subsequent plays which would feel that much more meaningful after all that had transpired, after all we'd been through.

AFTERWORD

A CRACK
IN THE DOOR

t's spring 2022, three months into the off-season. I'm in a good
state of mind. I'm caught up in the usual running around at this
time of year, catching up on all the many projects that were put
on hold during the season.

A couple of days ago I received my acceptance for the residency program in family medicine that I applied for last fall. It's
now time to decide whether to accept the offer.

There's been movement on the football side too. It's free
agent season in the NFL. Teams are calling. I have to decide. Am
I going to stick with the game for now? Is that going to be my
next move?

I want to embrace the fact that I have these options. I know
how privileged I am to have the opportunities I've had. And I'm
really proud of myself that I went back and played professional
football again after opting out, that I took the chance to do it
when I could.

I'm not great at making decisions when it means letting go of
an adventure, a goal or a dream. I never have been. Earlier in my

life, I felt a lot of stress over whether I'd make the right call. I've always taken my mom's advice and tried to open as many doors as possible. Now, for the first time, I feel as if I have to close a door, and I don't know for certain which one. Because, this time, there's no going back.

Once I walk away, I cannot go back to football. And I know what I'd be giving up. That endorphin high you get playing in front of 80,000 people, the rush, the excitement. How can you replicate that? You lose track of time. You're in the moment like at no other time in life. And football is not like hockey: after you retire, you can't play in a rec league at the local arena and go out for a beer afterward. It doesn't work like that. Football is 100 percent on, or it's nothing. You can't play without the stakes.

I've learned something about myself. For me, the best way to make a decision is to put myself in a place where I live with that choice for a little while and see how it plays out. Way back when I was a first-year med student at McGill and I quit football to study, it didn't feel right. It was a disaster. I began to fall apart. So I found a way to fix it, to make both things work. I know I can't make both things work forever. Pro football careers are finite, starkly so. In a not too distant future I will have to walk away from football definitively, completely. And I'll survive. I'll manage. I might even thrive. I'm older now, better equipped in all kinds of ways.

So. Is that time now? Probably. Most likely.

But absolutely?

Here's what I know, what I understand. I walked away from football when it felt important, necessary and right. Our world was in crisis, and I had training and skills to offer, so I tried to do my part. Then, against expectations, against odds, against what some might see as logic or even common sense, I fought my way back onto the field. I proved to myself that I belonged there.

Because I did both of those things, I feel at peace with whatever happens next. I can play football. I can go back to medicine. I can finish my master's degree in public health at Harvard. I will have to choose. It's going to be hard.

Here's as far as I've come. It's OK to want to do it, and it's OK to not want to do it. Time will tell me what's right.